Music, Social Media and Global Mobility

Routledge Advances in Internationalizing Media Studies

EDITED BY DAYA THUSSU, *University of Westminster*

Music, Social Media and Global Mobility

MySpace, Facebook, YouTube

Ole J. Mjøs

Routledge
Taylor & Francis Group

NEW YORK   LONDON

First published 2012
by Routledge
711 Third Avenue, New York, NY 10017

Simultaneously published in the UK
by Routledge
2 Park Square, Milton Park, Abingdon, Oxon OX14 4RN

*Routledge is an imprint of the Taylor & Francis Group,
an informa business*

First issued in paperback 2013

Typeset in Sabon by IBT Global.
Printed and bound in the United States of America on acid-free paper by
IBT Global.

Library of Congress Cataloging-in-Publication Data
Mjos, Ole J., 1970–
   Music, social media, and global mobility : Myspace, Facebook,
YouTube / Ole J. Mjøs.
      p. cm. — (Routledge advances in internationalizing media studies ; 7)
Discography: p.
   Includes bibliographical references and index.
   1. Music—Social aspects.   2. Music and globalization.   3. Social
media.   4. Online social networks.   I. Title.
   ML3916.M56 2012
   302.23'1090511—dc23
   2011035078

ISBN13: 978-0-415-88274-3 (hbk)
ISBN13: 978-0-203-12754-4 (ebk)
ISBN13: 978-0-415-71620-8 (pbk)

Contents

Figures and Tables

FIGURES

TABLES

Acknowledgments

Various individuals have contributed in different ways in making this book possible.

I thank my colleagues Hallvard Moe and Lars Nyre for reading and commenting on chapters and extracts and for help shaping the book, and Moe in particular for his continuous support and role in implementing a both humane and productive writing regime. I am indebted to Frode Guribye, Daya Thussu, Patrik Wikström, and John Urry for reading an earlier version of the manuscript and providing valuable feedback and suggestions for improvement. It goes without saying that any remaining inaccuracies and errors of fact or interpretations are entirely my own.

I am thankful to Monika Büscher as well as John Urry for letting me spend time and present my work at the Centre for Mobilities Research, Lancaster University, UK. I thank Joseph Turow and Monroe Price for giving me the opportunity to reside as visiting scholar at the Center for Global Communication Studies, Annenberg School of Communication, University of Pennsylvania, US.

I would like to express my gratitude to Daya Thussu, series editor, for continuous counsel, and Kjetil Rommetveit, Espen Sommer Eide, Vegard Moberg Nilsen, Birthe Skotheim, Ketil Mosnes, Kristian Stockhaus, Aksel Mjøs, Espen Ytreberg, Trine Syvertsen, Vilde Schanke Sundet, Karoline Ihlebæk, Gunn Enli, Jostein Gripsrud, Dag Elgesem, Astrid Gynnild and Knut Helland for comments, help, or advice on various parts and aspects of the book project at different stages.

I am grateful to my current employer, the Department of Information Science and Media Studies and the Faculty of Social Science, University of Bergen (UiB), Norway, for generously giving me the time and resources to complete this book.

I am thankful to everyone who kindly let me interview them for this project, to Felisa Salvago-Keyes, Julie Ganz and Erica Wetter at Routledge, to Elizabeth Thussu for editing the manuscript—for which I am most grateful, as well as Michael Watters at IBT, and Ingebjørg Braseth, master's student at the department, UiB, for great help with organizing the appendix and bibliography.

Finally, I thank my mother Kari, father Ole, and my sisters Hilde and Elisabeth Mjøs, and all my dear friends for continuous encouragement and warm support over the years.

Preface

The idea for this book project came about when as a former electronic music practitioner, I started to think about how this practice seemed to have changed over the last decades. I was involved in this part of the music sector throughout the 1990s, both as producer and as administrator—close to a decade. I contributed on records released by record labels based in Europe—in the UK, Belgium, and the Netherlands. Since 1997 I have been living in Bergen, a small city on the west coast of Norway, first as a music practitioner, before moving into television documentary production and then into academia. Since the turn of the millennium, a number of electronic music artists, producers, and DJs based in Bergen have experienced success internationally. Media on both sides of the Atlantic, *The New York Times*, *The Guardian*, *The Independent*, the *BBC*, *Billboard*, and *MTV*, have all given considerable attention to what particularly the press refers to as a Bergen scene. Today, still living in Bergen, but now working as a media researcher at the University of Bergen in the fields of international communication and global media studies, observing former colleagues and current friends involved in the electronic music scene, I have been struck by how different their music practice seems, particularly the increasing use of the internet. I observed how from the mid-2000s the internationally expanding social media, MySpace, seemed to have become a key tool and a new arena for many of them in a relatively short time. What fascinated me in particular was how MySpace facilitated audio and visual user participation for these electronic music practitioners in Bergen, while at the same time MySpace was controlled by the media mogul Rupert Murdoch's News Corporation. This local music scene had suddenly become part of a global social media service owned by one of the world's largest media conglomerates (for many years central in the international communications and global media discourses). News Corporation's acquisition of MySpace in 2005 was one of the conglomerate's key strategies for securing a position online. From these electronic music practitioners, I heard how they created profiles on MySpace to promote and access music and information, to get to know other musicians, to connect with music scenes, to distribute concert flyers and videos, and to communicate with fans and fellow practitioners—both in the local community and across the world in the UK, US, Australia, and Japan. At the same time, stories of the wonders of MySpace and its ability to 'break' music artists internationally began to appear in the mainstream press worldwide. This was very different from my professional experience in the 1990s as a music practitioner.

In the early 1990s, prior to the maturing of the internet and long before what we today know as social media, the physical movement of formats, objects, and persons was at the center of music practice. My colleagues and I had to send physical music demo tapes from Norway to record labels in London and continental Europe by ordinary mail. If we were lucky and got a record deal, we sent the finished recordings on tapes to the record company, and months after that, we received vinyl records in the post. CDs were an important format—particularly for albums. The physical distribution of flyers and posters person-to-person was the main means to promote club nights or concerts. You could read about new electronic music in British magazines such as *Mixmag, ID, DJ,* and *The Face,* but to hear such music, you had to either order records by mail or travel to cities with club venues and specialist record shops such as London.

The difference between the 1990s and today is striking. I became curious and wanted to understand how these electronic music practitioners experienced these recent developments and in particular the possible role that global social media seemed to play in their practice. I also wanted to explore to what extent this development could say something about general developments within the media and communications landscape.

Many researchers on 'new media' have feared that their object of study will 'disappear' or morph into something unrecognizable. I too worried about this, and to some extent my worries were realized. I had not grasped how quickly the social media environment could change. When I started to think about this project in 2007, MySpace was the focus of my study, and there existed few studies of the social media phenomenon in general. At that time, MySpace had more users than Facebook, both in the US and internationally. However, Facebook expanded rapidly after it opened to the wider public in 2006. By May 2008, Facebook had more users internationally than MySpace. Facebook's expansion continued at an astonishing rate. By the end of 2010, Facebook had been adopted by more than 500 million users. That year Facebook's prominence within popular culture was further highlighted when Sony Picture's feature film *The Social Network,* about the founders of Facebook, had topped the US box office. When interviewing with music practitioners in early 2009, the focus of the research project was on the role of MySpace. I realized that MySpace had been very important from the mid-2000s, but the internationally expanding Facebook was rapidly becoming a popular social media, for these music practitioners as well. I decided to talk to interviewees again in late 2010 to learn how their use of social media had developed. I also compared MySpace to other global social media, in particular to contrast the key historical and political economic aspects of their global expansion. The book, then, centers on the period 2005 to 2010, the seminal years of the development of a global social media environment, focusing on MySpace, Facebook, and YouTube—the online video-sharing service—and the take-up of these services by electronic music practitioners. YouTube has also been of major significance for music practitioners as a channel for music and concert videos, not least since it is possible to incorporate or embed the online video service on artists' MySpace profiles, and later on Facebook. It is difficult to study moving targets, but since I had decided to study the activity of electronic music practitioners that had been active over a long period of time, I aimed to examine the bigger picture. I therefore talked to the electronic music practitioners about their practice in the 1990s, and during the emergence and maturing of the internet and global social media, and after the social media phenomena had achieved a mainstream presence.

The book, then, explores the emerging global social media and music nexus in the period from 2005 to 2010, from both a corporate and a user perspective, using two methodological approaches. The user perspective is explored mainly through qualitative interviews with these practitioners—examining their experiences and practical work. To strengthen the study, and enhance the wider relevance of the book, also included is a historical and political economic exploration of the global social media environment emerging since the mid-2000s. The development of these online services is studied from a corporate perspective through the analysis of secondary sources: quantitative data, corporate strategies, marketing reports, and statistics on media use. This also includes the corporate relationship and collaboration between the music industry and these social media services. This approach aims to map the context and environment the music practitioners operate in from a corporate perspective. Throughout the book, I also show how the two perspectives, the user perspective and the corporate perspective, intersect and interrelate.

The book, then, has three take-aways. Firstly, it shows, from both a corporate and a user perspective, how the emerging global social media and music nexus represents a new space for electronic music practitioners, while at the same time the users of these services are, in various ways, being (or at least attempted to be) exploited commercially. Secondly, this development has theoretical consequences. It challenges, in particular, some political economic perspectives on international communication and media globalization, as much of our knowledge derives from the study of television and film—traditional audiovisual spaces, without such opportunities for user participation. Thirdly, the book suggests how we may theoretically grasp this development. Global social media facilitates unprecedented possibilities for practitioners to communicate and operate within the global communications infrastructure. By incorporating the theoretical 'mobilities' framework into the field of media and communications, we take this user activity and user movement into account and achieve a more nuanced understanding of the way media globalization unfolds and develops.

The book does not make claims that the experiences of this group of global social media users are generalizable, but the portrayal of these music practitioners' engagement with these online services, together with a detailed account of the central political, economic, and technological factors in the development of the global social media landscape, aims to give insight into an environment of which more and more people across the world are becoming a part of.

Ole J. Mjøs is Associate Professor at the Department of Information Science and Media Studies, University of Bergen, Norway. He is the author of Media Globalization and the Discovery Channel Networks (Routledge, 2010). His previous practical experience in the media and creative industries includes work in television documentary production, and contributions on many records within the wide genre of electronic music.

1   Introduction

In 2005, Skatebård (Bård Åsen Lødemel), the Bergen-based electronic music artist, producer, and DJ, and one of the subjects of the research in this book, started a profile on the social media service MySpace:

> I had been thinking about creating a 'website' for my musical activities for many years, but I could not afford to pay someone 20,000 Norwegian kroner (approximately \$3,500–4,000) to construct an html site. I did not even know how to rent a domain name on the internet. I am sure there were many in a similar situation that created MySpace profiles. It was easy to create a website (on MySpace) where you could present music and have direct contact with others, and have complete control over the site despite having no knowledge of web design. This was back in 2005. (Skatebård, March 2009)

Skatebård was not alone in signing up with MySpace. Music artists and bands not only in the US but in different parts of the world were flocking to the social media. Halfway through 2005, the American music magazine *Billboard* claimed 240,000 amateur and professional bands had created profiles on MySpace to promote their music. At that time, MySpace had reportedly around 15 million members, and new users continued to join at an astonishing rate, rapidly expanding the MySpace universe (Bruno, 2005; Cohn, 2005; News Corporation, 2005).

MySpace appealed particularly to young people, and American teenagers had started to use MySpace 'en masse' in 2004 (boyd and Ellison, 2007). Although bands and music artists "were not the sole source of MySpace's growth," as the pioneering social media researchers boyd and Ellison (2007) point out, "the symbiotic relationship between bands and fans" was vital for the services popularity and expansion especially among youth. Both parties benefited from the "bands-and-fans dynamic". The former was interested in reaching fans, while the fans wished to be noticed by their favored music artists and groups. MySpace enabled contact between the two as fans used the 'friend' function to "signal identity and affiliation" on their MySpace profile, and bands could communicate and distribute information to their network of fans' profiles (2007). MySpace, then, provided opportunities within the global media and communications landscape that had not been available previously and consequently many music artists and fans embraced the service.

While artists had relied on physically promoting themselves, distributing flyers, fanzines, videos, and music on CDs and hoping that their music videos were shown on local or national television shows or specialist television outlets such as MTV, the emergence and take-up of social media began to influence their practice. MySpace let artists create profiles where they could present their music, incorporate YouTube music videos, display band photos, and list upcoming concerts. They could distribute flyers to—or contact—other MySpace members. Importantly, it was also possible to link their MySpace profile to other profiles.

The usability of the pioneering MySpace appealed to millions of people, not only bands, and a growing preoccupation with the commercial potential of such online services soon caught the attention of the media and communication industry giants. In 2005, the same year as Skatebård, the Bergen-based electronic music practitioner, adopted MySpace, News Corporation, one of the world's largest media conglomerates, bought MySpace for $580 million—at the time, the largest sum paid for a social media entity (News Corporation, 2005; Siklos, 2005). With powerful new owners and increased attention in the international mainstream press, MySpace expanded fast. In January 2007 it was the most popular website in the US (Angwin, 2009: 254). Vast numbers of bands and artists were among the millions attracted to the multimedia online service. "I know we have 5 million bands," Chris DeWolfe, (former) CEO and co-founder of MySpace claimed in 2008: "Virtually every artist has a profile on MySpace" (DeWolfe quoted in Locke, 2008). However, these formative years of the global social media and music nexus are characterized by flux and shifts. Facebook was already outperforming MySpace globally in mid-2008, and the popularity of Twitter also grew rapidly in this period (Arrington, 2009b).

This book shows how these recent developments have consequences for our comprehension of how media globalization unfolds and develops. It focuses on understanding how these global social media have evolved, and how one group of users—electronic music practitioners—have come to take up and use these services in their music practice and work. These practitioners are part of the wider group of bands and artists that was of key importance in the development of MySpace. MySpace, along with YouTube, was the first to enable these practitioners to participate and operate within the global communications infrastructure in an unprecedented way. Later, Facebook and Twitter became part of the global social media milieu and were adopted by many music practitioners. It is clear that during the formative years of the global social media environment (2005 to 2010), these services facilitated an increased potential for communicative and virtual mobility for such music practitioners (Hannam, Sheller, and Urry, 2006; Elliott and Urry, 2010: ix). Still, several factors may influence or limit the users' virtual mobility—the ability to communicate, operate, and initiate within this online space. It is therefore vital also to explore the relationships between the users and the corporate strategies of these global social media as they roll out across the world—not least the services' monetization strategies, as they may all have an impact on the users' mobility. Therefore, to understand the impact and significance of the various components that drive this development, we need to examine it from both a user and a corporate perspective.

At the center of the book are electronic music practitioners in the city of Bergen, Norway, and the role global social media have in their practice. Since the late 1990s, Bergen's electronic music scene has been particularly thriving and outward-looking. This scene has been part of the international electronic and dance music scenes that emerged in several cities in the late 1980s and early 1990s in the US, UK, and continental Europe (Hesmondhalgh, 1998; Reynolds, 1999; 2008). These scenes, often seen as part of 'club culture,' soon became a 'global phenomenon' (Thornton, 1995: 3). The popularity and international expansion of electronic music was partly made possible through sampling techniques and low-cost technology that required no formal skills of writing or reading music. The term 'electronic music practitioners' used in this book is, like McLeod's term 'electronic/dance music,' an 'umbrella term' or 'metagenre' that is used "to label a heterogeneous group of musics made with computers and electronic instruments—often for the purpose of dancing. Electronic/dance is a metagenre name that is vague enough to describe the broad variety of musical styles consumed by a loosely connected network of producers and consumers" (McLeod, 2001: 60; see this and Reynolds, 1999: 398–436, for extensive lists of sub-genres). This book, then, applies the term 'practitioners' in a wide sense. It refers to artists, producers, DJs, club organizers, and promoters all working within this genre.

The most internationally well-known Bergen-based band is Röyksopp—an electronic music duo whose debut album *Melody AM* (2001) reportedly sold more than a million copies worldwide. Alongside Röyksopp, internationally known artists and DJs such as Annie, Datarock, Bjørn Torske, and Skatebård, together with both amateur and semi-professional DJs, club promoters, and music producers, have populated the small but highly active Bergen electronic music scene. These artists are key interviewees in this book (see Appendix for discographies of the interviewed artists). (Note: I worked with interviewees Bjørn Torske and Torbjørn Brundtland, the latter now part of the duo Röyksopp, in the 1990s and several of the interviewees are among my current acquaintances and friends.) Many of these practitioners have operated both locally and internationally for several years, and some (in particular the members of the Bergen-based Datarock, as well as Mikal Telle, record label owner, DJ, and event organizer) also have links to and within music genres such as indie rock. Since the turn of the millennium, these Bergen-based artists have achieved artistic or commercial success (or both) and received considerable attention, not only in the niche music press, but in the international popular and mainstream press. The electronic music practitioners in this book have frequently been described by the press as central in the Bergen music scene. The *Lonely Planet Guide* for Scandinavia points out how:

> (T)he so-called "Bergen Wave" was largely responsible for putting Norway on the world electronica circuit in the first years of the 21st century. Röyksopp (www.royksopp.com) in particular took the international electronica scene by storm with their debut album *Melody A.M.* in 2001 and they've never really left the dance-floor since. (Ham et al, 2008: 52)

In a piece on the artist Annie, the *The New York Times* points out the city is "one of Scandinavia's most peculiar and vibrant musical corners," and furthermore "in recent years, Bergen has produced a number of pop musicians of international stature" (Rosen, 2005). Along similar lines, in a review of Datarock's album, the *BBC* describes Bergen as "the seaside town with the ridiculously vibrant scene that spawned Annie, Royksopp, Erlend Oye and countless others" (Kutchinsky, 2007). The British newspaper *The Guardian* refers to the "'Bergen' scene that, as well as Röyksopp, has also given the world the like-minded Annie and the Whitest Boy Alive" (Hann, 2009). The *Huffington Post*, the influential American news website and blog, points out that "Bergen, Norway, nestled on the country's craggy west coast, is an unlikely hotbed for new music. But that's what it has become over the last decade" (Mohr, 2009), and the online music site *Clash Music* describes Bergen as having "one of Northern Europe's most vibrant music scenes" (Clash Music, 2009).

Some Bergen-based musicians have voiced skepticism about the label 'Bergen scene' or 'Bergen wave.' Tenold, in his historical study of the wider music milieu in Bergen (not limited to electronic/dance music) also points out that "the references to Bergen might be seen as a kind of branding, though one that the artists did not necessarily endorse themselves" (Tenold, 2010). It is easy for the press to slap the term on a group of artists, which risks exaggerating the cohesion between them and contributing to the hyping of an exotic and remote part of Europe. Still, there are a number of facts that relate specifically to the Bergen-based electronic music practitioners studied in this book. These artists have for longish periods been based in the same geographical area, they have all released key records on the Bergen-based label Tellé Records (founded by interviewee Mikal Telle), and many have done remixes of each other's work and collaborated in various ways (see Appendix for discographies of the artists). Furthermore, many of them know each other personally and professionally, and all have frequented and played at the same venues and club nights in Bergen run, in particular, by interviewee Vegard Moberg Nilsen (i.e., Electric Café, Straedet, Café Opera). Several of these practitioners have also organized and played at regular club nights in Bergen at the same venue, Landmark: Hot!Hot!Hot! (co-organized by Mikal Telle), Digitalo (organized by Vegard Moberg Nilsen and Skatebård), and Powerblytt (organized by interviewee Lars Jacob Tynes Pedersen, and Kjersti Blytt—also forming the duo The Work). Lastly, as we shall see, a number of these artists discovered MySpace through each other. The book, then, shows how this group of Bergen-based electronic music practitioners, as well as practitioners from a related electronic music scene in East London, worked before and after the arrival of global social media, how they adopted these services, and the role these services have in their music practice at both a local and an international level.

The rapid adoption of global social media by hundreds of millions of internet users across the world stands in contrast to the development of traditional media in a number of ways. From a user perspective, television, for example, has never been able to allow its users to create personalized profiles and communicate in the way global social media have done. From a corporate perspective, these new online services attempt to exploit user involvement commercially in unprecedented ways, employing surveillance systems to collect information on users for commercial purposes. At the same time, the global social media and music industry collaborate in an effort to reach potential customers among these users. Therefore, only an examination from both corporate and user perspectives can give us sufficient insights into the significance of the global social media and music nexus.

Drawing on interview-based research with these electronic music practitioners in Norway and the UK, together with the historical portrayal of the emergence of global social media, the book aims to situate this development in music culture within the wider transformations of the media and communications landscape; from analog to digital, from national to global, and from largely passive to more active media use. These changes also influence the making, promotion, distribution, and selling of music, although the extent of the impact is debated. Some point out how "the transformation is of such a magnitude that it is relevant to talk about 'new' industry dynamics" (Wikström, 2009: 4). What characterizes these changes is the dramatically declining significance of "physical music distribution" and the escalating role of the internet (Wikström, 2009: 5). Others claim that "the response of the music industry to Internet distribution, social networking sites, home-copying and the creation of non-commercial distribution mechanisms has been complex and even chaotic" (Lister et al, 2009: 193). Still, some argue that "digitalization hasn't yet killed the music business as we know it and there is little prospect that it will" (Hesmondhalgh, 2007: 254). For this reason, the example of the music industry indicates that one should be careful not to overstate the impact of the internet on "existing cultural industries" (Hesmondhalgh, 2007: 255). The examination of the connection between social media and music in a global context can therefore contribute to understanding these ongoing changes.

The popularity of the pioneering cross-national MySpace shows how the development of the social media environment can be unpredictable and characterized by sudden shifts and changes. Soon after it was established, MySpace faced extensive competition, first in the US and then across the world. When in 2006 Facebook ended its membership restrictions—inviting anyone with a working email address to join the service—and with Microsoft joining as minority owner in 2007, it soon surpassed MySpace as the most popular social media site in the US and internationally. In 2006, the internet-based enterprise Google followed fellow industry giants News Corporation into the social media environment by acquiring the popular video-sharing site YouTube for $1.65 billion. YouTube then also played a role in making MySpace popular, as the users of the social media could incorporate, or 'embed,' the video service on their profiles as an online video channel (Angwin, 2009; Burgess and Green, 2009). As with MySpace and Facebook, powerful new owners helped YouTube grow. By early 2008, web metrics services reported that YouTube was among the most visited websites worldwide (Burgess and Green, 2009). Meanwhile, MySpace was increasingly portrayed to be struggling by the press and scholars alike. Social media scholar danah boyd pointed out that "MySpace's status among teens had begun to fade" (2008: 62). The newspaper *Financial Times*, for example, published an article titled "The Rise and Fall of MySpace" (Garrahan, 2009). Similarly, scholars Patchin and Hinduja pointed out that "a significant number of youth appear to be abandoning their profiles or MySpace altogether" (2010) and the newspaper *The Guardian* claimed that, since early 2008, "Facebook secured its dominance over MySpace in the UK early last year, since when MySpace's user base has declined regularly" (Arthur and Kiss, 2009). In contrast, YouTube and Facebook have continued to expand—the latter attracting over half a billion users across the world at the end of 2010 (Facebook, 2010), among them many music bands and artists. Although Facebook has outgrown MySpace in terms of numbers of users and is described by the press as the winner in the race for worldwide social media dominance, in a wider perspective, MySpace was the first social medium to receive broad attention in the international mainstream press and experienced rapid adoption not only by bands, but also millions of internet users worldwide. The two, together with YouTube, therefore represent pioneering global social media services in the second half of the 2000s—the formative years of the global social media environment.

The rise of global social media, and their widespread adoption, is at the heart of the wider changes within the media and communications sector. This has consequences not only for how social media are studied, but also the terminology used to describe these services. Both MySpace and Facebook are described as "social network sites" (boyd and Ellison, 2007; Papacharissi, 2009). Boyd and Ellison define such sites as "web-based services that allow individuals to (1) construct a public or semi-public profile within a bounded system, (2) articulate a list of other users with whom they share a connection, and (3) view and traverse their list of connections and those made by others within the system" (2007). The way these sites have evolved since 2005 has consequences for how we label and define them. While communication between users and the enabling of users "to articulate and make visible their social networks" (boyd and Ellison, 2007) is at the heart of these services, their increasing inclusion of user-generated or corporate music, videos, and film clips to communicate makes, for the purpose of this book, 'social media' a more precise term to describe these evolving multimedia services. Still, the application of the term 'social media' does not dismiss the key characteristics of the term 'social network sites,' as pointed out above, but includes them as well.

The aim of this book is not to capture the day-to-day development and innovation and the seemingly eternal flux of the global social media landscape; instead, it tries to understand these changes as part of the wider developments taking place within the global media and communications environment: digitization, globalization, and user participation in various forms. Therefore, the book covers both the time before, the transition period, and the time after the emergence of social media and the adoption of such services by electronic music practitioners. It focuses on exploring the activity among a selection of electronic music practitioners that is taking place within a historical, political, and economic industry context. In order to explore this development, I have adopted two key methodological approaches: reflecting the user and corporate perspectives. The key approach for exploring the user perspective is qualitative interviews with the selected group of music practitioners, examining their experiences and practical work. This interview approach is commonly used as part of ethnographic studies of global social media (see boyd, 2008; Takahashi, 2010). Most of the interviewees are Bergen-based music practitioners, but they also include practitioners in the UK who are part of a local London scene, with connections to the Bergen scene. I knew most of the interviewees prior to this project since I have previously been part of this scene as a music practitioner and attended many events within this scene. As with all qualitative researchers, I also have to make reservations in regard to generalizability, as the study has a given focus and covers a limited time frame. Furthermore, the interviewees belong to a particular geographical area, are key members of physical 'real world' music scenes, and were early adopters of MySpace. For these reasons, they are particularly interesting to study. In addition, the examination of their use of global social media gives insight into the possibilities and limitations for social media users in a wider sense.

The electronic music practitioners were chosen according to the same criteria. First, the interviewees should have knowledge of "the cultural arena or the situation or experience being studied," second, "they should be willing to talk," and third, if the people within the studied sphere "have different perspectives," they "should represent the range of points of view" (Rubin and Rubin, 1995: 66). Importantly, all interviewees were active music practitioners over a long period and were therefore in a position to reflect on their practice prior to the maturing of the internet and emergence of global social media and after adopting this technology and these services. Therefore, conducting semi-structured interviews with people selected according to shared selection criteria allows for comparison between the possible roles of global social media in their individual music practice. Interviews were carried out in the period between February 2009 and December 2010. This is a long time in the changing social media and online environment, but such a challenge is not new for researchers of the online environment: "The evolving nature of the Internet makes it a moving research target. Almost all research can only describe what has been the situation, rather than what is now or what will soon be" (Hampton and Wellman, 2002: 351). boyd has also highlighted this in her study of social media. In late 2004, at the start of the fieldwork, boyd "traced the rise of MySpace" when "only a handful of teens had adopted MySpace" (boyd, 2008: 62). By the end of the study, Facebook had "become a significant competitor to MySpace and MySpace's status among teens had begun to fade" (boyd, 2008: 62). The focus of this project was initially MySpace, and I also experienced the shift within the global social media environment described by boyd. MySpace is particularly important because of its pioneering role, but the introduction and take-up (and dominance) of Facebook, as well as the growth of other global social media, are all part of the formative years of this milieu. To address and include this change in the study, I interviewed some people in the second half of 2010 to allow for comparisons and elaboration, as many of the interviewed electronic music practitioners had used these online media services since 2005.

The examination of the global social media and music nexus from a corporate perspective allows for a more general historical and political economic exploration of the development of these services. This also includes the corporate relationship and collaboration between the music industry and global social media. The corporate perspective, then, helps us to understand the environment in which the electronic music practitioners I studied operate. The approach consists of analyzing existing secondary sources such as media industry trade press and newspapers, corporate strategies, and public information and media user statistics. As with interviews of social media users, the analysis of such secondary sources is a common approach in the study of global social media (see, for example, boyd, 2008; Patchin and Hinduja, 2010).

OUTLINE OF THE BOOK

Chapter 2 introduces the way in which the internationalization and globalization of media have been studied historically as I set up a theoretical framework within which the book's chapters are situated. It goes on to show how global social media have become part of the research agenda and discusses how the nature of these online entities challenges aspects of our practical and theoretical understanding of the process of media globalization. The following five chapters investigate the key components of the global social media and music nexus, from both the corporate and the user perspective, and the relationship between them. From this, it becomes clear that the emergence of a global social media environment since 2005 has facilitated a new space for music practitioners in the study. In the final chapter, the components of the global social media and music nexus are addressed within the discourse of the internationalization and globalization of media, in order to gain insights into how media globalization evolves.

Chapter 3 examines the emergence of a global social media landscape by explaining key political, economic, and technological tendencies and factors paramount in the worldwide expansion of these services. As such, it traces the general developments underpinning the emerging global social media and music nexus from a corporate perspective. The chapter first examines the surfacing of social media within the US media and communications landscape in the late 1990s and early 2000s. It then explores MySpace's, as well as YouTube's, pioneering efforts to expand internationally in the mid-2000s, followed by Facebook along with Twitter's roll-out, through to 2010. The social media phenomenon was perceived as key to traditional media conglomerates such as News Corporation, Time Warner, and Disney, as well as the computer software giant Microsoft, to help tackle the radical transformations caused by digitization and secure a powerful corporate position online—both in the US and internationally. In particular, News Corporation's acquisition of MySpace contributed to the renewed belief in the financial potential of the internet after the dot-com bubble had burst at the turn of the millennium. As with traditional global media such as television, localization is the key corporate strategy for the expanding social media. However, new technology and the characteristics of the online environment make it possible for global social media to localize and personalize at an unprecedented tempo, often with the help of the services' own users, in order to anchor themselves in local cultures and societies.

Chapter 4 explores the relationship between global social media and music. It details this connection not only from the perspective of electronic music practitioners, but also from a corporate perspective, as the major operators within the music industry and social media have become intertwined. The chapter focuses on the early adoption of these services and gives insight into how bands, artists, and fans across the world became users of social media, as music is a cultural form that binds users together. In particular, the chapter considers the various ways in which the Bergen-based music practitioners, along with representatives of a London scene with connections to Bergen, have come to adopt social media. In 2005,

MySpace had a pioneering role and began to influence music practice and work as well as the way fans and music enthusiasts communicated and accessed music, through facilitating possibilities for local and cross-national communication. At the same time, the growing number of music practitioners and fans adopting these services attracted the music industry, which saw global social media as a way to help tackle the challenges facing the music sector. The music industry and these services, then, have in only a few years become allies and partners in various ways.

Chapter 5 examines the nature of the contact between the music practitioners and the way in which social media provide an online vehicle for, and encourage, communication among music practitioners and geographically dispersed music scenes. Their experience is linked to the theoretical metaphors of 'cosmopolitan fluidity' and 'transnational connections.' The first describes the ability to exist and live in the global and local—"the distant and proximate"—at the same time (Urry, 2003: 137). To what extent do global social media encourage such a way of living for music practitioners? The second metaphor relates to how these services facilitate transnational communication and interaction among users (Hannerz, 1996). While the first half of the chapter focuses specifically on the role of MySpace, the second half looks at Bergen-based artists' use of global social media in 2010. Many of them adopted these services in 2005, so by the end of 2010 they had been users for half a decade. The last part of this chapter, then, aims to show how such use had developed by the end of these five seminal years.

Chapter 6 explores the relationship between corporate influence and global social media on two levels: internally, within the social media environment, and externally, in relation to the outside media and communications environment. The chapter first examines global social media's monetization strategies. As with other electronic and digital media and communications systems, users' activity may be subject to a form of surveillance (Urry, 2007) and used for commercial purposes. MySpace and Facebook have embarked on major efforts to monetize their operations. As global social media do not charge any membership fees, these strategies involve the gathering and commercial use of information provided by the users on their profiles or more indirectly through their behavior when logged on to these services. The chapter then explores the global social media in relation to the outside environment—the very media and communications environment in which they exist. These global online entities differ from traditional global television and media outlets because the users' participation, contribution, and activity are at the heart of these services. The logic of global social media—the mixing of user-generated content and communication, and also traditional media content (e.g., News Corporation's early attempts to distribute some of its television programming through MySpace)—can represent a challenge for transnational audiovisual policy. Overall, then, the corporate influence on both the internal and the external level reflects the more general tendencies and trends: the general strong preoccupation among corporate and political stakeholders, as well as the media and press, with the possibilities for economic rewards and growth generated within the online sphere.

The concluding chapter synthesizes the findings of the previous chapters and explains how these challenge explanations of media globalization. The characteristics of the components of the global social media and music nexus mapped in the previous chapters are compared and contrasted to the traditional and common understandings of the relationship between media and globalization derived from the field of media and communications, and in particular perspectives from the political economy tradition. The chapter shows how over the last decades major traditional audiovisual operators have been at the center of discourses in several ways: influence within the relation between the global and local, the powerful position of the US media, and fears of cultural homogenization and the notions of cultural and media imperialism, as well as the increased flows of media content generated from regions other than the US. Although these new global media services follow the pattern of American media companies' overseas expansion, their utilization of online technology to culturally localize and personalize, and the users' communication and self-generated media content within these services, set them apart from traditional global media. While, for example, global television channels localize through dubbing and subtitling of programming, the inclusion of local advertising, and some local programming, global social media's opportunities for personalization and language translations, often done by the users themselves, are unprecedented. However, these services are commercial entities that attempt to create revenues and profit in numerous ways and compete with national social media services. Still, as the study of the music practitioners show, these services create new online space that traditional global media have never facilitated. Therefore, when placing the global social media phenomenon within the theoretical discourse, they challenge historical understandings of the relationship between the global and local within the media landscape.

2 Media Globalization and Global Social Media

Research on the relationship between media and globalization has been pre-occupied with exploring traditional audiovisual spaces created by the film and television industries. While an 'active audience' has been able to choose television programming from a rapidly growing number of television channels, and benefits from watching these media in numerous ways, these audiovisual spaces still provide very limited opportunities for individual media users' actual participation and input. However, the way the relationship between media and globalization has evolved has given rise to global social media as facilitators of new online spaces. While these spaces exist within corporate and contested environments, they provide increased potential for participation of the media audience and users. This development is particularly visible within the global social media and music nexus emerging since 2005. In order to grasp the theoretical consequences of these recent transformations within the media and communications industry and the emergence and take-up of global social media, it is important to look at how the relationship between media and globalization is understood and defined.

Media globalization is closely tied to how the development of a global media and communications infrastructure has facilitated increased opportunities for cross-national communication and the distribution of media and communication across the world (Katz, 2005; Kraidy, 2005; Rantanen, 2005; Thussu, 2000/2006; Flew, 2007). Drawing on Tomlinson's general suggestion that the "broad task of globalization *theory* is both to understand the sources of this condition of complex connectivity and to interpret its implications across the various spheres of social existence" (1999: 2), we can study the processes of media globalization—taking place within the media and communications' sphere—by answering the following questions: how is this condition created, and to what extent, and in what way, are the opportunities for global mediation and communication utilized? We thereby explicitly explore how the phenomenon of media globalization develops by examining the central economic, political, and technological processes creating a cross-national and increasingly global media and communications infrastructure and, at the same time, by studying the characteristics of the specific activity taking place within this infrastructure

(Mjøs, 2010a). This book follows this approach when examining the emergence of the global social media and music nexus from both corporate and user perspectives, by studying the historical, political, and economic factors pivotal in the development of global social media and, at the same time, the activity taking place within these services. The theoretical significance of the emergence and use of global social media, and their difference to traditional media, becomes visible when we look at the traditional theoretical approaches to the internationalization and globalization of media. By placing the global social media and music nexus within, in particular, the political economy research tradition and historical theoretical context, we see more clearly how the general characteristics of these online services represent not only transformation but also continuity with the past.

The enhanced possibilities for international and, increasingly, global production and distribution of media products, along with conglomeration within the media and communications sector, have given rise to discourses about influence and power and the wider consequences of this development. Historically, much of our knowledge of how the relationship between media and globalization evolves and what it leads to is based on studies of traditional media. The large US-originated media and communications conglomerates and players have been at the center of, first, the discourse on the relationship between internationalization and media and, later, on globalization and media. The critique of the strong position of the US within an internationalizing media and communications industry goes back to the 1960s. The US's political and economic self-interest when leading the development of an international communications industry at the cost of smaller states and cultures was the target of Schiller's early critique. Through cultural domination, US media exports, and television programming in particular, undermined and weakened indigenous and traditional culture (Schiller, 1969). Hence, the theoretical concept of 'cultural imperialism' emerged and "endured to become part of the general intellectual currency of the second half of the twentieth century" (Tomlinson, 1991:2). Mirroring the notion of domination within the media sector, Boyd-Barrett's concept of 'media imperialism' drew attention to the uneven distribution of power between countries and the dominating role of the US and primarily Western countries, specifically within the international media sphere (1977: 117). The concept of 'cultural imperialism' received considerable attention and was influential in the 1970s and 1980s (Thussu, 2000/2006). Dorfman and Mattelart's study of Disney products in South America attempted to show the 'cultural imperialism' thesis in practice (1975). The thesis was also supported by related concepts such as 'cultural synchronization.' In the early 1980s, Hamelink argued that transnational communications companies (TNCs) are central in this process as "(t)he principal agents of cultural synchronization" (1983: 22, 23).

Although the cultural imperialism thesis and cultural synchronization argument focused on the US/Third World relationship, Schiller warned against the consequences of uneven cultural power between the US and Western Europe (1985: 11). The European Commission also pointed out how American films and television programs dominated European media space, creating "a certain uniformity" on television screens (European Commission, 1984: 47). In the 1990s, as US-originated media companies were becoming globalized, Schiller's critique extended to this development as well: "Initially this could be seen as American cultural imperialism. More recently, it has become transnational corporate cultural domination" (1992: 39). Still, together, the US and increasingly these TNCs represent "systemic power and control" also within a global media sector, through support of both telecommunications and media and communications software and hardware (Schiller, 1998: 23, quoted in Thussu, 2000/2006). Similarly, Boyd-Barrett maintained that aspects of "media imperialism" are still relevant as "there is considerable evidence of unequal international media activity, coupling strong media exporters to heavy media importers, and the US still figures, unquestionably amongst the former" (1998: 160).

When American satellite television channels first expanded into Europe in the early 1990s, there was a belief in "corporate circles" that mirrored the notions of critical scholars; cultural differences were diminishing as "a global culture was emerging" and English was seen as the coming universal language, even in Europe (Chalaby, 2005: 53). However, such views underestimated the significance of local culture and language. Already in the 1970s, this was observed in relation to media products in South America. Local media products, de Sola Pool argued, have several benefits in comparison to imported media products:

(1) They are protected by barriers of language; people would rather see a film made in their own idiom than one with subtitles or even one that is dubbed.
(2) They are protected by barriers of social support. Much of the enjoyment of media is discussing them with one's friends. Reading this year's best-seller is a social experience. Top TV shows or movies provide grist for conversation the next day, and that is much of their drawing power.
(3) Local products are protected by barriers of culture. Domestic products portray characters eating foods the people eat, wearing the clothes they wear, celebrating the events they celebrate and gossiping about the celebrities they follow. (de Sola Pool, 1977: 143)

These observations were made decades prior to the expansion and consolidation of American-originated cable and satellite television channels but remain highly relevant for the activities of all global media and television outlets today and, as this book shows, also for the global social media entities. De Sola Pool's early observations, then, are a precursor to the concept of 'cultural proximity.' The growth of national and regional television and the cultural sector in Latin America from the end of the 1960s and throughout the 1980s showed how "audiences are seeking greater cultural relevance or proximity from both national and regional television programs" (Straubhaar, 1991: 276). Similarly, around the same time, but across the Atlantic, Collins pointed out that differences in language and also culture in Europe complicated the creation of transnational television and its audience (1990: 3, 4). So, although a global broadcaster like MTV thought the television channel's content had a universal appeal, by the mid-1990s managers at MTV realized the need to adjust to more local conditions (Chalaby, 2002: 195). In general, localization of television programming and channels is done through dubbing or subtitling of programming, by introducing some local television content, or by adding the name of a country or language to a global brand (i.e., Discovery Channel US, Discovery Channel India, CNN Español, or CNN Germany). These approaches have long been applied in order to appeal to segments of the national television audiences' cultural and linguistic preferences (Chalaby, 2005; Thussu, 2005; Mjøs, 2010a).

However, despite these localization efforts, neither MTV nor Discovery Channel have posed a threat to national broadcasters in Europe. Furthermore, television produced specifically for a national audience remains popular and continues to achieve higher ratings than imported programming. This contributes to explaining why the concept of cultural imperialism and the related media imperialism have increasingly been criticized.

On a general level, Tomlinson argued that in contrast to the much discussed dominant, one-way distribution flows of media products, "globalization may be distinguished from imperialism in that it is a far less coherent or culturally directed process" (Tomlinson, 1991). Similarly, Sreberny criticizes the 'cultural imperialism' thesis for expressing ideas of hegemonic media that are "frozen in the realities of the 1970s, now a bygone era" (2000: 96).

Others point out that the concept of 'imperialism' is inaccurate because "the model needs to take account of audiences, audience preferences; audience consumption of specified cultural products as a proportion of total media and non-media consumption" (Boyd-Barrett, 1998: 168). The continuing strong position of national and local culture, then, is closely tied to critiques of the view coming from different academic disciplines or schools that "globalization is eclipsing the nation" (Curran, 2002: 182). The localization of global media operators and the popularity of domestic media products remind us that national specificities are still a major force in the global media landscape. These are manifest through languages, political systems, and traditions that "find continuing expression in the media of different nation states" (Curran, 2002: 183). Still, although the cultural imperialism thesis has far less support today, the continuing differences seen in the trade of film and television programming and ownership structures remind us of uneven power relations existing within parts of the media industry (Morley, 2006: 35). Historically, then, the discourses on international communication and global media have been preoccupied with power relations within the television and film sector. However, the next section shows how the maturing of the internet and its logics over the last two decades, as well as the emergence of a global social media environment, represents a new space for participation by the media user. This development needs to be included in these discourses.

THE EMERGENCE OF GLOBAL SOCIAL MEDIA

MySpace and Facebook are the result of decades of corporate and public preoccupation with the possibilities for interaction and communication between individuals within the virtual environment. As such, the development of these global social media and the spaces for public participation they provide differ from the far more closed spaces of traditional audiovisual media, historically at the center of discourses on international communication and media, and globalization and media. Prior to the emergence of what we today know as global social media, research focused on personal representation and possibilities for action within the emerging 'cyberspace.' Many focused on the potential for such activity, often depicting the future in utopian terms. Cyberspace, yet to materialize in the late 1980s, was eagerly described as "a globally-networked, computer-sustained, computer-accessed, and computer-generated, multidimensional, artificial, or 'virtual' reality" (Benedikt, 1991: 122). In the future, individuals would be able to operate and create within this 'virtual reality': "In cyberspace the common man and the information worker—cowboy or infocrat—can search, manipulate, create or control information directly; he can be entertained or trained, seek solitude or company, win or lose power . . . indeed, can 'live' or 'die' as he will" (1991: 123). However, as Benedikt pointed out at the time, "This fully developed kind of cyberspace does not yet exist outside of science fiction and the imagination of a few thousand people," but due to the enormous activity and efforts of the computer industry, "one might cogently argue that cyberspace is 'now under construction'" (1991: 123).

By the mid-1990s, from being only available to the American military, the internet was "now available to anyone who can buy or borrow an account on a commercial online service" (Turkle, 1995: 11). In 1993 there were only 20 million internet users; by 2000 there were 400 million. Similarly, only 400 websites populated the web in 1995, but by 2000 there were 200 million such sites (Thussu, 2000/2006). In this early phase of internet development, Turkle, along with others, optimistically drew attention to the possibilities for the growing numbers of internet users to operate within this space declaring that for many of us "cyberspace is now part of the routines of everyday life" (1995: 9). The internet would facilitate an arena for human interaction and the creation of communities within this new space: "We have the opportunity to build new kinds of communities, virtual communities, in which we participate with people from all over the world, people with whom we converse daily, people with whom we may have fairly intimate relationships but whom we may never physically meet" (Turkle, 1995: 9, 10). Kollock and Smith, pioneering researchers on online communities and communication, shared this view, but expressed it in more cautious words: "It is clear that computer networks allow people to create a range of new social spaces in which to meet and interact with one another" (1999: 3).

However, at the time, Wellman and Gulia pointed out that "unfortunately, there have been few detailed ethnographic studies of virtual communities, no surveys of who is connected to whom and about what, and no time budget accounts of how many people spend what amount of hours virtually communing" (1999: 170). As the online environment has matured and expanded geographically and possibilities for individual participation have developed, research has increasingly focused on understanding online social ties, and the nature, meaning, and role of the relationships and communication between people for private or professional purposes within the virtual environment or 'virtual communities,' as well as the relationship between the online world and 'real world' (Hampton and Wellman, 2002, 2003; Haythornthwaite and Wellman, 2002; Haythornthwaite, 2005). In the last half of the 2000s, as global social media entities emerged and became widely adopted, research on these entities and networks has followed. As with previous research, many of these recent studies of social media are also preoccupied with studying the nature of the communication between online users now taking place within these services (Papacharissi, 2009).

While the creation of online identities had already begun in the mid-1980s, as people created pseudonyms and aliases when using electronic bulletin boards on the WELL (Whole Earth 'Lectronic Link), the technological development and expansion of the internet in the last half of the 1990s allowed people to develop increasingly advanced online identities (Rheingold, 1993/2000; Angwin, 2009: 51). A further key development was Friendster, one of the first social network services that received mainstream attention, which appeared in 2002. It aimed to compete with the dating site Match.com (boyd and Heer, 2006; boyd and Ellison, 2007). What separated Friendster from other dating sites was that it allowed for peoples' internet personas and profiles to be linked:

> Friendster's innovation was to add a feature linking people's online personas together. Each Friendster profile contained pictures not only of the member but of the member's friends. Clicking in the friend's picture would take you to the friend's profile page. While it seems like a small thing, this was a huge innovation. Suddenly all these stand-alone Web identities could be placed in an understandable context—the context of their friends. (Angwin, 2009: 51)

The linking of online identities, in the form of personal profiles, was therefore crucial in creating today's social media landscape. From a corporate point of view, these new spaces for mediation and communication also represented large groups or 'communities' of internet users that could be sold to advertisers (Spurgeon, 2008). In 2003, just a year after Friendster, MySpace was launched. Facebook appeared in 2004 and YouTube in 2005. So in just a few years MySpace, Facebook, and YouTube achieved cross-national presence, received press attention, and became the most used and noticeable global social media. As such, boyd and Ellison argue, MySpace and Facebook, together with Friendster, were three key social network services "that shaped the business, cultural, and research landscape" (2007).

The worldwide adoption of these services among all age-groups, not only young people and music practitioners, shows how social media and network services have become arenas for online activity and various forms of communication. From 2007 to 2008, the number of users of these forms of services in selected countries increased by over 5.4 percent—to an average of 67 percent. The highest reach was in Brazil, with 80 percent, and the fastest growth was seen in Germany, from 39 percent to 51 percent (see Table 2.1; adapted from Nielsen Online, 2009).

This development has continued. By 2008, two-thirds of the world's internet population visited social networking or blogging sites—an activity that accounted for 10 percent of all internet time. In December that year alone, the average Australian spent nearly 7 hours on social media

Table 2.1 Germany Has Seen the Greatest Increase in Online Reach of Member Community Websites (% of the online population)

	December 2007	December 2008
Brazil*	78	80
Spain	65	75
Italy	63	73
Japan	67	70
UK	59	69
USA	64	67
France	64	67
Australia	55	59
Germany*	39	51
Switzerland	41	51

*Home only
(Adapted from: Nielsen, 2009.)

sites, while Americans and users in Britain followed with over 6 hours of use. On average, from December 2008 to the same month in 2009, the use of social media services, the most used being Facebook, Twitter, and MySpace, increased with an average of 82 percent in the US, UK, Australia, Brazil, Japan, Switzerland, Germany, France, Spain, and Italy (Nielsen Online, 2009, 2010a).

The increased use of these services, as internet users entered and utilized the global media and communications infrastructure, is also reflected in the rapidly growing body of research on the global social media. The early ethnography of Friendster gave insight into the "tensions that emerge as users participate in a public/private social application with varying expectations, values and experiences" (boyd, 2004). A later study showed how Friendster profiles changed "from being a static representation of self to a communicative body in conversation with other represented bodies" (boyd and Heer, 2006). However, as boyd pointed out, only two years after its launch, Friendster experienced a drop in popularity. Although the 'early adopters' of Friendster still had a presence, their active use had declined dramatically, and by 2004, the service "was dominated by individuals living in Singapore, Malaysia and the Philippines" (boyd and Heer, 2006).

Shklovski and boyd's report *Music as Cultural Glue: Supporting Bands and Fans on MySpace* was one of the early writings on the relationship between music practitioners and music fans and MySpace. The study concluded that "MySpace has created an environment that supports consumption and production of music while providing for the communities that exist around music" (2006). In 2007, the first overview of social network services was published, detailing their history and development. The study also drew attention to how quickly the popularity of such services could shift (boyd and Ellison, 2007). Boyd's pioneering ethnographic study showed how teens use services like MySpace and Facebook "as spaces to mark identity and socialize with peers" (boyd, 2008). And as MySpace expanded outside the US, research began to reflect this. In Japan, the study of a group of young people showed how they vary between the global MySpace and Mixi—a Japanese social networking site (Takahashi, 2010). Van Doorn's study of a group of Dutch MySpace users showed how "a group of interconnected 'friends' on MySpace engage in gendered and sexualized interactions through the use of various semiotic resources (i.e., text, images, video)" (2010). In contrast to the 'negative attention' MySpace received in the media and parents' concern about adolescent use of the service, a study showed how careful young people are when sharing personal information on MySpace, as well as not giving everyone access to their MySpace profile (Patchin and Hinduja, 2010). As with Boyd's (2008) earlier study, Patchin and Hinduja also pointed out how MySpace was losing out in popularity to Facebook toward the end of the 2000s.

Facebook opened to the general public in 2006 and, parallel to its expansion, received increased attention from the research community. The early study *The Benefits of Facebook "Friends"* gave an account of the relationship between the use of Facebook, and the "formation and maintenance of social capital" (Ellison, Steinfield, and Lampe, 2007). A comparative study of Facebook, LinkedIn, and ASmallWorld explored how the structure and makeup of these services "may set the tone for particular types of interaction" (Papacharissi, 2009). Similar to earlier studies on MySpace, Mendelson and Papacharissi studied Facebook members' "use of photo galleries as an instrument of self-presentation and a means of visual autobiography online" (2010). Research has also come to include political and economic aspects of MySpace and the emergence and impact of YouTube (Burgess and Green, 2009; Wasko and Erickson, 2009; Mjøs, 2010b). Together, the rapid worldwide take-up of—and research on—global social media underlines what Haythornthwaite and Wellman called for close to a decade ago, "a new way of thinking about the internet: not as a special system but as routinely incorporated into everyday life" (2002: 6). In sum, global social media is receiving increased attention from researchers and disciplines—just as other popular forms of media such as television, film, and radio have for many decades. Therefore, the next section details how this book contributes to this growing body of work by incorporating these major transformations in the discourses on media and globalization.

THE RELATIONSHIP BETWEEN GLOBAL SOCIAL MEDIA AND MEDIA GLOBALIZATION

Global social media have emerged as a consequence of the processes of media globalization, digitization, and the growth of the internet and Information and communication technologies (ICTs) within the media and communications industry. In contrast to traditional users of media and media audiences, these services have facilitated new online spaces that enhance the potential for user activity. Users of these services can now have a presence within the global media landscape in a way never seen before in media history. The theoretical significance of global social media becomes visible when placing the phenomena within the 'mobilities' framework. It becomes clear that these services facilitate an increased potential for communicative and virtual mobility (Hannam, Sheller, and Urry, 2006; Elliott and Urry, 2010: ix) for the studied music practitioners. Virtual and communicative mobility relates to virtual travel, often taking place "in real time and thus transcending geographical and social distances," and communicative travel, consisting of "travel through person-to-person messages via messages, texts, letters, telegraph, telephone, fax and mobile" (Elliott and Urry, 2010: 16). As we shall see, global social media therefore differ from traditional media by providing a new space for media users.

The rise of global social media can be seen as part of a wider 'mobility turn' in society that is underpinned by the emergence of 'mobility systems' throughout the twentieth century (Sheller and Urry, 2006). These systems include national telephone systems, low-cost air travel, mobile phones, and networked computers (Urry, 2007). The media and communications sector is central in this development: "Such virtual communications and mobile telephony is calling into being new ways of interacting and communicating within and across societies" (Urry, 2007: 5). The internet and MySpace, Facebook, and YouTube are the result of the development of such 'mobilities systems' and are themselves services that create spaces and arenas that increase the potential for user activity and participation.

In what way do these services differ from other media? In contrast to traditional media, global social media embody a duality that becomes visible when examining the development of the phenomenon from both the user and the corporate perspective. This duality is what facilitates the enhanced potential of social media users' virtual mobility.

The User Perspective

Global social media facilitate increased opportunities for communication; for example, music practitioners can use these services to get in touch with each other and their fans, and fans may link or communicate with bands. A band's MySpace or Facebook profile may include information about the band and upcoming concerts, the opportunity for fans to listen to the group's music and watch videos, and importantly, to link their own social media profile to the band's profile and become one of the band's 'friends.' The users may then receive information about the band and will be able to signal their musical taste and interest in the band to other users. In general, this also means users can present their lists of 'friends," and making one's online social network visible is what makes these services unique (boyd and Ellison, 2007). As with MySpace, Facebook and Twitter have increasingly become part of the music and global social media nexus, as many music practitioners have become adept at using the services. Furthermore, Facebook collaborates with, for example, the commercial online music streaming service, Spotify. Users of Facebook and Spotify may post playlists from the music service on their social media profiles. Also, bands and artists may embed videos and songs on their Facebook profiles, and fans can link their profiles to bands' profiles. While MySpace has been outperformed by Facebook, MySpace nevertheless led the way in facilitating an online environment with features that previous media and communications services lacked. These features were important for music practitioners and their take-up and use of these services.

The Corporate Perspective

The increasing number of social media users soon caught the attention of media and communications conglomerates. These large companies were searching for ways to generate profit within the online environment. Some believed that these services could help create a much sought after content synergy between the conglomerates' traditional media players (film, music, and television) and 'new media' ventures (the internet and mobile telephony). Investment by the largest media and communications companies allowed for the extensive development of the social media environment and improvement of their usability, as well as corporate collaboration and alliances, not least within the international music industry. The music industry soon sought to reach potential consumers of music among the millions of social media users. Furthermore, the self-disclosure of information by users on the millions of MySpace and Facebook profiles and their behavior and activity online are considered as having an enormous commercial potential. The services develop systems that target advertising according to the information provided by users. However, Facebook's efforts to map its users has regularly led to fierce protests.

The corporate and user perspectives, then, allow us to understand the role and functions of the components of the global social media and music nexus. As such, the approach resonates with the call for studies that take into account both macro perspectives and micro perspectives and combine the study of political economy of the media and the study of reception among media users. In the early 1990s, Morley called for a such nuanced approaches:

> Which can deal both with the global-local dynamic of these cultural processes at a substantive level, and with the need to articulate the micro- and macro-dimensions, so as to integrate more effectively our analyses of the domestic, the local, the national and the international aspects of communications. (Morley, 1991: 15)

A decade and a half later, a similar critique is found in Curran and Morley's call for the use of interdisciplinary approaches within media and communications research:

> Nowadays, some of the debates that characterised this field in the 1990s (. . .)—such as that between political economy and reception studies, concerning whether the Holy Grail was to be found in institutional structure of the media or in the conditions of their reception—do (happily) seem to have worn themselves out. (. . .) The business in hand is then how better to articulate the insights produced by these different perspectives. (Curran and Morley, 2006: 1)

The emergence of a global social media landscape and the global social media and music nexus allows us to respond to such calls.

It is the emergence of global social media and the music practitioners' activity within this new online space that challenges theoretical perspectives, particularly from a political economic tradition. While a preoccupation with uneven power and domination within the media and communications sector also extends to the online environment (Boyd-Barrett, 2006; Wasko and Erickson, 2009), the way the relationship between media and globalization has evolved has given rise to these new online spaces for media users.

The US media conglomerates and large players, for half a decade at the center of studies within international media and media globalization, have strong gate-keeping functions in their media content and services, and distribute similar media products and service offerings globally, all in line with a defined brand (Hamelink, 1983; Schiller, 1985; Roe and De Meyer, 2001; Chalaby, 2002; Katz, 2005; Mjos, 2010a). However, although the US continues to dominate the world's media market sales, strong national and regional television and media players coexist with global media outlets (Hafez, 2007; Straubhaar, 2007; Thussu, 2000/2006; 2005; 2007a). This has resulted in increased representation to local, national, and regional culture, voices, and society.

The music industry is also characterized by conglomeration. The sector is dominated by a handful of big corporations. In recent years, the 'big four' (Universal Music Group, Sony Music Entertainment, Warner Music Group, and EMI Group) control 70 to 80 percent of the global music recording market (Thussu, 2000/2006: 173; Wikström, 2009: 69). Three of these companies are again part of media conglomerates: NBC Universal, Sony, and Time Warner (Hesmondhalgh, 2007). However, as within the television industry, not all music companies are owned or controlled by the 'big four.' Numerous independent and smaller players operate both locally and internationally (Hesmondhalgh, 2007).

While global social media and the traditional global audiovisual operators such as CNN and Discovery Channel, as well as the majority of large music operators, originate from the US, share worldwide commercial ambitions, and are becoming part of—or are themselves evolving into—large media conglomerates, the peculiar logic of the global social media sets them apart as the social media rely entirely on the contributions of their users around the world. They are the key actors in the expansion, as well as contraction, of social media entities. The music practitioners in this book were also among numerous users across the world who switched from MySpace to Facebook—resulting in the growth of the latter. The internet therefore introduces to the media and communications landscape a logic (as exemplified by the nature of the global social media) characterized by less control, non-linearity, and a greater degree of unpredictability (Urry, 2003, 2007); however, as a consequence, the internet also increased the potential for virtual and communicative mobility for social media users (Elliott and Urry, 2010), i.e., music practitioners.

The corporate/user duality characterizing these global social media creates a paradox preoccupying both the industry and critics alike. Adam

Bain, EVP at Fox Interactive Media (part of News Corporation, the owner of MySpace), points out: "For users, MySpace is a platform for public self-expression. For advertisers, it's now a platform for understanding user behavior" (quoted in Kaplan, 2007). Similarly, Bell drew attention to this duality, pointing out that on the one hand, the possibilities for the individual user have "opened the door for many users to become producers, to write their own blog or build their own MySpace page" (2007: 5), but that on the other hand, one may consider user-generated content as "free media content that allows producers to express themselves but that ultimately benefits the entrepreneurs of this new dotcom economy (and as their sites are bought up by media conglomerates, worries about profit motives escalate)" (2007: 6).

This corporate/user duality is part of wider changes taking place within media and communications. Scholars are preoccupied with attempting to theoretically capture the role and significance of the 'new media' user through terms such as 'participatory culture' (Jenkins, 2006), 'produsage' (Bruns, 2008: 5) and 'mass self-communication' (Castells, 2009). Jenkins argues that 'participatory culture' describes the situation where "rather than talking about media producers and consumers as occupying separate roles, we might now see them as participants who interact with each other according to a new set of rules that none of us fully understands" (Jenkins, 2006: 3). The concept of 'produsage' attempts to describe a "move beyond the commonplace assumptions associated with traditional concepts of producers, products, and production, and to develop a systematic understanding of the processes, principles, and participants of produsage" (Bruns, 2008: 5). And Castells' concept of 'mass self-communication' aims to describe the "new form of interactive communication (that) has emerged" that is both 'mass communication' and 'self-communication' (2009: 55). In contrast to traditional mass communication that is 'one-directional,' internet users can "potentially reach a global audience, as in the posting of a video on YouTube" and at the same time "it is self-communication because the production of the messages is self-generated" (Castells, 2009: 55).

Global social media is at the heart of the development these scholars address. The study of the global social media and music nexus, the development of these services, and their collaborations with the music industry, along with electronic music practitioners' take-up and use of them, aims to contribute to the body of work on the development of these services in relation to the discourse on media and globalization.

3 The Emergence of the Global Social Media Environment
MySpace, Facebook, YouTube

In less than a decade, a global social media environment has evolved within the media and communications landscape. Since the turn of the millennium, a plethora of local, national, regional, and global social media and networking services have come to populate the online milieu, where they compete and coexist, grow and fade. This chapter explores the political, economic, technological, and cultural tendencies and factors influential in the development of this environment. It shows how the global social media services MySpace and Facebook, along with YouTube and Twitter, have exploited the factors associated with media globalization—the increased linking and intertwining of the global media and communications landscape—to expand. The chapter, then, traces key general developments underpinning the global social media and music nexus from a corporate perspective.

Throughout these formative years, the take-up and time spent on social media have increased across the world. In the year from December 2008, the general use of social media services, the most used being Facebook, Twitter, and MySpace, increased with an average of 82 percent in the US, UK, Australia, Brazil, Japan, Switzerland, Germany, France, Spain, and Italy (Nielsen Online, 2009, 2010a). This development has continued, according to market research company Nielsen. Internet users across 10 countries spent around five and a half hours a month on social networks such as Facebook, Twitter, and MySpace, in February 2010. Although the American online environment has the largest number of unique social network users, internet users in Italy and Australia spent most time on such online services that month (Table 3.1).

By 2010, according to market research company Nielsen, the overall time spent on social media services had increased generally, and the largest amount of time by far was spent using Facebook (see Table 3.2).

This chapter first examines the surfacing of social media within the US media and communications landscape in the late 1990s and early 2000s. It then explores MySpace's pioneering efforts to expand internationally in the mid-2000s, followed by Facebook, along with Twitter's rollout, through to 2010. Through localization strategies, these global entities aim to anchor

Table 3.1   Social Network Usage by Country; February 2010 (Home and Work)

Country	Time per person (hh: mm: ss)
Average	5:27:33
Italy	6:27:53
Australia	6:25:21
United States	6:02:34
United Kingdom	5:50:56
Spain	4:50:49
Brazil	4:27:54
France	4:12:01
Germany	3:47:24
Switerland*	3:26:00
Japan	2:37:07

*Home only
(*Data source:* Nielsen Online, 2010b)

Table 3.2   Global* Social Network Traffic; February 2010

Website	Sessions per person	Time per person (hh: mm: ss)
Facebook	19.16	5:52:00
MySpace.com	6.66	0:59:33
Twitter.com	5.81	0:36:43
LinedIn	3.15	0:12:47
Classmates Online	3.29	0:13:55

*United States, Brazil, Australia, Japan, France, Germany, Italy, Spain, Switzerland, and United Kingdom.
Unique audience represents active usage, not overall membership of social networks.
(*Data source:* Nielsen Online, 2010b)

themselves in local culture among internet users to reduce corporate risk and create more stable and predictable conditions for corporate activity within the global online environment. However, the global social media's different approaches to localization and personalization help explain why

Facebook in recent years has become the world's most used social media and Twitter has experienced rapid growth, while MySpace is struggling both financially and in its ability to keep and attract users.

THE RISE OF GLOBAL SOCIAL MEDIA

The digitization process and a maturing online environment cause uncertainty and opportunities for traditional media organizations. Digitization revolutionized the possibility of and capacity for the production and distribution of media content. In Europe, this has led to a dramatic rise in the number of local, national, and regional television channels and media outlets targeting the culturally and linguistically varied and distinct parts of the region. By 2010 there were more than 6,500 television channels in the European Union and candidate countries (Mavise, 2010). At the same time, regional centers for film and television production have developed outside Europe and the US. Now, news and entertainment satellite television channels originating outside the Western world create media contraflows. ICTs such as broadband, mobile telephony, and the internet have—in addition to facilitating new possibilities for communication—given rise to numerous new audiovisual distribution possibilities through video-on-demand, online video streaming, and downloading of professional as well as user-generated media content (Thussu, 2000/2006, 2007a; Castells, 2004, 2009; Goggin, 2006; Arsenault and Castells, 2008).

Out of these transformations, new forms of media and communications entities and services have emerged and, in the mid-2000s, particularly within the online environment. While many of the online outlets are extensions of traditional media such as newspapers and television channels, there was a striking emergence of a particular kind of internet-based online service and enterprise. As this chapter shows, News Corp's willingness to pay $580 million for MySpace was considered by many as something more than a conventional acquisition. It represented a major corporate response to the ongoing changes within the sector and was part of the resurgent commercial belief in the internet. The social media phenomenon began to move into the mainstream as the acquisition was widely reported in the international mainstream press, and the financial sector and analysts embraced these new online media forms. Several of these new online-based players became popular and valuable, strengthening belief in the financial potential of the online environment. This helped reignite corporate investment that had more or less vanished since the dotcom bubble burst at the turn of the millennium, not least among traditional media and communications companies, seeking to position themselves to commercially exploit the online milieu. As a result of these developments, together with the rise of the internet search engines Google and Yahoo!, social media such as MySpace, Facebook, Twitter, and the video-sharing service YouTube have in a short time become part of everyday life for users of the internet across the world.

An Emerging Social Media Environment: Politics, Technology, Economics

Although people had already started creating an 'online identity' in the mid-1980s, using aliases to identify themselves on electronic message boards on the WELL (Whole Earth 'Lectronic Link) (Rheingold, 1993/2000), the development of what we today refer to as the internet increasingly facilitated the creation of more advanced 'online identities,' or personas. GeoCities, launched in 1994, allowed for users to develop free web pages "describing themselves through photos and text, and by affiliating themselves with groups of like-minded people." The year after, the dating service Match.com was launched with personal profiles (Angwin, 2009: 51). Sixdegrees.com, the early social networking site launched in 1997, let users develop profiles and list their friends, and the year after allowed them to surf friends' lists. While the idea of a profile already existed and some services had lists of friends, although not accessible to other users, boyd and Ellison point out that "Sixdegrees.com was the first to combine these features" (2007). However Sixdegrees.com was "ahead of its time," according to its founder, A. Weinreich (quoted in boyd and Ellison, 2007). While Sixdegrees.com attracted "millions of users," boyd and Ellison point out that the majority of them lacked "extended networks of friends who were online. Early adopters complained that there was little to do after accepting friend requests, and most users were not interested in meeting strangers" (2007). However, between 1997 and 2001 a number of 'community tools,' originating outside the US, began to appear online. Cyworld was launched in Korea in 1999 and included social network functions in 2001. In 2000, LunarStorm, a Swedish online community, included social network functions (see detailed figure in boyd and Ellison, 2007). However, as boyd and Ellison emphasize, the three services Friendster, MySpace, and Facebook were particularly important for the social media environment, as they influenced both the internet industry and research (2007).

Friendster launched in 2002. While most such sites were preoccupied with allowing people to be introduced to others they did not know, but with shared interests, Friendster differed, as "it was designed to help friends-of-friends meet" (boyd and Ellison, 2007). Furthermore, Friendster allowed for users' internet personas and profiles to be connected and become part of "an understandable context—the context of their friends" (Angwin, 2009: 51).

While it could be difficult to attract visitors to ordinary websites, Friendster allowed members to link their online identities and thereby create an audience for each other. As a consequence, Angwin argues, "Friendster was inadvertedly [sic] building a more powerful network" (2009: 51). However, the popularity of Friendster began to fade for several reasons. One of them was the appearance of 'Fakesters'—people who created aliases that were Friendster personas different to their real-life identity (boyd and Ellison, 2007; Angwin, 2009). The owners of Friendster did not like this and discouraged it. There were protests among 'Fakesters' and Friendster users. In contrast, MySpace, launched in 2003, welcomed aliases and 'Fakesters' (boyd and Ellison, 2007; Angwin, 2009). Another reason for the gradual demise of Friendster was, according to Tom Anderson, co-founder of MySpace, a rumor that Friendster would start to charge money from members. This also led to protests, and Friendster users distributed messages that promoted the idea of joining other services such as MySpace (boyd and Ellison, 2007).

MySpace had launched in 2003 and quickly became popular, especially among young people, for a number of reasons. In contrast to Friendster and other existing social network services, MySpace welcomed teenagers, facilitated more advanced personalization of user profiles, and grew rapidly outside the attention of mainstream press throughout 2004. The service soon acquired a status for being popular, and "one particularly notable group that encouraged others to switch were indie-rock bands who were expelled from Friendster for failing to comply with profile regulations" (boyd and Ellison, 2007). MySpace appealed to young people that had not been members of Friendster. Many joined to "connect with their favorite bands" and "as teens began signing up, they encouraged their friends to join. Rather than rejecting underage users, MySpace changed its user policy to allow minors" (boyd and Ellison, 2007). In addition, there were technological developments that MySpace could exploit. MySpace appeared at a time when broadband became affordable not only for adults but also for younger people. This, together with higher data capacity, allowed users to include more pictures on their MySpace profiles (Angwin, 2009: 59).

MySpace experienced explosive growth. In 2005, around a quarter of a million amateur and professional bands had created profiles to promote their music; halfway through the year, the service had close to 30 million members. At the time, these users spent on average more than triple the time on MySpace as users of Facebook, and five times more than users of Friendster. MySpace's young users, many between the ages of 16 and 24, were extremely attractive to advertisers but difficult to reach through newspapers and television. In addition, it cost nothing to create a profile and use the MySpace network, nor was any subscription fee required (Bruno, 2005; News Corp, 2005; Siklos, 2005; Naughton, 2006; La Monica, 2009). MySpace's usability and increasing popularity among young people and its potential as a vehicle for advertising caught News Corporations attention.

In the same year, 2005, YouTube was officially launched. The video-sharing service was adopted by a vast number of internet users and was soon branding itself as the "the world's most popular online video community" (Wasko and Erickson, 2009: 373). Along with a number of competing web-based video services, YouTube aimed "to remove the technical barriers to the widespread sharing of video online," as the service allowed users to "upload, publish, and view streaming videos without high levels of technical knowledge, and within the technological constraints of standard browser software and relatively modest bandwidth" (Burgess and Green, 2009: 1). By late 2005, YouTube was the most well-known service among a group of web-based services that hosted videos, according to the technology online news site, Techcrunch (Arrington, 2005a).

There were a number of reasons for YouTube's growing popularity. YouTube was free to use and users could upload as many videos as they liked on the service, in different formats. Techcrunch pointed out that "YouTube converts video to a Flash format, and therefore upload and playback is extremely fast. In our tests, videos uploaded significantly faster than in other services" (Arrington, 2005a). In addition, YouTube not only "offered basic community functions such as the opportunity to link to other users as friends" but also, importantly, "provided URLs and HTML codes that enabled videos to be easily embedded into other websites, a feature that capitalized on the recent introduction of popularly accessible blogging technologies" (Burgess and Green, 2009: 1). This feature was particularly popular among MySpace users, including bands and artists, and it helped create a relationship or symbiosis between YouTube and MySpace in this early phase. This contributed to the growth of both: "YouTube was the equivalent of Photobucket. Since MySpace didn't have the capacity to store videos, many MySpace users stored their online videos on YouTube and provided a link to the YouTube videos on their MySpace profiles. At the time, YouTube was just six months old and displaying three million videos per day" (Angwin, 2009: 187). The popularity of both MySpace and YouTube among internet users grew rapidly, and this development contributed to renewed interest in internet-based companies from investors.

The Corporatization of Social Media

Media conglomerates spent enormous sums of money on various internet ventures and entities during the end of the 1990s. At the turn of the millennium, most of these investments proved to be far less lucrative than initially thought. The dotcom bubble burst, as the unrealistically high value of internet-based enterprises plummeted. Similarly, such "speculative boom(s)" have been observed throughout history from tulipomania in the Netherlands in the 1630s to financial crashes on Wall Street. Such crashes are the result of "speculative investment [that] has risen like a rocket and come down again like a stick" (Lister et al, 2009: 188). This was certainly the case with numerous internet-based companies or dotcoms as the

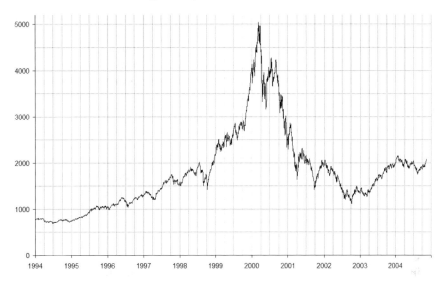

Figure 3.1 NASDAQ—dot-com bubble.

technology-heavy Nasdaq stock exchange, in which many such companies were listed, rose and dropped at dramatic speed (Figure 3.1).

Why did this happen? In hindsight commentators point out that throughout the 1990s and beginning of the 2000s, some investment funds tempted customers with 100 percent returns on investments. However, such "promise was based on little more than enthusiasm and technophilic passion—very few direct consumer service providers were able to demonstrate that their sites could actually maintain secure income streams" (Lister et al, 2009: 188). Furthermore, people began to realize that the development of 'net retailing' would take both time and considerable investment, in contrast to the speculative approach that led to the dotcom crash in 2000 and 2001 (Curran and Seaton, 2010: 271). Some even pointed to this at the time of the dotcom boom: "What makes many internet company valuations baffling for seasoned observers is that many have yet to make a profit, and show little sign of ever doing so" (Hunt, 1999).

The major media companies took part in the dotcom frenzy. Between mid-1999 and the beginning of 2001, News Corp invested a reported £1.3 billion in internet projects (Milmo, 2001). A major joint venture between News Corp and website Healtheon/WebMD was formed in 2000. News Corp provided $700 million in media services, but the collaboration was disbanded the same year. News Corp's decision to move the production of the websites Foxnews.com, Foxsports.com, and Fox.com away from its US internet unit, News Digital Media, to the control of the traditional homes of these brands, was described by the *BBC* as "a nail in the coffin of

News Corp's internet strategy" (BBC, 2001). Similarly, other media giants' early online ventures proved expensive. Disney acquired the internet search engine, Infoseek, and changed and rebranded it into the internet portal Go Network (www.go.com). Launched in 1998, the company hoped that Go Network would generate $350 million per year, but the portal did not manage to attract an audience and was closed in 2001. In total, Disney lost $790 million on the Go Network operation (Blevins, 2004). Perhaps the most spectacular casualty of the dotcom crash was AOL's (formerly America Online) acquisition of Time Warner. The internet service provider AOL bought the traditional media conglomerate Time Warner for more than $150 billion in 2000. This deal became a symbol of the new era as it represented the merger of the 'new' and the 'old' as underlined by Stephen M. Case, a co-founder of AOL: "This is a historic moment in which new media has truly come of age" (quoted in Arango, 2010). However, as the dotcom bubble burst, the value of the new company AOL Time Warner diminished at dramatic speed (Arango, 2009). Again, in hindsight, some argue that the merger between AOL and Time Warner was "driven by the manoeuvres of the financial markets" and not the demands among the media audience and consumers: "Despite looking like the Holy Grail this particular example of corporate convergence became more of a poisoned chalice—falling victim at least in part to the disillusion with digital media that followed the dotcom crash" (Lister et al, 2009: 204).

Media conglomerates, then, were not untouched by these developments. These internet investments were partly to blame for the subsequent reorganization of companies like AOL Time Warner and Vivendi (Curran and Seaton, 2010: 271). However, seen in a historical perspective, the internet economy did not disappear for good as "history remained on its side" (Hartley, 2002: 77). The escalating enthusiasm for the internet and the subsequent dotcom bubble and crash has numerous historical parallels. Key events in the development of the transport sector such as the railways in the 1850s and later the arrival of cars in the 1920s "were both followed by horrific stock market collapses in the US, but neither railways nor automobiles went away" (Hartley, 2002, 77, 78). In the long run, then, Hartley predicted that the technological innovations underpinning the development of the internet will result in a viable industry sector (2002: 78).

By the mid-2000s, new and expanding internet companies had yet again become increasingly visible in the US and throughout the world. Traditional media companies were cautious, but many, including News Corp, were once again enticed to invest enormous sums in internet entities, afraid of losing out on the strategic and financial potential of the internet. News Corp's and other traditional media companies' resurgent interest in internet companies in the mid-2000s is ascribed to the rise of one particular internet-based phenomenon: Google. Google's idea of selling advertising linked to internet searches was key to legitimizing the internet as a medium for attracting advertising on a large scale (Kafka, 2007; La Monica, 2009).

Google's advertising revenue increased dramatically in a very short time—from around $70 million in 2001 to around $1.4 billion in 2003 (Google, 2009). The global internet search engine went public in August 2004, and only a few months after the public launch, the market value of Google surpassed that of News Corp. The following year, the Google enterprise was considered more valuable than the traditional media conglomerates Walt Disney and Time Warner (La Monica, 2009). Although the rapid escalation of the value of internet entities mirrored the late 1990s, their seemingly viable advertising business model and large number of existing users could now more easily justify the valuation of these companies (Croteau and Hoynes, 2006; Schifferes, 2006).

The same year that Google was listed on Nasdaq, the term Web 2.0 was launched. This was to become the buzzword epitomizing the revival of the internet, fronted by Google. Web 2.0, generally claimed to have first appeared at the Web 2.0 Conference, organized by O'Reilly Media in San Francisco, US, in 2004, was partly launched in an attempt to revive business and financial interest in the web (Web 2.0 Conference, 2004; O'Reilly, 2005). O'Reilly Media, founded by Tim O'Reilly, published books, organized conferences, and provided online services. The emergence of Google and its technological characteristics did not go unnoticed by Tim O'Reilly. In his Web 2.0 manifesto, *What is Web 2.0?* (2005), O'Reilly pointed explicitly to how Google signified the new era of the web, and the web browser Netscape represented the old: "If Netscape was the standard bearer for Web 1.0, Google is most certainly the standard bearer for Web 2.0." O'Reilly attached the term Web 2.0 to one of the most significant internet technology-related inventions to date. The Google phenomenon certainly served the interest of both technological, financial, and political stakeholders—strengthening belief in the internet after the dotcom crisis (Mjøs et al, 2010).

At the time of the skyrocketing of Google and the launch of the Web 2.0 term, Rupert Murdoch, the powerful chairman of News Corp, along with several competing media conglomerates, again wanted to join the apparently lucrative internet:

> It was clear, three or four years ago, that there was a lot happening on the internet, and revenues were going there. So we thought we'd better get in there pretty fast and look for opportunities. So we looked around at a lot of things and rejected most of them as too expensive or limited in their capacity to expand. And then we found MySpace. (Murdoch, 2008)

The rise of Google, Yahoo!, and other popular advertising-based internet companies based on promising new technology were therefore key in restoring the belief in the financial potential of the internet (Schifferes, 2006; La Monica, 2009). All the major media conglomerates plunged into costly new

Table 3.3   Acquisitions of Social Media

Year of Acquisition	Social Media	Acquiring Company	Price (in millions)
2005	MySpace	News Corp	$580 (est.)
2006	YouTube	Google	$1.650
2007	Facebook	Microsoft	$240 (1.6 percent)
2008	Bebo	AOL/Time Warner	$850

(*Data sources*: Google.com, 2006; Stone, 2007c; Angwin, 2009, Sabbagh, 2008.)

internet ventures, rushing to acquire certain internet properties, and in the second half of the 2000s, the social media and networks in particular (see Table 3.3). Services like MySpace, Facebook, and YouTube, or websites that facilitated the building of online communities, were particularly attractive as investors hoped to be able to "translate potential captive audiences into advertising revenue" (Wasko and Erickson, 2009: 378).

In 2005, News Corp bought MySpace for around $580 million dollars. In the run-up to the acquisition, Viacom and its MTV Networks were also interested in MySpace. Viacom and its global media youth brand saw the social media as a potentially vital part of their digital strategy, but eventually lost out to News Corp in a bidding war (Angwin, 2009). On 9 October 2006, Google announced its acquisition of YouTube. The deal was worth $1.65 billion. Internet users viewed around 100 million videos on YouTube per day, and this motivated Google's acquisition (Wasko and Erickson, 2009: 378). In 2007, Disney acquired Club Penguin, a virtual world for children with nearly a million paying users, for up to $700 million. Facebook, with roughly 15 million monthly visitors in mid-2006, generated interest—and offers—from both Viacom and Yahoo! that year, but Facebook declined both (Wasko and Erickson, 2009: 377). Still, in 2007, Microsoft paid $240 million for 1.6 percent ownership of Facebook—an investment valuing Facebook at $15 billion (Stone, 2007c). The year after, Time Warner paid $850 million in cash for Bebo, the third largest social internet network in the US, with more than 40 million users worldwide (Olson, 2008; Sabbagh, 2008).

The investment made by Microsoft and consequently the estimations of Facebook's total value also had wider consequences for valuation estimates of MySpace and the global social media phenomena in general. An Equity Research Report from Credit Suisse, the international financial services group, gives insight into the financial sector's reflection on the value of these suddenly emerging online entities:

> Outlook: Despite the strong growth Facebook is achieving internationally, MySpace remains very dominant in the US. The growth in

both platforms over the past two years suggests growth in the social networking phenomenon rather than cannibalization. (Credit Suisse, 2007: 1)

Therefore, Credit Suisse argued, if Facebook was valued at $15 billion, MySpace was worth far more than the sum News Corp. had paid to acquire it. This, the international financial services' group argued, should be reflected in the value of News Corp. Still, Credit Suisse questioned whether the acquisition of a small share, just 1.6 percent, of Facebook could be a yardstick or represent a precise measure of the value of the whole company. A valuation of $15 billion equals $204 per unique Facebook user, and such a valuation would have implications for MySpace and News Corp: "Applying the same value per unique user to MySpace would give a value for MySpace of close to $22bn or $8.28 per NWS share" (see Table 3.4).

The sum of nearly $22 billion stands in stark contrast to the $580 million acquisition of MySpace (Credit Suisse, 2007: 4). These enormous figures, and Credit Suisse's difficulty in reaching precise valuations, show how the financial sector grappled with assessing economically the global social media phenomenon.

Viacom's $160 million acquisition of the online game for children, NeoPets.com, with nearly 25 million members in 2005, and Disney's acquisition of the game developer Playdom in 2010, for up to $763 million, gives further proof of the belief in the financial potential of online services catering to a wide range of customer communities. The last acquisition also shows how global social media and social game services are becoming integrated. Playdom creates a range of game titles for Apple's iPhone, MySpace, and Facebook (Boston Globe, 2005; Disney, 2010).

In the years around the MySpace acquisition in 2005, News Corp. reportedly spent more than $1 billion on internet-related investments (Kafka, 2007; Angwin, 2009). With these investments, and in particular MySpace, Rupert Murdoch pointed out that his company "has begun to rival and in some cases surpass the internet elite" (2006). News Corp. and MySpace managements considered the online service to be a key digital media and communications entity for helping News Corp. extend its power in the online environment, where so many media companies had failed previously. It was believed that MySpace could expand globally

Table 3.4   Facebook and MySpace Implied Valuation

	Valuation ($M)	Unique users (M)	Value/unique user ($)
Facebook	15,000	73.5	204
MySpace	21,834	107.0	204

(*Data source:* Credit Suisse, 2007.)

online attracting millions of young users whose profiles could then be sold to advertisers. News Corp also thought it was possible to generate online traffic from MySpace to the company's other internet entities, and, importantly, there were hopes for synergy between MySpace and the company's traditional media holdings, such as television programming and films (BBC, 2005; Scott-Joynt, 2005; Angwin, 2009; La Monica, 2009; Maney, 2009).

Around 2006 then, MySpace, Facebook, and YouTube all wanted to expand beyond the US. However, these plans for expansion were only implemented after News Corp took control of MySpace in 2005. Similarly, as we shall see later in this chapter, Facebook's growth overseas intensified after the investments from Microsoft, in 2007.

The Global Expansion and Localization of MySpace

As News Corp took over MySpace, Rupert Murdoch expressed global aspirations for MySpace. He wanted to create an online 'global portal' for young people, according to Angwin (2009: 231). Such ambitions should not come as a surprise. News Corp is the only traditional media conglomerate that does not originate in the US. It has therefore always had a more global outlook than other media conglomerates and is described as "one of the most developed examples of a global media strategy" (Croteau and Hoynes, 2006: 139, 140). Similarly, media scholar Turow suggests that executives of the company would claim that "News Corporation has globalization in its genes" (2009: 241). Despite the references to 'global' media companies, it is important to keep in mind how "the centre of gravity of each of these companies is in the developed world. More than that, it is clearly in the USA" (Sparks, 2007: 144). Still, while the US remains the most important market for the major media conglomerates, the share of News Corp's turnover derived from the US is the lowest among them. In 2005, 54 percent of News Corp's turnover came from the company's operations in the US, while as much as 78 percent and 79 percent of Viacom and Time Warner's, respectively, were made in the US (Sparks, 2007: 143).

One could say that MySpace was already 'global' due to its online presence. In 2005, the number of internet users had already reached more than a billion (Clickz, 2005). In theory, any user could access websites such as MySpace. In contrast, at the time Facebook was only open to students at Harvard and a few other universities. However, just as with traditional commercial media outlets, it is the actual number of subscribers and measurable viewers or users that is crucial for commercial media business models to work. MySpace could document the numbers creating profiles on MySpace, as well as the number of visits to the web service. This made the service particularly attractive. Still, MySpace's rapid growth, followed by Facebook's overtaking of MySpace as the world's most used social media, underlines the volatility characterizing the social media environment.

Therefore, these services have attempted to affix themselves among their users and audiences through catering for their local culture and language. Their localization programs aim to create the links between the local and the expanding social media that are required to conduct corporate activity. Furthermore, MySpace, and in particular Facebook, users' opportunities for personalizing their profiles show how the service creates a link between the individual user and the expanding entity.

Despite the difference between global television and the internet, there are several corporate lessons to be learned from the traditional media players and brands. Just as within the television sector, the social media landscape is characterized by the negotiation between the global and the national or local: between globalizing trends and the specific interests of culturally and linguistically diverse markets. Similar to the television channels MTV, Discovery Channel, and CNN that have been able to secure a worldwide presence since the 1990s, the most ambitious social media rolled out through regional or country-specific versions. While localization is also the key strategy of the expanding social media, their approach to localization differs in several respects. The possibilities for swift and detailed localization within the online environment, in the case of Twitter and Facebook with the help of thousands of social media users, are unprecedented. Furthermore, when users log on to global social media, they enter their personal version of the service consisting of their personal profile placed within the network of their friends' profiles. This, along with the ability to localize, helps explain the rapid expansion and adoption of the largest social media.

News Corp is no stranger to localization. The company's pan-Asian television network, STAR (Satellite Television Asian Region), has 330 million viewers for its 50+ television services in seven languages across 53 Asian countries. In India, STAR's popularity and reach are ascribed to localization strategies. The television network has "skillfully prioritized the local over the global" by incorporating local content, using Indian languages, and promoting the network's closeness to the Indian nation (Thussu, 2007b: 596). Similar to STAR, MySpace decided to launch regional or country-specific versions. Chris DeWolfe, co-founder of MySpace, expressed the need for such an approach soon after News Corp took over the service: "The idea behind internationalization is localization" (DeWolfe, quoted in Levine, 2006b). While global television channels took decades to localize their services across large parts of the world, MySpace expanded at unprecedented speed. Within only a six-month period, between June 2006 and January 2007, MySpace launched services in the UK, Ireland, Australia, France, Germany, Japan, Spain, and Italy, and aimed to have a presence in 28 countries by 2008 (Barrett, 2007; News Corp, 2007; Angwin, 2009).

As MySpace began to expand its services throughout the 2000s, Facebook started to plan overseas expansion through localization as well. Facebook, allowing the wider public to join the service in 2006, was by 2007 the second largest social media in the US after MySpace, but having become the most popular social media in other English-speaking countries including Canada, Facebook also began to translate its service into non-English languages. The localization plan was, according to *Financial Times,* an attempt to "capitalise on the explosive growth." (Allison and Van Duyn, 2007) Furthermore, Facebook had caught the interest of Microsoft, which was considering investing in social media. The computer software giant decided to invest in Facebook later in 2007. This meant that MySpace and Facebook were backed by two of the biggest players in the global media and communications industry. Facebook's plan for international expansion was also motivated by the growing interest in these kinds of services across the world, not least by MySpace's early expansion efforts.

The first localized version of MySpace was a UK version. The UK, and London in particular, has historically been a bridgehead for expanding US-originated media companies. American cable and satellite television channels launching pan-European networks have benefited not only from the UK's liberal media regulatory regime and the well-developed media and related service sector, but also from the fact that the European headquarters of large multinational advertising clients and agencies have traditionally been based in London (Flynn, 1992; Tunstall and Machin, 1999: 72). After setting up its first overseas office in London, MySpace expanded throughout the rest of Europe. MySpace's European managing director, David Fisher, emphasized how MySpace aimed to be a global brand that "engages with its users on a local level," and it was focused on creating "more content tailored to European users" (Fisher, quoted in Sweney, 2006). However, despite the localization efforts and the aim of creating "local communities, with local staff and local music," Fisher points out that the "users are still plugged into the MySpace global community" (Fisher, quoted in Levine, 2006a). This underlines the corporate preoccupation with localization and shows how a expanding media company wishes to communicate its concern for the local. Still, despite such sentiments, just as with localization of global television channels, the localization of global social media 'accelerates the process of globalization' as global media enterprises are able to operate cross-nationally despite national cultural differences. The global players can thereby establish themselves in a number of markets and compete with national television and media outlets (Chalaby, 2002: 199).

The degree of MySpace's early localization varied, but the front page of a localized version of MySpace was usually in a national specific language, and the content often featured national and local bands and artists. In Europe, MySpace collaborated with the local music, film, and fashion sectors, and new launches of localized MySpace portals were accompanied by concerts and collaboration with local radio and television shows. Although the west European versions that launched throughout Europe in 2006 were localized in terms of language and some content, the MySpace concept did not differ very much from the original American version. However, local differences in territories outside the US and Europe posed other kinds of challenges for MySpace, according to the newspaper *The Wall Street Journal*. In India and parts of Latin America, the capacity of internet connections is often limited. The MySpace versions in these territories must therefore be less technically advanced. Furthermore, a version of MySpace in Hebrew would need to take into account that the language is read from right to left (Vascellaro, 2008). The expansion into these territories may not be profitable in the short term, but the service is "placing strategic bets" for the long term, according to Travis Katz, International Managing Director of MySpace (Katz, quoted in Vascellaro, 2008).

In China, MySpace applied a more extensive form of localization: "We have to make MySpace a very Chinese site," Rupert Murdoch said in 2006. "I have sent my wife across there because she understands the language" (Murdoch, quoted in Van Duyn and Chaffin, 2006). News Corp has tried for decades to secure a strong presence particularly within the Chinese television industry, and Murdoch's wife, Wendy Deng, has an important role as the company aims to establish MySpace China. Deng is Director of MySpace China Holdings Limited (MySpace China)—a joint venture of which News Corp owns 51.5 percent. MySpace China "licenses the technology and brand to the local company in China that operates the MySpace China website" (News Corp, 2008: 125).

Around the same time as MySpace began to roll out overseas, YouTube launched its localization program, also at a fast pace. In 2007, the year after Google acquired YouTube, the video-sharing service announced that it was to create 'local versions' of YouTube for countries like Ireland, Brazil, France, Italy, Japan, Netherlands, Poland, Spain, and the UK. First, the country-specific sites would be translated into local homepages, and at a later stage, localization would include a range of additional country-specific functions: "With our announcement today we are expanding upon our already global platform to make it even more relevant for our local communities," said YouTube co-founder and CEO Chad Hurley. As part of the localization plans, YouTube formed partnerships with public and commercial television and media content producers in these countries. These included BBC (UK), France 24 (France), Antena 3 (Spain), RTP (Portugal), and VPRO (Netherlands) (Errity, 2007). By the end of 2007, YouTube had launched in 14 different language versions (Nicole, 2007).

The early global expansion efforts of MySpace clearly mirror some of the aspects of the way the global television players have approached localization, and how global media have come to coexist and compete with national and regional players. From the late 1990s, the European television industry saw a rapid increase in television channels. This also included a growth in 'proximate television'—regional and local television channels adapting to Europe's cultural, linguistic, political, demographic, and geographic diversity (De Moragas Spa and Lopez, 2000: 43). As a result of competitors launching local imitations toward the second half of the 1990s, the American thematic cable and satellite television channels were forced to localize and adapt to diverse local audiences (Chalaby, 2002: 192).

While the global television channels dub or subtitle programming into different languages, the popularity of global television formats marked the arrival of a more extensive form of localization. As with global television channels, these program forms have an ability to travel across the world while appealing to local or national cultural specificities. However, the local or national cultural content is inserted into a defined and copyrighted global television format concept: "Domestic producers can incorporate local color and global audiences can paradoxically feel at home when watching them. Locality needs to be evicted so it can be reintroduced as long as it does not alter the basic concept" (Waisbord, 2004: 378). Still, while global television channels can only adjust to local preferences—at least in smaller television markets—television formats represent an unprecedented localization within the television industry.

MySpace's relationship with localization has both similarities and differences to global television channels and formats. They are all global media services that attempt to exploit the connection between the local and the service. They show how global cultural producers reach "differentiated global market" through the "strategy of glocalisation" (Robertson, 1995: 40) However, a central difference between global social media and global television lies in their treatment of the local and the space they give to cultural and linguistic expression. As with global television channels, the logic of formats limits the possibilities for local input, as "copyright holders ultimately determine what changes can be incorporated; they remain 'the author' of the text despite a variety of national adaptations and audiences' interpretations" (Waisbord, 2004: 380). However, while MySpace and Facebook do set the rules and decide the possibilities of action within the services, the speed and extensive language localization is unprecedented. In fact, these services rely on the users in various localities across the world as providers of the service's content. However, as the next section shows, the global social media's choice of localization strategy differs. This helps explain why Facebook and Twitter have been able to reach and tailor their services to so many different localities around the world and outperform both MySpace and several national social media.

The Battle for 'World Domination': MySpace vs. Facebook

In 2006, the same year MySpace started to localize, Facebook opened up to the public. Facebook's increased popularity and use grew at an astonishing rate. The international press showed its preoccupation with the competition with stories such as *Is Facebook the New MySpace?* (*PC World*, Sullivan, 2007) and *As Facebook Takes Off, MySpace Strikes Back* (CNN.com, Kirkpatrick, 2007). In fact, since announcing News Corp's acquisition of MySpace in 2005, to Facebook's dominant position in 2010, the two social media have been protagonists in press coverage of the emergence of the global social phenomenon. The press' portrayal of the two social media and competition between them have served as a narrative device introducing social media to a wider public beyond technologically oriented audiences. 'MySpace vs. Facebook' represented a battle between Rupert Murdoch, perhaps the world's most powerful media mogul, and Mark Zuckerberg, a young industry outsider.

When starting out, the member policy of the two services differed. While MySpace was open to the public to join when launching in 2003, Facebook was first only open to students at Harvard, then gradually to students at Yale, Stanford, and Columbia University in 2004. At the time, *Harvard Crimson*, the Harvard student newspaper, described Facebook as a very modest startup operation. The founder of Facebook, Mark Zuckerberg, paid $85 per month for using servers and was quoted as saying, "It might be nice in the future to get some ads going to offset the cost of the servers" (Schneider, 2004). In 2006, as Facebook opened its service to users outside colleges and universities, the mainstream press followed developments closely. By reducing its restrictions for membership, Facebook was aiming to "compete more directly with bigger rival MySpace," according to the British newspaper *The Guardian* (Sweney, 2006). Soon after opening, Facebook became popular with internet users, and its growth rate outpaced MySpace (Table 3.5).

This development continued into 2008 as Facebook's popularity escalated. Still, in mid-2008, MySpace had the most users in the US—76 million—but Facebook increased its user base to around 55 million in the US that year. While MySpace had more users than Facebook in the US in 2008, Facebook had far more users outside the US. MySpace had 125 million users across the world, while Facebook had 222 million at the end of 2008. This dramatic shift happened in just a few years (Arrington, 2009a, 2009b).

However, by 2008, the global social media environment was populated not only by MySpace and Facebook. At the time, the two giants co-existed with a plethora of smaller regional, national, and local social media. In Germany, the network Studivz.net proved popular. Hives was a popular national social media in the Netherlands, and in Poland the adoption of the service Grono increased. Hi5 had become popular in countries in Latin America and Europe, and Friendster and Cyworld had been taken up in

Table 3.5   Facebook Growth Outpaces MySpace (Unique Audience in Millions)

	2006 October	2007 October	Change
MySpace	49,516	58,843	19%
Facebook	8,682	19,519	125%

(Adapted from Fortt, 2007.)

parts of Pacific Asia. Orkut was popular in both Latin America and Pacific Asia (Le Monde, 2008). Still, MySpace was the first social medium to implement major global localization strategies.

Despite MySpace's aggressive expansion and preoccupation with localization, in 2007 and 2008 the service began to reduce its operations in parts of Europe and Asia. Due to reduced financial growth globally and bleaker prospects for advertising revenue, as well as severe local competition in some places, local MySpace offices in the Netherlands, Poland, Norway, and South Korea closed down. In early 2008, less than a year after opening, the MySpace office in the Netherlands closed. The day-to-day handling of MySpace Netherlands was transferred to the Berlin office in Germany. MySpace had reportedly attracted an additional 250,000 users after opening the local office, attracting a total of 650,000 users in the Netherlands. However, MySpace was dwarfed by Hives, the national Dutch social media service that claimed to have more than 5 million registered users in the country (Wauters, 2008). MySpace opened an office in Norway in mid-2006 due to the rapid rise in users, particularly music bands. At the time, around 30,000 Norwegian-based music artists and bands were registered on MySpace. However, in March 2009 this office was also closed down as part of a larger international restructuring and centralization of MySpace. This was also partly due to the global financial situation and reduced potential for advertising revenue. A Nordic regional office took over the control of MySpace Norway. The portal continued to be in the Norwegian language, but without providing the same local Norwegian content and services (Thorkildsen, 2009). Also the Polish and the South Korean MySpace offices were closed in early 2009. Similarly to both the Norwegian and Dutch MySpace portals, the South Korean operation was to be run from a MySpace office abroad. In South Korea, MySpace faced intense competition particularly from Cyworld—a social network service launched as early as 1999. By 2009, up to 90 percent of South Koreans in their 20s were reportedly members of this service (Kincaid, 2009). Similarly, MySpace closed its Polish office also due to strong local competition from, among others, the social network nasza-klasa.pl (Warsaw Business Journal, 2009). However, the expansion and contraction of the social media's localization efforts is not new.

Traditional media outlets aiming to expand globally have been faced by strong local competition. MTV Europe's early operations in Europe exemplify the complexity of targeting a large geographical region, consisting of many countries, numerous national and local languages, and extensive cultural diversity. The pan-European television channel experienced fierce local competition in Belgium, Netherlands, and Luxembourg (Roe and De Meyer, 2001: 42). Similarly, as the youth music channel The Voice was introduced in Norway with Norwegian-speaking hosts, MTV Nordic split into MTV Norway, MTV Sweden, and MTV Denmark. The splitting of video signals allowed pan-European television channels to insert programming and advertising for specific countries in contrast to the whole European territory. Both global television outlets and social media, then, show how both financial and cultural factors, as well as competition, influence the degree

Table 3.6   The Localization of MySpace

Americas
MySpace Argentina
MySpace Brazil
MySpace Canada (English)
MySpace Canada (French)
MySpace Latin America (Spanish)
MySpace Mexico
MySpace US (English)
MySpace US (Latino)
Europe
MySpace Austria
MySpace Denmark
MySpace Finland
MySpace France
MySpace Germany
MySpace Ireland
MySpace Italy
MySpace Netherlands
MySpace Norway
MySpace Poland
MySpace Portugal
MySpace Russia
MySpace Spain
MySpace Sweden
MySpace Switzerland (French)
MySpace Switzerland (German)
MySpace Switzerland (Italian)
MySpace Turkey
MySpace UK
Asia
MySpace Australia
MySpace India
MySpace Japan
MySpace Korea
MySpace New Zealand
MySpace China

(*Data source:* MySpace.com, 2009.)

of localization. The closure of the European MySpace offices was part of a larger international or global strategy to focus on the nine countries that generate 95 percent of the advertising revenue, and where the service might become market leader (Wauters, 2008).

Despite the reduced resources devoted to localization, by 2009, only three years after launching its overseas rollout, MySpace had localized its service in close to 30 territories in Europe, the Americas, and Pacific Asia (see Table 3.6).

The localization process of global television and online-based media is also reflected within the structure of these organizations. As Discovery Channel expanded overseas, the television channel soon introduced new job functions and titles such as 'reversioning specialist' and 'global commissioning editor.' The former oversees 'language customization of programming.' According to a job advert for this position for Discovery Latin America/Iberia, the responsibility includes "Audio and editorial quality control of all translated, dubbed, and/or subtitled programming," as well as "monitor(ing) editorial content and inappropriate cross-cultural words, gestures, or symbols in regional productions." Among the further requirements are "hands-on experience and in-depth knowledge of social and cultural sensitivities in Brazil" (Discovery, 2004). Similarly, MySpace seeks to employ 'localization managers' and 'localization coordinators.' The job advert for the first position points out how "the localization manager is responsible for managing the localization of MySpace's social networking website." The responsibilities of this position include to "drive localization operations at MySpace, making strategic decisions on localization processes, standards, tools, technologies, and resources." Similarly, the localization coordinator's responsibilities include the management of translations and 'linguistic testing' of any MySpace-supported languages such as French, Italian, Spanish, and Portuguese (Jobs.Climber.com, 2010).

However, as MySpace scaled back its original localization infrastructure and local presence, Facebook continued to expand at a dramatic pace. The shift in the social media environment is reflected in Nielsen's statistics from 2008 to 2010. While MySpace had more unique users in 2008, Facebook

Table 3.7   Top Social Network Sites; March 2010—US Home & Work (Unique Audience in Millions)

	Facebook	MySpace	Twitter	LinkedIn
2010	117,109	42,147	20,109	13,876
2009	68,151	55,914	13,858	15,815
2008	24,940	61,285	520 (thousand)	7,877

(Adapted from Nielsen Online, 2010c.)

Table 3.8   Facebook Language Localization—2010

Locale	Language
Afrikaans	Afrikaans
Albanian—BETA	Shqip
Arabic	ةيبرعلا
Armenian—BETA	
Azeri—BETA	Azərbaycan dili
Basque–BETA	Euskara
Belarusian—BETA	Беларуская
Bengali	
Bosnian—BETA	Bosanski
Bulgarian	Български
Catalan	Català
Croatian	Hrvatski
Czech	Čeština
Danish	Dansk
Dutch	Nederlands
English (UK)	English (UK)
English (US)	English (US)
Esperanto—BETA	Esperanto
Estonian—BETA	Eesti
Faroese—BETA	Føroyskt
Filipino	Filipino
Finnish	Suomi
French (Canada)	Français (Canada)
French (France)	Français (France)
Galician—BETA	Galego
Georgian—BETA	ქართული
German	Deutsch
Greek	Ελληνικά
Hebrew	
Hindi	
Hungarian	Magyar
Icelandic—BETA	Íslenska
Indonesian	Bahasa Indonesia
Irish—BETA	Gaeilge
Italian	Italiano
Japanese	
Korean	
Kurdish—BETA	Kurdî
Latin—BETA	lingua latina
Latvian—BETA	Latviešu
Leet Speak—BETA	Leet Speak

Continued

Table 3.8   Continued

Leet Speak	Leet Speak
Macedonian—BETA	Lietuvių
Malay	Македонски
Malayalam	Bahasa Melayu
Nepali—BETA	
Norwegian (bokmal)	Norsk (bokmål)
Norwegian (nynorsk)—BETA	Norsk (nynorsk)
Pashto—BETA	پښتو
Persian—BETA	فارسی
Polish	Polski
Portuguese (Brazil)	Português (Brasil)
Portuguese (Portugal)	Português (Portugal)
Punjabi	
Romanian	Română
Russian	Русский
Serbian	Српски
Simplified Chinese (China)	
Slovak	Slovenčina
Slovenian	Slovenščina
Spanish	Español
Spanish (Spain)	Español (España)
Swahili—BETA	Kiswahili
Swedish	Svenska
Tamil	
Telugu	
Thai	
Traditional Chinese (Hong Kong)	
Traditional Chinese (Taiwan)	
Turkish	Türkçe
Ukrainian—BETA	Українська
Vietnamese	Tiếng Việt
Welsh	Cymraeg

(Facebook, 2010a)

had nearly three times more users by 2010. Also, in the US, Twitter had in a short time nearly half as many users as MySpace (see Table 3.7).

Mirroring the actions of MySpace, Facebook implemented localization programs fast. Facebook established an international headquarters in Dublin, Ireland, in 2008 to develop its business in Europe, the Middle East, and Africa (Facebook, 2008b). The company boasted that its Tokyo office was the first Facebook office with dedicated localization engineers working to adapt the service to Japanese culture and customs (Facebook Careers, 2010). By 2010 Facebook global language localization proved to be unprecedented, also in comparison to MySpace. The service localized into not only the major languages, but also several minority languages (Table 3.8).

Table 3.9 YouTube Globalization Continues with Four New Languages

	Language
2005	English
2006	Dutch, English (UK), French, Italian Japanese, Polish, Portuguese (Brazilian), Spanish (Spain)
2007	Chinese (Traditional), Spanish (Latin America), German, Russian, Korean
2008	Chinese (Simplified), Czech, Swedish
2009	Hindi, Portuguese
2010	Danish, Finnish, Greek, Hungarian, Norwegian, Croatian, Filipino, Serbian, Slovak

(Adapted from Van Buskirk, 2010)

Table 3.10 The Localization of YouTube

Country	URL	Language
Australia	au.youtube.com	English
Brazil	br.youtube.com	Portuguese
Canada	ca.youtube.com	English, French
Czech Republic	cz.youtube.com	Czech
France	fr.youtube.com	French
Germany	de.youtube.com	German
Hong Kong	hk.youtube.com	Chinese
Israel	il.youtube.com	English
India	in.youtube.com	English, Hindi
Ireland	ie.youtube.com	English
Italy	it.youtube.com	Italian
Japan	jp.youtube.com	Japanese
South Korea	kr.youtube.com	Korean
Mexico	mx.youtube.com	Spanish
Netherlands	nl.youtube.com	Dutch
New Zealand	nz.youtube.com	English
Poland	pl.youtube.com	Polish
Russia	ru.youtube.com	Russian
Spain	es.youtube.com	Spanish
Sweden	se.youtube.com	Swedish
Republic of China (Taiwan)	tw.youtube.com	Chinese
UK	uk.youtube.com	English

(Data from Nicole, 2007; Sayer, 2007; Joshi, 2008; Wikipedia, 2010.)

As with MySpace and Facebook, YouTube created localized versions and the service's localization escalated from the start of 2007. By 2010, the video-sharing service had created 28 country-specific versions (Van Buskirk, 2010; see Table 3.9). The localized version of YouTube is selected according to the IP address of the user (see Table 3.10).

Twitter launched around the same time as YouTube in 2006. Since then, users of Twitter have been able to create personal profiles and post 'tweets'—messages of a maximum length of 140 characters. The majority of Twitter profiles are accessible to the public, and users may register to follow the activity of fellow Twitter users. As with other global social media,

Table 3.11   The Global Mobile Expansion of Twitter

Country	Number to send SMS	Telecom
Argentina	89338	Movistar and Personal
Antigua	176	Digicel customers
Anguilla	176	Digicel customers
Australia	0198089488	Telstra customers
Bhutan	40404	B-mobile
Brasil	40404	TIM customers
Bolivia	40404	Viva customers
Bermuda	176	Digicel customers
Canada	21212	
El Salvador	40404	Digicel and Tigo customers
Fiji	40404	Digicel
Grenada	176	Digicel customers
Guyana	1443	Digicel customers
Haiti	40404	Digicel customers
Honduras	40404	Digicel customers
India	53000	Bharti Airtel customers
Indonesia	89887	AXIS, 3, Telkomsel, XL, Axiata, TelkomFlexi, Bakari and Indosat
Iraq	71117	Zain
Ireland	51210	O2 customers
	51644	Vodafone customers
Jamaica	176	Digicel customers
Jordan	90903	Zain customers
Kuwait	89887	Zain customers
Kyrgyzstan	4040	Megacom
Macedonia	40404	VIP customers
Madagascar	40404	VIP
Malaysia	28933	Maxis

Continued

Table 3.11 Continued

Mexico	6464	Telcel customers, only supports sending updates to Twitter
Nauru	40404	Digicel customers
New Zealand	8987	Vodafone and Telecom NZ Customers
Nicaragua	89887	Movistar
Nigeria	40404	Zain customers
Panama	3010	Digicel customers
Papua New Guinea	40404	Digicel customers
Paraguay	40404	Personal
Romania	89338	Vodafone customers
Saudi Arabia	8 40404	STC customers
Sri Lanka	40404	Dialog customers
St. Lucia	176	Dialog customers
St. Vincent	176	Dialog customers
St. Kitts	176	Dialog customers
Sweden	71017	3 customers
Tonga	40404	Dialog customers
Trinidad and Tobago	40404	Dialog customers
Turkey	2444	Vodafone customers
UK	86444	Vodafone, Orange, 3 and O2 Customers
United Arab Emirates	335640404	Zain
US	40404	

(Twitter, 2010.)

Twitter has also expanded into mobile telephony. The service has rolled out globally in collaboration with local or national telecom companies in each country (see Table 3.11).

The users can choose among the available languages in their Twitter settings. Having localized into French, German, Italian, Japanese, and Spanish, Twitter is also preoccupied with expanding the number of language options (Twitter, 2010).

In China, American-originated global social media have all faced fierce competition, as Chinese services had achieved dominance in key demographic groups by the time the US services arrived. By 2009, News Corp's ambitious attempts to launch MySpace in the Chinese online sphere had still not succeeded. Furthermore, Google, along with Facebook, YouTube, and Twitter, has been either completely or partially blocked by Chinese authorities. Instead, QQ, an instant messaging and chat program, and the social networking site Xiaonei (now called RenRen) are by far the most popular services among Chinese internet users (Nielsen Online, 2009). The table below gives a snapshot of the situation in China in 2009 (see Table 3.12). However, it also exemplifies the challenge in trying to define 'social

Table 3.12   Social Internet Networks in China

Ranking	Name of Social Network	Users in China (in millions)
1.	QQ	378
2.	51	130
3.	Baidu	110
4.	Xiaonei	40
5.	Baidu Komgjian	27
11.	MySpace	6
16.	Facebook	1.452
17.	Friendster	1.100
18.	LinkedIn	1.026

(Deleon, 2009.)

internet networks' or 'social media.' While QQ is mainly an instant messaging service, QZone, which has the same owners as QQ, is considered a
social network, and Baidu is a Chinese online search engine. By 2009, then,
MySpace's and Facebook's reach and appeal among Chinese internet users
were dwarfed by these services (see Table 3.12).

However, it is difficult to compare how the social media environment
develops in different parts of the world. This is underlined by the internet technology news site, Techcrunch: "To be frank, we're not sure where
QQ the communication (IM) (instant messaging) service ends and where
QZone the social network begins" (Wauters, 2009). Therefore, the actual
number of users of the Chinese services is difficult to estimate. In mid-
2010, the market research company Nielsen Company and the consul-
tancy company McKinsey attempted to map some of the characteristics of
internet use in parts of the Asia Pacific region. The report pointed out how
blogging is popular in Japan, and how Twitter has become very popular
among internet users in the country. Sixteen percent of Japanese internet
users use Twitter, compared to 10 percent in the US (Nielsen, 2010d).
Mixi, a Japanese social medium where users create a profile and connect
with other profiles, had 15 million users in mid-2008. In India, Orkut is
still more popular among internet users, but Facebook increased its market share. In South Korea, as many as 95 percent of internet users use
the social media service Naver, but Twitter has also gained in popularity
(Nielsen Online, 2010d).

In just a few years, from 2005 to 2010, a global social media environment
has evolved, and as we have seen, it is characterized by shifts and volatility
and the coexistence of national, regional, and global services. Facebook and
MySpace particularly, along with YouTube and Twitter, represent key services, as they have global ambitions and have implemented extensive localization strategies throughout this period. Why did MySpace first expand so
quickly only to be outperformed by Facebook and a fast-growing Twitter

service? There are several suggested answers. Some draw attention to the relationship between both MySpace and Facebook and the concept of 'critical mass.' After reaching a certain number of users, the adoption of these services is self-sustaining (Rogers, 2003; in Guribye, 2007). People want to be where others are. In the piece *Is Facebook the New MySpace?* trade publication, *PC World* compared these services with social clubs:

> (A)s the people at Friendster learned, things can change quickly in Web culture. Social networking sites appear to be unusually transient businesses—a bit like social clubs in the real world. Every couple of years or so a different club becomes incredibly popular, and everyone starts going there, leaving the previous year's hot spot nearly empty. That's human nature, and it dominates the virtual world, too. (Sullivan, 2007)

The coverage in the mainstream press of the battle between the two social media certainly also played a role in promoting not only MySpace and Facebook, but also the social media phenomenon in general. The coverage of the two became a focus of both niche publications on technological development and general press reporting on social media (see Table 3.13). *The New York Times* was among the many mainstream news outlets

Table 3.13   The Press: MySpace and Facebook

Year	Title of News Story	Newspaper
2005	"News Corp to Acquire Owner of MySpace.com"	(The New York Times, Siklos, 2005)
2006	"Murdoch Unveils Plans for MySpace.com"	(The Guardian, Timms)
2007	"Is Facebook the New MySpace?"	(PC World, Sullivan)
2007	"As Facebook Takes Off, MySpace Strikes Back"	(CNN.com, Kirkpatrick, 2007)
2008	"Facebook 'Is Beating MySpace in Popularity Contest'"	(ZDNET.com, McCarthy, 2008)
2009	"Social Networking: Will Facebook Overtake MySpace in the U.S. In 2009?"	(Techcrunch.com, Arrington, 2009a)
2009	"Facebook Now Nearly Twice the Size of MySpace Worldwide"	(Techcrunch.com, Arrington, 2009b)
2009	"MySpace Is Forced to Slash Workforce as Social Network Users Flock to Facebook"	(The Guardian, Teather, 2009)
2009	"How Facebook Beats MySpace"	(McWilliams, The Guardian, 2009)
2010	Once-Fading MySpace Focuses on Youthful Reincarnation"	(USA Today, Schwartz, 2010)

(Siklos, 2005; Timms, 2006; Kirkpatrick, 2007; Sullivan, 2007; McCarthy, 2008; Arrington, 2009a, 2009b; McWilliams, 2009; Teather, 2009; Schwartz, 2010)

that reported on News Corp's acquisition of MySpace in 2005. The British newspaper *The Guardian* covered MySpace's plans for overseas expansion, and American newspaper *USA Today* reported on how MySpace attempted to fight back after restructuring in 2010. The two global social media, then, have been protagonists when the press has introduced the phenomenon to a wider public (see Table 3.13).

Still, perhaps the main reason for Facebook's and Twitter's popularity is their approach to localization: this differs from MySpace. As pointed out, localization is the key corporate strategy for traditional global television operators and online entities alike. The choice of localization strategies, then, has consequences for the competition between both local and fellow global operators. When looking closely at the localization strategies of MySpace on the one hand, and Facebook and Twitter on the other, we see how their approaches differ. This helps to explain the explosive growth of Facebook and Twitter.

Soon after the launch of the term Web 2.0, the buzzword at the center of the resurgence of the internet industry, a number of related terms followed. One of them is 'crowdsourcing.' The term, coined by journalist Jeff Howe, in the piece "The Rise of Crowdsourcing," in *Wired* magazine, in 2006, aimed to describe 'the age of the crowd.' The idea behind the term was that "distributed labor networks are using the internet to exploit the spare processing power of millions of human brains," according to Howe, who pointed out that the web services Wikipedia, eBay, and MySpace all relied on the "contribution of users" (Howe, 2006). The term was promoted as describing a key characteristic of the 'new web,' or Web 2.0, by books such as Howe's own *Crowdsourcing: Why The Power of the Crowd is Driving the Future of Business* (2009). The idea and the term spread and were soon adopted and promoted in numerous publications particularly for business purposes such as *Crowdsourcing Customer Service: How May We Help We?* (Libert and Spector, 2010a); *Crowdsourcing Your Sales: Let Customers Sell Themselves (and Others)* (Libert and Spector, 2010b); and *Crowdsourcing Your Brand: How to Tap Customer Desire* (Libert and Spector, 2010c). Some of the global social media quickly picked up on this concept and implemented it in their plans for localization.

All global social media rely on the contributions, input, activity, and communication of their participants and users in the form of postings of written messages, pictures, and video clips. However, MySpace's approach has clear parallels with the traditional global television channels' localization that its owner, News Corp, has successfully implemented across the world for many years: "(MySpace) tend(s) to put a team on the ground locally (...) and then build the site not only in the local language, but promote local artists and other popular culture as well" (Arrington, 2008). However, as pointed out, several of MySpace's offices closed as the service reduced its physical presence and activity in a number of localities. In contrast, Facebook has relied on a more online-based and user-led approach to localization:

Facebook is taking a radically different approach—tapping users to do all the hard work for them. They are picking and choosing markets (Spanish was opened first, two weeks ago; today German and French were launched) and asking just a few users to test out their collaborative translation tool. Once the tool is perfected and enough content has been translated, Facebook will offer users the ability to quickly switch the language on the site, per their preference. (Arrington, 2008)

When Facebook localized the service into German, more than 2,000 German-speaking Facebook users contributed to translating the site from English. The translation process took less than two weeks (Facebook, 2008c). Facebook used the same approach when translating the site into Spanish. Close to 1,500 Spanish-speaking Facebook users were involved and helped translate the site in less than four weeks (Facebook, 2008a). According to the company Inside Facebook, which tracks the development of the social media, Facebook allows users to utilize a 'translations' application' to translate all phrases on the Facebook service. The application is available to all users with the aim to translate the site into "every major language on earth" (Smith, 2008). In 2008, as the localization of Facebook gathered speed, users could join the translation project in the following way:

1. Add the Translations app and choose your language. (Currently, there are translation projects going on in English, Français, Deutsch, Español, Català, Čeština, Dansk, Euskara, Galego, Italiano, (. . .), Magyar, Norsk, (. . .), Nederlands, Polski, Português do Brasil, Română, Русский, Slovenščina, Suomi, Svenska, (. . .), Türkçe, (. . .)
2. Turn on in-line editing. This will highlight every word on Facebook that needs translating. You can click on each phrase and vote on translations submitted by others or submit a new translation yourself.
3. Browse the translations directory to view and translate more phrases. You can browse and vote on any of the 24,000 phrases. Facebook's top translators have had thousands of translations accepted!

(Smith, 2008)

By 2010, Facebook claimed that more than 300,000 Facebook users have contributed to the translation of the site into many languages (Facebook, 2010d). In fact, Facebook has not only been translated into the major languages but also caters for minority languages and thereby has, in an unprecedented way, adapted to the different cultural and linguistic specificities across the world (see Table 3.8).

Twitter also decided to start to localize its service with the help of its users: "Following a lead from Facebook, Twitter announced that it was crowdsourcing the translations through Tweeter volunteer linguists" (Grunwald, 2010) Still, Twitter has taken a cautious approach. At first, in 2009, the service invited a selection of them to participate in translation, and then gradually increased the number of translators. The aim was to make Twitter available in Japanese, French, Italian, German, and Spanish (Twitter Blog, 2009).

Facebook's and Twitter's internet-based strategy seems to be less costly and more efficient than that of MySpace. The idea of 'crowdsourcing' is accepted by many users of these services despite the fact that they are helping the expansion of a commercial media entity. The service's immersion in local cultures is done mainly through language and text, utilizing online and computer technology. This stands in contrast to traditional global television channels, as well as to MySpace's approach to localization, relying on a more traditional physical engagement with local culture. As MySpace has scaled back its operations and presence, this may also have had an effect on its ability to attract users and activity and to generate advertising revenue (Garrahan, 2009).

While the linguistic localization of global social media has enabled them to reach linguistically diverse audiences, the personalization of these services has made them able to come even closer to the individual internet user. With the arrival of advanced multimedia mobile telephones—smart phones—social media were gradually introduced on them as well. Both a MySpace Mobile and Facebook Mobile feature was launched in 2006, and the Facebook Platform for mobile was launched in October 2007 (Facebook, 2011). The ability to create a link between the individual user and the service, then, makes these global social media stand out even more compared to traditional global media. Also, there are differences in the opportunities for personalization provided by social media services, and as with the approaches to language localization, this is also the case with MySpace and Facebook. Users log onto personal profiles that contain information provided by the user and these are to various degrees organized and designed by the user depending on the format and architectural structure of the social media (Papacharissi, 2009). MySpace profiles in the mid-2000s allowed for the inclusion of text, pictures, and importantly music. As such, it resembled a website. As Facebook opened up to the public, it introduced a user profile format that differed from a MySpace profile. At the center of the Facebook profile is the user's 'wall' where the user's 'friends' post messages and make their communication visible. The newest posts appear at the top of the wall, and when a new post appears, the older ones are moved down. The user and his or her friends can comment on these posts. When Facebook emerged, MySpace profiles did not have such facilities for visualizing interaction and communication between users. Also, in contrast to Facebook, the postings were at the very bottom of a MySpace user's profile. As such, the format of the Facebook profiles represented a more dynamic website, putting the ongoing posting and communication between the users at the center, compared to the more static MySpace format. The differences in format between the two global social media have also been observed by researchers: "(MySpace's) format has remained relatively stable over time (as compared with Facebook, which more frequently adds features and shifts its architectural format)" (Davis, 2010: 1105). The differences in personalization therefore also help explain why Facebook became so popular among a wider social media audience.

Facebook's extensive localization and personalization made it extremely competitive in many parts of the world. Even in France, traditionally sceptical of American media, competition with the national French language web service Skyrock was significant, according to Peter Bellanger, chief executive and founder of the service. "Prior to Facebook, the landscape was simple," Bellanger points out. "We were the absolute dominant player in France. People used Skyrock for their blogs and MSN for chatting. Now we are no longer alone, we are in an ecosystem where we have to fight hard for market share. We are sharing the time of our users with Facebook" (Bellanger, quoted in Palmer, 2010). Similarly, in Norway, the national social network, Nettby, decided to close down its service after four years. At its height, it had more than 800,000 registered user profiles, and more than 70 percent of Norwegian teenagers had created a profile. Since around 2008, the service experienced a continuous decline in activity. Despite the implementation of a range of measures to turn things around, including a complete redesign, the competition from Facebook, in particular, has been too great, Nettby claimed. This is not only happening in Norway, according to Nettby's press release when announcing its closure: "National social networks also in for example Denmark, Sweden and France, are experiencing strong reduction in user activity. The winner is Facebook" (Nettby, 2010).

The development and competition between the different services show how rapid change takes place within this online milieu. In just five years, from 2005 to 2010, a global social media environment emerged and established itself. By 2010, Facebook reportedly had more than 500 million users across the world. The sheer number of users makes Facebook the 'winner' of the race with MySpace. At the end of the 2000s, MySpace allowed users to synchronize part of their activity with other social media. This meant that users of Facebook were able to view their friends' MySpace activity without leaving Facebook. MySpace had already allowed its users to sync with Twitter and vice versa. Some suggest that this signaled MySpace's attempt to "carve out a niche that is no longer about competing with Facebook but co-existing. MySpace users will also be able to share music, videos, game applications, links and photos across both social networking sites." (MSNBC, 2010) This was considered part of MySpace's response to its diminishing advertising revenue and lack of growth in user adoption (2010).

In less than a decade, a social media landscape has evolved with remarkable speed and was rapidly perceived by traditional media conglomerates such as News Corp, Time Warner, and Disney, as well as the computer software giant Microsoft, as vital to help them secure a position online.

To expand globally and compete with regional, national, and local social media services, MySpace and Facebook launched ambitious localization strategies. These strategies show how, also within the online environment, the process of media globalization is characterized by continual negotiation between the global and local. However, as we have seen, the differences in localization approaches, as well as the different approaches to personalization, help explain why Facebook and Twitter have become so popular.

4 The Global Social Media and Music Nexus

Who needs major labels, marketing, or airplay? A social networking site is getting more hits than Google—and turning invisible bands into mini entertainment networks. How MySpace became the MTV for the Net generation. (*Wired*, Howe, 2005)

One reason we've been so popular on the music side is because there's all these artists out there that didn't really have a voice. They'd have their own website but no traffic. You can create a high-quality CD for a couple of thousand bucks but there wasn't the way to get that to the masses (. . .). The band in Manchester starting up couldn't reach fans in Dublin or Iowa or Australia. Now, it's totally globalised the fanbase for emerging artists. (Chris DeWolf, CEO and Co-founder of MySpace, quoted in *The Guardian*, Gibson, 2006)

The new version of Spotify (online music streaming service) is really pretty amazing—it shifted the experience so now you connect with your Facebook account to see what all your friends are listening to and all the different music they like and subscribe to. It adds a new element on top of the experience and almost makes it a completely different experience. I'm using it so much more. (Mark Zuckerberg, Founder of Facebook, quoted in *The Guardian*, Kiss, 2010)

By 2010, there were reportedly around 2 billion internet users—nearly 30 percent of the world's population (Internet World Stats, 2010), and an increasing number of these users adopt global social media. Building on the previous chapter's mapping of the development of this social media environment, this chapter shows how a significant relationship between global social media and music has emerged. While the preceding chapter explored the rise of global social media from a general historical, political, and economic perspective, this chapter examines the global social media and music nexus from both a corporate and a user perspective. It shows how the global social media and music connection is at the center of the ongoing changes within the media and communications landscape—characterized by digitization, globalization, conglomeration, and an expanding online landscape. The chapter examines first how global social media and music became linked. It then shows how representatives of one of the key groups of users, music practitioners, adopted social media and thereby became a part of this nexus and goes on to explore from a corporate perspective the global social media and music relation as these services and the music industry have increasingly become intertwined.

GLOBAL SOCIAL MEDIA AND MUSIC

MySpace was the first globally expanding social medium to receive wide attention, particularly for its connection with music. By 2008, the number of bands and artists across the world with registered profiles had reached 5 million, according to MySpace (DeWolfe, quoted in Locke, 2008). The myriad bands and artists had 'friends'—registered MySpace users from across the world—linked to their profiles. The number of these linked 'friends' could be anything from a few hundreds to, in the case of international mainstream artists and bands such as Madonna or Metallica, hundreds of thousands or even millions. Since 2006, when Facebook opened up to public use, the connection between global social media and music has strengthened further, as artists have also taken up this service. As with MySpace, the number of fans and 'friends' of bands' Facebook profiles may vary from just a few to millions. Twitter was launched in 2006 and was also quickly adopted by music practitioners. This chapter focuses on mapping the users' take-up of MySpace in the time from 2005, but also the corporate relationship between these services and the music industry, while part of the next chapter examines these electronic music practitioners' use of the global social media by late 2010.

Although MySpace was the first global social medium to facilitate musicians' and artists' opportunities to express themselves and reach audiences and communicate with fans and fellow musicians, there are both corporate and personal struggles for influence within the global social media and music nexus. These emerge and can be observed both in the relationship between the social media users themselves and increasingly between the global music industry and the users. Some users have more influence than others. They function as nodes of influence and can have an impact on the activity of others. The global social media environment is also seen as a key area for a music industry attempting to adjust to the process of digitization and the challenges represented by the online environment. As we shall see, the influence of the large music industry players extends within these services as they attempt to capitalize on the users' music interest.

The music industry organization International Federation of the Phonographic Industry (IFPI) describes the current situation and challenges of the industry by drawing attention to the shifts in the global sales of music. The total global revenues for sales of recorded music in 2009 fell by 7.2 percent to US$17 billion. As much as 80 percent of this reduction took place in two markets: Japan and the US. Sales of physical music formats were down 12.7 percent worldwide from 2008 to 2009 (see Table 4.1).

Over the same period, sales of digital music increased by 9.2 percent to US$4.3 billion, 10 times the value of the digital music market in 2004 (see

Table 4.1   Recorded Music Sales 2008–2009 (% Change by Region)

	Physical	Digital	Performing Rights	Total
North America	-17.9	1.1	20.3	-10.4
Europe	-8.9	29.7	4.1	-4.1
Asia	-15.4	10.4	11.9	-9.2
Australia/ New Zealand	-2.4	41.4	8.6	3.5
Latin America and Caribbean	-4.7	17.6	23.2	-0.7
Global	-12.7	9.2	7.6	-7.2

(Adapted from IFPI, quoted in Andrews, 2010.)

Table 4.2) (IFPI, quoted in Andrews, 2010). However, IFPI argues that "piracy continued to erode legitimate music sales worldwide" (IFPI, 2010). Still, the actual impact of such 'piracy' is difficult to estimate, as music industry scholar Wikström points out: an illegally downloaded music file or song "is not necessarily corresponding to one track purchased at a single-song-download service" (2009: 151). Furthermore, Hesmondhalgh emphasizes, the music industry has "always had to fight over the boundaries between 'legitimate' forms of musical consumption—those involving income flows to them—and 'illegitimate' ones" (Hesmondhalgh, 2009: 61). While the possibilities for copying have increased, not least through online technology, "file-sharing is extremely unlikely to lead to a collapse of the

Table 4.2   Global Recorded Music Sales 1997–2009 (US$ Billions)

	Physical	Digital	Performance Rights
2009	11.9	4.3	0.8
2008	13.7	3.9	0.7
2007	16.1	3.0	0.6
2006	18.5	2.2	0.6
2005	20.5	1.2	0.5
2004	22.0	0.4	0.5
2003	22.5	—	0.4
2002	24.3	—	0.4
2001	26.1	—	—
2000	26.5	—	—
1999	26.9	—	—
1998	26.8	—	—
1997	25.6	—	—

(Adapted from IFPI, quoted in Andrews, 2010.)

idea that huge amounts of money can be made through music" (Hesmond-halgh, 2009: 61). Therefore, while sales of recorded music have 'suffered' in recent years on a global scale, "rather than the outright collapse of the music business, the big issue facing capital seeking to invest in culture over the next decade is how to find new ways of making money from music" (Hesmondhalgh, 2009: 61).

When mapping the global social media and music nexus, then, one needs to be aware of the continuity with the past. As in the analog era, the music industry continues to be dominated by a handful of big corporations. In recent years, the 'big four'—Universal Music Group, Sony Music Entertainment, Warner Music Group, and EMI Group—have controlled 70–80 percent of the global music recording music market (Thussu, 2000/2006: 173; Wikström, 2009: 69). Furthermore, the music industry is part of the process of conglomeration of ownership characterizing parts of the media and communications industry. Three of these four dominant music companies are part of global media conglomerates: NBC Universal, Sony, and Time Warner. Since 2005, the previous chapter showed how no one of the strategies of media and communications conglomerates has been to move into the global social media environment, investing huge sums in MySpace, Bebo, and Facebook. The rapid adoption rate of these services, not least by artists, music enthusiasts, and fans, soon also caught the attention of the major music players. Therefore, the largest social media services and the music industry now collaborate in a number of ways. Global social media, then, has become part of the music industry's efforts to create profit in the digital and online era. This recent development is explored here, but to understand the significance of this global social media and music nexus, we have to go back in time.

MYSPACE AND MUSIC

The relationship between music and the internet is often characterized by controversy. At the heart of this association is peer-to-peer (P2P) networking technology. The ability to circumvent rights holders of music and other media products from the distribution chain, as individual internet users share MP3 files of music as well as other media content, is considered by some as "perhaps the single most important technological concept which has pushed this process forward" (Wikström, 2009: 148). As the capacity and speed of personal computers increased and were utilized in the developing online environment, P2P networking became more and more prominent among users. In 1999, the technology reached the attention of the wider audience as the Napster software for file sharing became popular and the subsequent legal controversy between Napster founder Shawn Fanning and music companies intensified. Although Napster had to close, P2P has since developed into ever more advanced and powerful software and services (Wikström, 2009: 149). P2P software such as Grokster and

Kazaa appeared allowing internet users to "search each other's computers for music files" (Hesmondhalgh, 2009: 60). Gradually, P2P technology also reached within the global social media environment: "Peer-to-peer sharing is now becoming part of everyday media experience, via sites such as MySpace, Bebo and YouTube" (Hesmondhalgh, 2009: 63).

Still, while the internet was, from early on, 'blamed' by the music industry for web-based illegal distribution of music, it soon became a space for the promotion of music in various ways and social media came to play an important role. Angwin points out that while several larger American artists such as Madonna and Britney Spears used the major internet portals AOL, MSN, and Yahoo! to promote their music, lesser-known bands did not have access, or "get onto the AOL lineup," in the same way. The website MP3.com had served as a site for smaller acts to distribute their music, but as with Napster, the site was closed in late 2003 due to copyright issues (Angwin, 2009: 85). Social media researchers Shklovski and boyd point out that "MP3.com had just closed its doors and emergent bands were desperate to have a space to promote their music and gigs" (2006: 1).

The launch of MySpace marked the arrival of a marketing tool for these smaller and unsigned bands and often provided a way for them to link with fans (Angwin, 2009: 85). Soon after its launch in 2003, MySpace began to acquire a reputation for being popular among bands within certain music genres in the Los Angeles area (boyd and Ellison, 2007). According to Shklovski and boyd, "Having learned from mistakes made by MP3.com such as its reliance on downloading apps and Windows media, MySpace built a Flash player that allowed all users to stream music directly from the profile page. Musicians could upload up to four songs and make these songs available for download or streaming within the site" (2006: 1). MySpace, then, appealed particularly to young people, and American teenagers had started to use MySpace 'en masse' in 2004 (boyd and Ellison, 2007). This did not go unnoticed by the press. In mid-2005, music magazine *Billboard* reported:

> With its focus on 16 to 34-year-olds, MySpace has become a power house for online music promotion. Acts such as Nine Inch Nails, Weezer, the Black Eyed Peas, Queens of the Stone Age, Foo Fighters have used the service to host 'listening parties,' exclusively streaming upcoming albums in their entirety weeks before street date. (Bruno, 2005: 14)

At the time *Billboard* claimed "More than 240,000 bands have MySpace profiles, using the system to promote and distribute their music through the digital word-of-mouth the site offers" (Bruno, 2005: 14). Not only the music press, but also the technology trade press, in particular the magazine *Wired,* soon picked up on MySpace. MySpace, having been acquired by News Corporation in 2005, was therefore a hot topic for the magazine at the end of the year, and *Wired* drew attention to the relationship between MySpace and music:

> (MySpace is) a community website that converts electronic word of mouth into the hottest marketing strategy since the advent of MTV. Massively popular, MySpace is nominally a social networking site like Friendster, but nearly 400,000 of the site's roughly 30 million user pages belong to bands. The rest belong mostly to teens and twenty-somethings who attend the groups' shows, download their songs, read their blogs, send them fan mail, and enthusiastically spread the word. (Howe, 2005)

In this early phase, MySpace founders Tom Anderson and Chris DeWolfe got local artists and music venue owners to create MySpace profiles, and other users could then become their 'friends.' The recruitment of participants in the music business helped promote MySpace: "All these creative people became ambassadors for MySpace by using us as their de facto promotional platform," DeWolfe said to *Fortune* magazine, adding, "People like to talk about music, so the bands set up a natural environment to communicate" (DeWolfe, quoted in Sellers, 2006). MySpace was not launched primarily to attract bands, but the relationship between bands and fans was central to MySpace's development:

> Bands were not the sole source of MySpace growth, but the symbiotic relationship between bands and fans helped MySpace expand beyond former Friendster users. The bands-and-fans dynamic was mutually beneficial: Bands wanted to be able to contact fans, while fans desired attention from their favorite bands and used Friend connections to signal identity and affiliation. (boyd and Ellison, 2007)

The fact that it was easy and free to create a profile made it appealing to bands to adopt the service, co-founder of MySpace, Tom Anderson, pointed out to news website, *Msnbc.com*; "Bands are going to MySpace because it's free and they don't have to know how to do a website" (quoted in Belzman, 2006). The magazine *Business Week* pointed to how MySpace's early popularity in the US was also due to the take-up by 'marquee names'—well-known American bands and artists: "Black-Eyed Peas, My Chemical Romance, and ex-Smashing Pumpkins leader Billy Corgan joined. That pulled in fans and their friends, who all found that MySpace offered loads of options that other sites lacked" (Rosenbush, 2005). MySpace, with its ability to attract music artists and fans, soon began to receive favorable attention across the Atlantic.

This was partly due to the worldwide news coverage in 2005 of News Corp's acquisition of the—for most people—unfamiliar social media phenomenon. At the time, and coinciding with News Corp's investment, the

British mainstream press in particular reported of bands suddenly becoming popular and reaching the top of the official national music chart through the use of MySpace. Stories of the 'magic' of MySpace spread throughout the media. In the UK, the *BBC* claimed that the rapid popularity of British artist Lily Allen and the band Arctic Monkeys in the mid-2000s was largely due to their presence and activity on MySpace:

> In 2003, a site was unleashed on the net that would change everything; a site so popular and influential it has launched the careers of pop stars and was purchased by Rupert Murdoch's News Corporation for $580m (£310m). That site is, of course, MySpace. The inclusion of music on Myspace has been one of the biggest reasons for the site's success. Unknown artists have demonstrated that social networking sites can be an effective means of promoting themselves. Artists like Lily Allen and the Arctic Monkeys have used MySpace as a springboard to success. (Cieslak, the *BBC*, 2006)

Similarly, the newspaper *The Independent* hailed the unknown 20-year-old US artist Kate Nash as the "new queen of MySpace" (Caesar, 2007). MySpace was also credited with playing a role in the launch of albums by major established artists such as REM, according to the *The Guardian*, "In 2004, the American band (REM) revived its fortunes and recaptured a youthful US audience by making its 13th major album—*Around the Sun*—available on MySpace.com for two weeks before its release date. The move was encouraged by the band's ailing record label, Warner Bros" (Forrest, 2005). Similarly, the press was giving MySpace part of the credit for the commercial success of Madonna's album released in 2005: "The multi-millionaire used her profile page on MySpace.com to promote *Confessions on a Dancefloor* by posting personal 'audio confessions' with which fans could interact and send in their own offerings" (Forrest, 2005). Along with several such stories, MySpace was portrayed by the press as an online promotion tool that could take bands and artists from obscurity to stardom—or at least to an audience.

Such belief was also promoted in numerous books and guides that emerged in 2006 and 2007. In various ways, these publications promised to show artists how to use MySpace to succeed within the music industry (see Table 4.3).

These publications picked up on the relationship between MySpace and music and aggressively promoted its significance. One of the user guides, *MySpace Music Profit Monster: Proven Online Marketing Strategies for Getting More Fans Fast*, describes the relationship in the following way:

> If you have always dreamed of a career in music, you're about to discover exactly how you can leverage over 100 million MySpace users to market your music. The internet has leveled the playing field, offering

Table 4.3 MySpace User Guides and Books

MySpace for Musicians: The Comprehensive Guide to Marketing Your Music Online (Vincent, 2007)
MySpace Maxed Out: Explode Your Popularity, Buzz Your Band, and Secure Your Privacy on MySpace (Editors of Bottletree Books LLC, 2006)
MySpace Music Profit Monster: Proven Online Marketing Strategies for Getting More Fans Fast (Kalliongis, 2008)
Hacking MySpace: Customizations and Mods to Make MySpace Your Space (Pospisil, 2006)
Amp Your MySpace: Essential Tools for Giving Your Profile an Extreme Makeover (Butow and Bellomo, 2008)
MySpace Music Marketing: How to Promote & Sell Your Music on the World's Biggest Networking Web Site (Baker, 2006)

more opportunities than ever before to expose you to the world. (Kalliongis, 2008: 13)

In a similar fashion, the book *MySpace Maxed Out: Explode Your Popularity, Buzz Your Band, and Secure Your Privacy on MySpace,* promotes MySpace's role in relation to music:

> Become MySpace royalty. Explode your career. Lock down your privacy. With over 120 million users MySpace is the world's largest social networking site. Feel lost and overwhelmed? Don't be! *"MySpace Maxed Out"* is an extensive guide to all areas of MySpace. Dominate it instead of being just part of it. Got a band? Learn 75 ways to get thousands of fans. (Editors of Bottletree Books LLC, 2006)

A third book, *Hacking MySpace: Customizations and Mods to Make MySpace Your Space,* emphasizes MySpace's standing within the music industry:

> Another factor behind MySpace's success is its credibility in the music industry and the fact that it has been a launching pad for a number of emerging bands such as Hollywood Undead (www.myspace.com/hollywoodundead), West Grand (www.myspace.com/westgrand) and Fall Out Boy (www.myspace.com/falloutboy). Canadian metal band Time is the Enemy (www.myspace.com/tite) was discovered by its label INgrooves on MySpace. More than half a million bands have MySpace web pages where they provide music clips and band information, and talk to fans. (Pospisil, 2006: 7)

However, others were less convinced—claiming that the connection between MySpace and music was more of a hype. The influence of the social media service is far less magical than suggested by the media and these publications. MySpace's ability to create overnight success for bands unaided is exaggerated, according to Johnny Bradshaw, representative of Domino, the record company of the British band Arctic Monkeys—one of the bands that the press claimed had become popular thanks to MySpace: "The media need to make the populace join the dots and this is a very easy way of doing that—so people think that MySpace and Arctic Monkeys makes sense, even though it's not true," (Bradshaw, quoted in Webb, 2006). Commenting on Arctic Monkeys' breakthrough, and the perceived role of the internet, journalist Webb pointed out in the British newspaper, *The Guardian*: "Beneath the online hyperbole, the more traditional elements behind the band's success (record label, management, press agent, distribution, major publishing deal) have been overlooked" (Webb, 2006).

But MySpace was not alone in being hyped. YouTube was subject to a similar celebratory treatment and 'mythologized' (Burgess and Green, 2009: 22). As with MySpace, YouTube was portrayed as a service that, through the distribution of amateur videos, could lead to success within the music industry. This idea was particularly promoted in the mainstream media through "individual success stories that appear to realize this promise" (Burgess and Green, 2009: 22):

> Chicago alternative rock band OK Go has become more popular on the video-sharing website YouTube than it ever was on MTV. The band's treadmill video has been viewed millions of times on the internet and featured on news programs around the world. Music industry watchers can learn from OK Go's experience, which shows that web users can catapult a band to fame, challenging the popular assumption that videos need to cost thousands of dollars or be directed by Hollywood film directors. (*The Sidney Morning Herald*, 2006)

Similarly, at the time, musician Terra Naomi reportedly "secured a recording contract after becoming one of the most subscribed artists on YouTube musicians' channel" (Burgess and Green, 2009: 22) And, just as with MySpace, guides and books appeared that promised to show how the use of YouTube could promote musicians: *YouTube: An Insider's Guide to Climbing the Charts* (Lastufka and Dean, 2008), and *15 Minutes of Fame: Becoming a Star in the YouTube Revolution* (Levy, 2008).

The hype surrounding Web 2.0 also affected the online services that were seen as services that characterized the 'new web.' Both MySpace and YouTube have been tied to the term Web 2.0—generally claimed to have first appeared at the *Web 2.0 Conference* organized by O'Reilly Media in San Francisco in 2004 (Web 2.0 Conference, 2004; O'Reilly, 2005). *YouTube: An Insider's Guide to Climbing the Charts* was one of the books O'Reilly Media published (Lastufka and Dean, 2008). The attention given to the idea of Web 2.0 reached perhaps its peak with *Time Magazine's* announcement of 'You' as 'Time's Person of the Year' in 2006. This underlined the idea that individual internet users, and their collaboration in services like Wikipedia, MySpace, and YouTube, were at the center of the development of the 'new' internet (Web 2.0) and that new technology would empower the user in unprecedented ways:

> It's a story about community and collaboration on a scale never seen before. It's about the cosmic compendium of knowledge Wikipedia and the million-channel people's network YouTube and the online metropolis MySpace. It's about the many wresting power from the few and helping one another for nothing and how that will not only change the world, but also change the way the world changes. [. . .] The tool that makes this possible is the World Wide Web. Not the Web that Tim Berners-Lee hacked together (15 years ago, according to Wikipedia) as a way for scientists to share research. It's not even the overhyped dotcom Web of the late 1990s. The new Web is a very different thing. It's a tool for bringing together the small contributions of millions of people and making them matter. Silicon Valley consultants call it Web 2.0, as if it were a new version of some old software. But it's really a revolution. (Grossman, 2006)

Time Magazine's description for the 'new web' in contrast to the 'overhyped dotcom Web' clearly resonates with O'Reilly's notion of Web 2.0. By resolutely distinguishing between the new and old web, exemplified by both YouTube and MySpace, *Time* joined in the promotion of the idea of the transformative qualities of Web 2.0 (Mjøs, Moe, and Sundet, 2010).

Still, there is no doubt that a large number of music practitioners—from small amateur acts to major global artists—took up MySpace in the mid-2000s. The significance of the relationship is further underlined when comparing the topics discussed on MySpace according to Nielsen Online. In 2008, one topic in particular stood out on MySpace when compared with Facebook: "Music's importance for MySpace versus Facebook is shown though an analysis of social media conversations—music is the biggest difference between topics discussed. It's mentioned in 20% of posts about MySpace compared to just 7% in posts about Facebook" (see Table 4.4).

The significance of music in discussions among social media users not only within MySpace but also within Facebook, the attention given to the global social media phenomenon, and the number of bands, artists, musicians, and fans taking up these services, together with the publication of the numerous 'how-to' books, show the significant role of music within global social media. However, the way music practitioners adopt these services and the nature of the music-related activities are far less clear. The next part of the chapter explores how electronic music practitioners discovered and

Table 4.4   Music is a Major Difference in Discussions around Facebook and
MySpace (% of Online Social Media Posts Mentioning the Network)

	Facebook	MySpace
Friends	22	27
Photos	14	12
Music	7	20
Problems	8	10
Video	6	9
Application	5	2

(Adapted from Nielsen Online, 2009: 10.)

started using MySpace, and thereby became a central part of the emerging
global social media and music nexus.

DISCOVERING MYSPACE

After launching in the US in 2003, and particularly after being acquired by
News Corp in 2005, MySpace's popularity soon increased in Europe. Norway, along with the other Nordic countries, is one of the countries in the
world with highest penetration and take-up of new media and communications technology and forms such as mobile telephony and the internet as
well as social media (Global Information Technology Report, 2010–2011).
Along with Facebook, by far the most popular social media, the adoption of
MySpace, as well as national competitors, has been fast and extensive in the
country. With a population of only around 5 million, by early 2009 there
were 1.5 million Facebook profiles with addresses in Norway (Midtsjø,
2009). As in other parts of the world, bands and artists based in Norway
also began to adopt MySpace. By 2009, around 30,000 Norwegian-based
bands and artists had registered on MySpace (Thorkildsen, 2009). As the
next section shows, electronic music practitioners were among the early
adopters of MySpace.

The electronic music scene in the city of Bergen, Norway, has been
prosperous and particularly internationally oriented. Bergen-based artists, club organizers, producers, DJs, and managers were part of the
international electronic music and dance music scenes emerging in certain cities in the late 1980s and early 1990s in the US, UK, and continental Europe. The most internationally well-known Bergen-based duo,
Röyksopp, helped place Bergen on the world map of electronic music.
Internationally known artists such as Annie, Datarock, Bjørn Torske, and
Skatebård together with amateur and semi-professional DJs, club promoters, music producers, and artists have for many years been a highly
active electronic music milieu. Many of these practitioners have operated

locally and internationally for several years, and some have musical connections to genres such as indie rock. Throughout the last decade, several of these Bergen-based artists received considerable attention not only in the niche music press, but also in the international mainstream press. Media on both sides of the Atlantic, *The New York Times* (Rosen, 2005), the *BBC* (Kutchinsky, 2007), *The Guardian* (Hann, 2009), the American online news outline *The Huffington Post* (Mohr, 2009), as well as specialist media outlets such as the online music site *Clash Music* (Clash Music, 2009), have all given considerable attention to these Bergen-based electronic music practitioners.

The next section shows how these electronic music practitioners worked prior to the arrival of global social media, how they took up these services, and how these online entities have come to influence their music practice and work.

In 2005 around a quarter of a million amateur and professional bands had created MySpace profiles to promote their music (Cohn, 2005). Around that time, music practitioners in electronic music and related genres in Bergen began to create MySpace profiles. These people were early adopters of the global social media service. The take-up happened in various ways, and there are several parallels to the way MySpace was adopted in the US.

The music practitioners interviewed have all been central and influential in the electronic music milieu in Bergen, and they share certain characteristics. All were active in the 1990s prior to the maturing of the internet and the emergence and popular take-up of social media. They come from Bergen or have been living there for a long period, and most know each other. All of them have played at the same venues and clubs nights in Bergen run in particular by interviewee Vegard Moberg Nilsen (Electric Café, Straedet, Café Opera). Several have organized and played club nights at the same venue, Landmark: Hot!Hot!Hot! (co-organized by interviewee Mikal Telle), Digitalo (organized by Vegard Moberg Nilsen and Skatebård), and Powerblytt (organized by interviewee Lars Jacob Tynes Pedersen with Kjersti Blytt—also forming duo The Work). Many of them have collaborated, and all the artists have released key records on the Bergen-based label Telle Records (see Appendix for discographies of the artists).

Mikal Telle is a Bergen-based manger, record label manager, DJ and club promoter. Telle, the owner of the Tellé Records label, became a central figure in the Bergen electronic music environment when releasing the first, or at least early, records in the late 1990s and early 2000s by the most influential Bergen-based electronic music artists. These records were for the most part released on the main Tellé Records label (and some on the smaller Ellet or Tellektro labels): Bjørn Torske (1998, 1999, 2000; 2001, 2002), Röyksopp (1998, 2001), Annie (1999, 2000), Skatebård (2002), and Datarock (2003) (see Appendix). All these artists are interviewed in this book.

Mikal Telle set up his first MySpace profile in November 2005. This was early compared to the general take-up of MySpace in Europe and Norway, and for Telle the service provided a platform to re-launch his small record labels from the analogue era:

> First, I started MySpace profiles for all my five record labels. By giving them a MySpace profile each they were brought back to life online. On these profiles, I embedded music that I had previously released. However, after a while I reduced the number of profiles. Now I have one MySpace profile that includes all five record labels. (Mikal Telle, February 2009)

Annie (Anne Lilia Berge), music artist and DJ, released her first album *Anniemal* in 2004. This included collaborations with British producer Richard X and fellow Norwegians Röyksopp, among others. The following year, she toured internationally—in both the UK and the US. During that period she started using MySpace:

> At the time I was touring with my first album, so it was a very convenient way for me to promote my concerts, and DJ-gigs and in general. I have an audience that is interested in what other artists I like, what I am doing, and what clothes I like. So, it became easier to update (such information on MySpace) than on a web homepage, and easier to reach more people. (Annie, November 2010)

The service, then, was instantly useful to her. Annie utilized MySpace to promote her music and in particular her concerts to a potential audience. MySpace allowed her to reach people and incorporate personal tastes for music and clothing when promoting her professional artist persona. Prior to the album release, Annie had received considerable coverage from, amongst others, the influential web-based music publication *Pitchfork Media*. One of her songs featured as number one on Pitchfork's Top 50 Singles of 2004, and her *Anniemal* album was featured as number 15 on the Top 50 Albums of 2004—both lists published on 30 December:

> For me, MySpace was important. I was quite early on referred to as an 'internet artist', because Pitchfork was very preoccupied with my music that I released. So, I was very early referred to as an 'internet artist'. At the time, I did not know what Pitchfork was, and I was perhaps one of the people who knew the least about different websites. But, I soon realized that it was a good thing to have knowledge about it. (. . .) I do not think that I used it (MySpace) the most, but I was absolutely using it particularly when on tour. (Annie, December 2010)

Annie points out how she was considered an 'internet artist'—an artist who had become known through, or by utilizing, the internet. This clearly resonates with the earlier references to the British band Arctic Monkeys as a

"MySpace band," and Kate Nash as the "new queen of MySpace" (Caesar, 2007). As previously shown, the press described these artists as the proof of the promotional power of the internet and MySpace.

Formed already in 1998, Röyksopp released its debut single *So Easy* (1999) and *Eple* (2001) both on Tellé Records (Mikal Telle's record label). The duo then signed to the British record label Wall of Sound and Röyksopp's debut album, *Melody AM*, released in 2001, became a major artistic and commercial success and established the duo in most parts of the world. The follow-up album *The Understanding* was released in 2005. However, at the time, and in contrast to Annie, MySpace was not important to the duo's music practice. Band member Svein Berge explains:

> I remember when MySpace emerged, and it was a bit like: "Aren't you on MySpace? Are you not up-to-date?" But, I think that the reason why we have not used MySpace (personally) is that we established ourselves prior to the arrival of (social media). So, we were already established (Svein Berge, December 2010)

Torbjørn Brundtland, the other half of the duo, points out how Röyksopp had, prior to the arrival of not only social media, but the mainstream take-up of internet, become well-known throughout the world:

> We had in a way already done the part when you try to get 'inside' (getting contacts and establishing oneselves as artists). And that happened before the internet became so popular that everyone used it. We did not use it much in the period when we established contact with Wall of Sound (the band's record company), around 2000 or thereabouts. (Torbjørn Brundtland, December 2010)

Röyksopp did secure the internet domain name www.royksopp.com very early but did not use it actively at first. The site was a static site with a news article or biography of the band: "From what we heard there were incredible high numbers of visitors, but there was not any content there then, so people disappeared. Later, we began to develop the website, and we were in a position that people soon visited the site. We did not have to work hard for that to happen" (Torbjørn Brundtland, December 2010).

Skatebård, on the other hand, a fellow Bergen-based music producer and artist operating internationally, joined MySpace in 2005. As with Mikal Telle and Annie, Skatebård saw MySpace as an opportunity to establish an online presence, and emphasizes that the service was free to use: "It was easy to create a 'website' (on MySpace) where you could present music and have direct contact with others, and have complete control over the site despite having no knowledge of web design. This was back in 2005." Prior to MySpace, Skatebård did not have an online presence for his artistic activities apart from his discography on the discogs.com web site (Skatebård, March

2009). Bjørn Torske, an influential Bergen-based DJ and producer for close to two decades, came across MySpace by word of mouth in 2005:

> A fellow electronic musician asked me, "Have you heard about MyS-pace?" This was in 2005. I did not know what this was, but he showed me how it worked. But it was quite new at that time, so I don't know how many were using it then. It took a year until I finally registered, and made a profile and began to upload music. In the beginning it was very much like: "This is something new and exciting. It is a way of getting in touch with people. You can present yourself. In a way it is a window to the world." And then you get friends. You establish contact with people—both musicians and people who are interested in music. It was a dedicated music profile account (you could register on). You can register on a (regular) person profile account or a music profile account—where you can upload and display music and people can lis-ten or download. (Bjørn Torske, September 2010)

Bjørn Torske, then, also saw the potential of MySpace for his music prac-tice and points out how, in the mid-2000s, there was a buzz around the ser-vice among both music practitioners and people interested in music. Also Vegard Moberg Nilsen, the Bergen-based DJ and central club organizer and promoter for over 15 years, emphasizes how he got to know about MySpace through word of mouth. All the Bergen-based artists interviewed in this book have been DJing at his club nights since the mid-2000s, and some since the late 1990s. Moberg Nilsen has also booked numerous well-known and lesser-known international DJs to play at his clubs. In 2005, he first created a profile for his DJ persona, DJ Baltazaar, and later for the club Straedet that he was promoting from 2006 to 2008:

> It was word of mouth: 'Have you seen this website MySpace where people can embed music?' First, people talked about it, and we started using it quite early. Then it was mentioned in the national (Norwegian) newspapers, but that was after we had started using it. And then, when it was in the media, it started to grow very fast. But before that it was only in a very defined environment, among people very interested in music. (Vegard Moberg Nilsen, February 2009).

Vegard Moberg Nilsen, along with Skatebård and Bjørn Torske, all got to know about MySpace from other people, and from then went on to join the service. However, as Moberg Nilsen points out, this was around the time that News Corp acquired MySpace, and the social media phenomenon had also begun to appear in the Norwegian national press and media coverage of MySpace was also picked up by music practitioners.

The same year, in 2005, Bergen-based band Datarock also created a MySpace profile. In 2001, Datarock released its first record—a split record with fellow Bergen-based artist Stockhaus on the Tellé Records label. The original members of Datarock were Fredrik Saroea and Ketil Mosnes, and the band has since toured worldwide and gradually become an internationally recognized electronic music/rock band. However, it was an associated member of the band that first heard about the MySpace phenomenon through colleagues active within a particular scene of music—punk and hardcore (the indie music genre). He decided to create a MySpace profile. Musicians within indie music had been particularly active MySpace users since it first launched in the US (boyd and Ellison, 2007; Angwin, 2009). Artists within this genre have traditionally cultivated a strong do-it-yourself culture, according to former Datarock band member, Ketil Mosnes:

> He (the associated Datarock member) had a background from punk bands and hardcore bands and that kind of music, and was therefore very interested in that culture, and he heard about this (MySpace). I don't know exactly how, but from his contacts within this community (punk and hardcore). It was he who came to Fredrik and me (the original Datarock duo) and said: 'Now there is a MySpace profile for Datarock'. It must have been in August or September 2005. MySpace had already existed for some time, but I had maybe only just about heard of it. (Ketil Mosnes, February 2009)

While many music practitioners began to take up MySpace, others were more reluctant. Lars Jacob Tynes Pedersen, DJ and co-organizer of the Bergen club, Powerblytt, and electronic music duo The Work (with Kjersti Blytt), explains how his colleague, Mikal Telle, tried to convince him to take up MySpace, in 2005:

> Here (on MySpace) you could become friends with the musician Vincent Gallo online! And, the question was: 'Was it really him and not some of his fans?' Mikal (Mikal Telle) was very enthusiastic about this, and he proved to be right when saying that this was the future of communication between music practitioners, and between practitioners and the audience. He recommended us strongly to become members here (MySpace). At that time, I was in general skeptical to the digitization and all this. I was quite conservative and fond of vinyl records, and felt that the music industry was threatened in a way. So, I was very skeptical, and we did not become members at first. (Lars Jacob Tynes Pedersen, March 2009)

This indicates how the new phenomenon raised concern not only about trust, but also how the degree of usability of MySpace was not evident to everyone. However, in January 2006 Pedersen changed his mind. A friend told him how he had come in contact with a large number of musicians internationally, and offered to create a MySpace profile for the club

Powerblytt in Bergen. This profile later became the profile for Powerblytt Records. A profile for the band, The Work, was created in the first half of 2006, and a The Work Remixes profile was created in 2008.

In the mid-2000s, then, word of mouth was clearly important in the take-up of MySpace among the Bergen-based electronic music practitioners. As with bands and artists in other parts of the world, these music practitioners were among the early adopters of the service. At the time, MySpace was still not well-known to a wider public.

Across the North Sea in London members of the electronic music community also noticed MySpace. (As we shall see later, the link between the club scene in East London and Bergen serves as an example of global social media's role in connecting music scenes). In East London, DJ Arno (Arno de Beaufort) and DJ Fonteyn (Clive Kelly) were discovering MySpace. DJ Fonteyn has promoted clubs and been DJing in London and in Europe since the early 2000s. In 2007 Fonteyn co-established the club Nuke Them All, and prior to that he ran the Italo disco/electro pop club Computer Blue.

> MySpace came along—probably about 2006 I would say. There was a massive hype about MySpace. What happened was really that there were big success stories. Initial signings on MySpace, and it became an industry buzz, and it kind of gave a false illusion that if you were doing something without any connection to the music industry, but if you were doing something really good, people would just pick up on it and magically whisk you off to some kind of success. That happened to a few people—probably the Arctic Monkeys was one of the first. They got a multimillion record deal with absolutely no record industry support, and became a huge phenomenon. And, then following that, everyone was looking at MySpace. It was immediately transplanted into the conscience of the young generation in Britain at the time. (DJ Fonteyn, March 2010)

Just as Bergen-based Vegard Moberg Nilsen pointed out, DJ Fonteyn also refers to stories in the press about MySpace. This further emphasizes the role of the traditional media in making MySpace known. Stories were picked up by members of the electronic music community both in Norway and the UK who then formed an opinion on the significance of MySpace in relation to music. DJ Fonteyn's colleague in East London, DJ Arno, who has been a DJ since the 1990s, also reflects on the role of MySpace within music in the UK at that time.

> I think the first social media that really made a difference was MySpace. Before that, there was Friendster, but it did not have so much of an aspect with music. It was very much just a friend thing. MySpace came along in 2004, 2005, and really started to explode in the UK in 2005. MySpace was not only a social media for linking up with your

friends, but also to put your music out there, and to discover other people's music. (DJ Arno, March 2010)

So a mix of recommendations from fellow music practitioners and a curiosity and desire among practitioners to explore the usability of MySpace, as well as the fact that MySpace was free, led to the adoption of the service in 2005 and 2006. The various ways in which they became familiar with and gradually took up MySpace shows how the US-originated phenomenon quickly spread out and became known and adopted within different local music milieus. The next section goes one step further by examining how the practitioners started using MySpace in their music practice.

USING MYSPACE

MySpace soon became a tool for many of the music practitioners. The service was seen as an online tool that enhanced the potential for the distribution of information between MySpace users. This section shows how MySpace, then, made it possible for users to operate on various levels online. Such issues have been addressed in relation to the internet previously. In the years preceding the rise of global social media, Hampton and Wellman's pioneering research on Netville, "an experimental 'wired suburb'" in Toronto, explored "how the internet affects neighborhood community" (Hampton and Wellmann, 2003: 278). The study showed that "Netville is a harbinger of 'glocalization,' being simultaneously globally connected and locally involved" (Hampton and Wellman, 2003: 306). The maturing and take-up of the internet and the subsequent arrival of global social media have accentuated this issue as the potential for such contact increased substantially. As such, referring to work by, for example, Hampton and Wellman, Papacharissi points out, "Social network sites represent a natural extension of this work, as they connect networks of individuals that may or may not share a place-based connection" (2009: 201) As the next section shows, MySpace represents such a glocalization device as it is possible to use the service at both a local and global level.

The Local and Global

MySpace was utilized in the promotion of local clubs to people in the Bergen area with MySpace profiles, and also to artists around the world who potentially could be booked to play at the clubs. Vegard Moberg Nilsen, DJ and club organizer and promoter of his Bergen-based club Straedet (running from 2006 to 2008), pointed out that many artists have their own MySpace profile and administered these sites themselves. In his experience, you could therefore approach artists directly and sometimes avoid paying fees to the artists' management:

It was very important to have this page (the MySpace profile for the club Straedet) as a reference and as a way of communicating when booking artists. (The MySpace profile of Straedet had) two very important functions. One: pure marketing. You can send messages to all your friends, and post flyers on their profile. Two: you can send emails internally in the MySpace system to anyone. You can send a message directly to any artist. When you do that to the biggest artists, then they have people who administer for them, but medium artists (in popularity) and underground artists often administer it (their MySpace profile) themselves, and then you often get an answer from this person (the artist). We booked many artists from abroad. It was a bit half-anarchistic as you could avoid the management and save money or the artist could get more money. It is almost a parallel to the way music is distributed digitally; that the world is becoming smaller. Then you have a unique possibility to get direct contact with artists—that was impossible before—because you exist in this community that is a very defined arena where you can talk together. (Vegard Moberg Nilsen, February 2009)

On the one hand, this shows how MySpace could be used to communicate between a single user to many users—from Moberg Nilsen to potential guests for the club Straedet. On the other hand, communication could also take place between single users—from one music practitioner to another. This communication took place within the MySpace universe, but the users could be based anywhere geographically. One of the artists that Moberg Nilsen contacted was DJ Fonteyn, part of the East London electronic music scene. Through MySpace, Vegard Moberg Nilsen got in touch, the London-based DJ remembers: "Vegard, my friend over there, he was obsessive about this kind of thing. He wanted to stay in touch with what was going on internationally, and he found it very easy to do that (using MySpace), and also to promote his nights in Bergen" (March 2010). Similarly, DJ Arno, DJ Fonteyn's colleague in London, points out how MySpace made it possible to connect with and become visible to other MySpace users both locally and internationally:

I think social media not only linked you to the rest of the world, but also helped you understand your direct environment (East London). You could find out who everybody was in an instant, other music practitioners but also your fans. With MySpace, it seemed you suddenly knew every Londoner who shared your music taste. And, everybody knew you as long as you did something worthy of attention. I think that was the first thing. Then, it (MySpace) opened the door for you to discover people on the other side of the world, and for them to discover you. (DJ Arno, March 2010)

Together with DJ Fonteyn, then, DJ Arno was booked "completely out of the blue" after meeting "someone on MySpace" for clubs abroad, including Bergen:

> The same thing (booking) happened in Bergen, Norway. A friend of mine linked up (through MySpace) with someone there, because they liked their record. We then got invited to perform. And this turned into a regular job (at the club Straedet in Bergen), where we would fly in and play every month. Similar events happened in other countries as well, just as quickly and unexpectedly. This would have never happened without the social media that was mainly MySpace at the time. (DJ Arno, March 2010)

Similarly, Lars Jacob Tynes Pedersen—the Bergen-based DJ and music producer—also emphasizes the local and international use of MySpace. Just as the club Straedet, run by Vegard Moberg Nilsen and where the East London-based DJs Fonteyn and DJ Arno played, the Bergen club Powerblytt was promoted to local MySpace users using virtual club flyers. It was Tynes Pedersen's music production activity that had a more significant international dimension on MySpace. A Japanese record company released a record of his (and Kjersti Blytt's) band The Work, and suddenly, Friend requests from Japan to the band's MySpace profile increased substantially:

> Suddenly a small following of people in Tokyo emerged. (They) contacted us, and especially the The Work's profile on MySpace. Incredible responses—and a large number of responses—from Tokyo especially. This has meant that Tokyo is the city we have sold the most records. We were also included on a compilation record in Japan (that was) mixed by a person who we came in contact with on MySpace. We have now many contacts there (in Japan) and this is solely due to MySpace. We would never have made contact with them if not for MySpace. (Lars Jacob Tynes Pedersen, March 2009)

However, the connection between Japan and Norway had been established prior to MySpace. The Tokyo-based record label, Escalator, had previously released records by music artists from Norway: "So the first node was not MySpace, but from there on it spread like fire through dry grass throughout the MySpace network," according to Lars Jacob Tynes Pedersen. As with Moberg Nilsen, Pedersen points out how MySpace allowed for communication both on a local and international level:

> (S)o there is a local aspect in relation to the marketing of our club night (Powerblytt) in Bergen. And, then, after we started to focus on the band profile (The Work) it became much more international. (. . .) The Powerblytt profile was a convenient vehicle for transporting information (individual club flyers) from one place to the other (locally). The artist

(The Work) MySpace profile has gone beyond our expectations of what we thought might happen when starting a website. (Lars Jacob Tynes Pedersen, March 2009)

Bergen-based artist and DJ Skatebård produces electronic dance music and records with an international appeal. Since 2002, he has released around 15 records and these sell up to 2,000 copies each. He is increasingly performing internationally. After adopting MySpace in 2005, it became an important tool for promoting his activity, and he used all the functionalities of the site. With around 6,000 MySpace Friends based in different parts of the world, the 'bulletin' feature of MySpace is important to him:

> I (send a bulletin) if I have a new record being released or something big going on, or if I have participated in a radio program and want to tell (MySpace friends) about the link to the podcast. The bulletin is a common space, or bulletin space—a page (within MySpace) where all my friends' bulletins appear. It (a bulletin from Skatebård) can often drown, because there are many who send out a lot, when you have as many friends (as I do). (In addition, you can include) music and pictures, and there is a blog where one can publish news and other things that happens in the Skatebård world. (Skatebård, March 2009)

In a similar fashion, Mikal Telle, Bergen-based manger, DJ, and record label manager of Tellé Records, used MySpace to promote his bands in Norway and overseas. He also used all the features of the MySpace profile, including the incorporation—or embedding—of YouTube videos, to create an interesting and appealing image and impression of bands he was managing:

> If you have a band that you want to get noticed, then you try to combine YouTube and MySpace. You film a concert and find the two minutes that are "hottest," and place it on YouTube, and then embed this video file on MySpace. So, when people visit the band's MySpace profile, they will at once see that "They are good live!" and here (next to the video on the MySpace profile) are some music tracks we can listen to. Then it is very often impressive if you have a very, very long list of tour dates that shows that you are a hard-working band. This is an impression you want to give as well. (Mikal Telle, February 2009)

MySpace, then, increased the music practitioners' ability to promote themselves and communicate with either single users or large numbers of users of MySpace both locally and internationally, and at low cost. In practice, we see that this takes place in a number of ways and through a combination of approaches. Some may distribute virtual flyers among other MySpace users or incorporate YouTube videos of bands on a MySpace profile to present a band. Others contact artists directly or send bulletins to other

MySpace users. Also, we see how traditional media played a role in promoting MySpace in general and the relationship between MySpace and music specifically. However, traditional media may also direct attention specifically to a band's MySpace profile. This happened to Datarock.

Datarock started out in 2000 as a local band in Bergen, but has in a few years become internationally known. Ketil Mosnes, former member of the band, explains the significance of MySpace, adopted by the band in 2005: "This was a specific way for us to get in touch with other bands and other people within our field of interest, and of course across the whole world" (Ketil Mosnes, February 2009). Australia was the first country outside Norway where the band became known. This happened after an Australian radio station picked up one of Datarock's songs and started to play it frequently, Mosnes recalls:

> So, completely beyond our control the recognition of the band and name grew quite significantly in Australia. We noticed this first and foremost through MySpace. We started to get a very high number of friend requests from Australia, and many 18-year-old girls who said, "We love you! You have to come to Australia," and that kind of talk. This was at a time when we still thought this (MySpace) was so amusing that I think we answered every one who wrote to us personally. It was very many. Around 70 or 80 percent of the queries came from Australia. This happened autumn 2005 and developed gradually into 2006. So, we traveled to Australia in February 2006 and experienced our little version of Abba in Australia in the 1970s, with fans standing outside the concert venue before the sound check, yelling at us. (Ketil Mosnes, February 2009)

A traditional radio station played one of Datarock's songs and this was noticed by people with MySpace profiles who contacted the band. Here, MySpace served as a connection between the offline and the online world. It facilitated the communication between Datarock in Norway and fans in the geographically distant Australia. The band considered the increased attention from MySpace users as an indicator of the band's popularity in Australia:

> So for us (Datarock), this MySpace thing was especially relevant in relation to Australia and the career we had there. It was very noticeable. I think it was a clever thing to answer personally everyone who contacted us for quite a long time. Because 17-year-olds who send a message to a band they are fans of are not used to getting an answer. From their perspective, these youths probably thought we were a bigger band than we were since we came from Europe to tour in Australia and play some of the big venues in the country. (Ketil Mosnes, February 2009)

Around New Year 2007, Datarock had also played a few concerts in the US and had signed deals with a Canadian manager and a Canadian record label. The band was also starting to get contacted by fans in the US through MySpace:

> I got the impression that some of them (US fans) had heard about us from their Australian friends. So, it went a bit like: Norway to Australia, and then Australia to the US. If you are an 18-year-old sitting in the US, and then your cousin who is studying in Australia tells you, "Yeah, you have to check out this band Datarock on MySpace!" then you do it. Then he becomes a fan of the band and sends us a message, and at that time, we still answered personally all the messages we received. (Ketil Mosnes, February 2009)

Soon after, Datarock's manager told the band's two members to stop personally responding to messages. It would take up too much of the band's time. This, again, shows how music practitioners may use different strategies when incorporating and utilizing MySpace in their music practice. Some artists ran their own MySpace profile, while others hired people to do it.

MySpace, then, came to play a significant role in a variety of ways for Datarock and most of the other Bergen-based electronic music practitioners. However, although MySpace facilitated increased opportunities to promote and connect with other MySpace users both locally and internationally, there are elements of influence within the service that need to be scrutinized.

Aspects of Influence within the Network

Although MySpace offers a range of opportunities for its users, there are relations within the service and between users that may determine to what extent users succeed in attracting attention and connect with other users. This is particularly relevant for music artists and practitioners. As such, we see how some users have greater influence than others within MySpace, and since the mid-2000s, the international music business has attempted to increase its influence within the global social media environment in a number of ways.

While a MySpace profile could have thousands of friends, each profile had a 'Top list.' A Top list consists of the icons of a small group of friends (usually from 8 to 20). The list is placed on the front of the MySpace profile's interface. A visitor to this profile will easily see this list but will have to laboriously click through the hundreds or thousands of other friends not on the list, as they are hidden behind the front of the profile. If your MySpace profile is featured as a friend on the Top list of someone whose profile is much visited, it is likely that you will receive attention in the form of people clicking on your profile icon and visiting your profile. You are thereby promoted by being endorsed by someone else in the MySpace universe. Vegard Moberg Nilsen, club promoter and DJ, experienced this when his Straedet club profile was featured on the international Bergen-based artist Annie's MySpace profile's Top list.

You use it (the MySpace profile) almost like a website, but the big difference is that it already exists in an environment where the users already are. They do not click themselves to your profile. They come to your profile via links. You place on the front of your profile the ones that you are most interested in promoting or showing that you are linked to. That is the trick. The more MySpace users who put Straedet (the club Moberg Nilsen promotes) on the Top list the more traffic (visitors to the Straedet profile) we got. Who you have good relations with (in real life) is very important, as well as who puts your name as a main friend or prioritized friend. You can put a number of friends on the front page. So, for example, when we were placed on the front (Top friends list) of Annie, whose profile has many thousands of hits each day, the traffic on our profile (Straedet) increased enormously. Very important. (Vegard Moberg Nilsen, February 2009)

Similarly, Lars Jacob Tynes Pedersen explains how, as a newcomer to MySpace, it was important to be featured on the Top list of local popular music practitioners who attracted the audience Pedersen also wanted to reach:

MySpace became a formidable way of becoming part of this environment. Mikal Telle, Skatebård, Datarock, Ungdomskulen (Bergen-based rock band) all had profiles. But (generally) there were still few people who had taken up MySpace, so at the time, if you became friends with one of these, then you were suddenly on their Top list. (The club Powerblytt) received many friend requests from people in Bergen who went to our club night, and they received a digital flyer for the club (via MySpace). There were maybe 50 at first, and then it increased as more and more people became part of it (MySpace). (Lars Jacob Tynes Pedersen, March 2009)

In a similar way, the British artist Kate Nash benefited from being placed on the 'Top 8' list of a much more popular artist. British pop artist Lily Allen, often seen as an artist having benefited enormously from MySpace, placed Nash on her 'Top 8' list. "It definitely helped," Nash claims, as "she has such a spotlight, and she brought that spotlight on to me" (Nash, quoted in Caesar, 2007).

Another way of receiving attention was to be placed as 'Featured Artist' on the front page of MySpace portals. Once the localization of MySpace started, regional and national MySpace versions could place local music-related information, news, and features of bands on the front of the various MySpace portals (see Chapter 3). By being on, for example, the front of the MySpace Mexico portal, an artist would reach Mexican users who might start surfing the MySpace service at the regional service's front page. Prior to localization, there was only one MySpace front page or portal for the whole world—the American version, according to Ketil Mosnes, former

Datarock member. Mosnes remembers the effect it had when the Bergen-based band he was part of suddenly became the featured band on the front of MySpace US:

> This was before MySpace Norway existed. There was only one MyS-pace. It is possible that there was a MySpace UK, but Norway was very much under the US. Suddenly one day, when I logged on to the Datarock profile (. . .). I think it must have been in January/February 2007. It was a relatively short time before we were traveling to *South by South West* and (other) music conventions (in the US). Then, I suddenly saw that we were the 'Featured Artist' on the front of the MySpace portal. We did not understand why, but we received more friend requests than I managed to approve. Once every five seconds, a friend request arrived, and my computer was a bit slow, so it took me six to seven seconds to press 'Approve.' (Ketil Mosnes, February 2009)

Datarock was 'Featured Artist' on the global MySpace portal for between three and four days, and after some time Mosnes had to get assistance in order to manage to approve all the friend requests:

> We were 'Featured Artist' for three to four days, and after a while, I got help from Fredrik (the other half of the Datarock duo) and our manager and some others. I could not sit around the clock. But, if I remember correctly, I think we got around 10,000 friends over those four days. And this is like a snowball, because these 10,000 persons tell their friends again. So, the flow of requests continued quite significantly also after we were removed from the MySpace front page. (Ketil Mosnes, February 2009)

Mosnes does not remember exactly how many friends Datarock had before this happened but claims that the number of friends quadrupled within a month after Datarock had been 'Featured Artist':

> Now, this is an estimate. I do not remember exactly, but from around 10,000 to 40,000 friends. It was an explosion (when we became 'Featured Artist') just a few minutes afterwards. I do not know how long we had been there when I first noticed it, but it cannot have been for many hours. It was quite extreme. Maybe I am not remembering exactly correct, but I think that MySpace had around 90 million users, and I think all 90 million got (the same) MySpace front page when they logged on. It was interesting to see this, but also a bit frustrating. (Ketil Mosnes, February 2009)

Mosnes does not know for sure the reason Datarock was given the coveted 'Featured Artist' position. However, one possible explanation could be that a record label based in Los Angeles was planning to release a record by

Datarock, and the influential head of this label contacted people within MySpace who were his friends: "I have also seen later that other bands that (the record label manager) is working with appear there (on MySpace). (These are) bands that from the outset are not very well-known. I don't know for a fact, but it seemed to me that this could be the case" (Ketil Mosnes, 2009). In retrospect, current sole member of Datarock, Fredrik Saroea, emphasizes the importance of being 'Featured Artist':

> The point is that Datarock has almost not sold any records. But, still we have been booked to play 700 concerts in 33 countries. We are not talking about one concert per country, but 17 tours in the US, and 6 tours in Australia. It is crazy. And, there is no link between our fan base or audience and sales of records. Rather, I think it is because (of) MySpace. The cool thing about MySpace, or used to be, was that it was just something that suddenly emerged. So, for example, we suddenly were the international 'Feature Artist' (on MySpace). (Fredrik Saroea, 2010)

Datarock clearly benefited from the structure of MySpace. Being on the front of the global MySpace portal gave the band significant exposure. This clearly connects with Papacharissi's general reflections on the consequences of the way social media are built: "The architecture of virtual spaces, much like the architecture of physical spaces, simultaneously suggests and enables particular modes of interaction" (Papacharissi, 2009: 200). The architecture of MySpace, then, influenced the music practitioners use of the service in different ways. Being the 'Featured Artist' brought the band many new friends. A large number of friend requests gives an indication of the popularity of bands. Also, as pointed out by Vegard Moberg Nilsen, and as was the case with Datarock, sometimes a band's friends may communicate directly with members of the band. Furthermore, becoming a friend of a band signals musical tastes and interests to other users of MySpace. Also, as several of the Bergen-based artists have pointed out, the Top friends list on the front of the MySpace profile, as well as the localization of MySpace, influences the nature of communication, as Mikal Telle explains:

> They (MySpace) have had an office (in Norway) that we have made great use of, so I think it has both advantages and disadvantages. I think it is not good when it fragments too much. For example, now when MySpace ha(s) their own office in Norway, then we have had a lot of things (bands and artists) on the front page of MySpace (Norway), but the point is that when we have had things on the front page of MySpace in Norway, then: "Who cares?" It is exactly the same thing as when MTV became MTV Norway: 'Who cares?" That attention only has a value in Norway. But, of course, you can continue to communicate internationally (on MySpace). If it had been international, then I think it had been more valuable. But, as soon as it is on the front page of Norway,

then you don't really care that much about the effect. I remember from when MTV fragmented. (Mikal Telle, February 2009)

In addition to MySpace, Mikal Telle and Fredrik Saroea have been using Underskog—a Norwegian invitation-only social network in Norwegian—particularly popular among people involved in the country's cultural and creative sector. The site was launched in 2005 and served as a noticeboard for events and discussion forum for members. By 2010, it had around 20,000 members. But this service did not have an international dimension:

> At the same time as MySpace, we had Underskog in Norway. It was more closed, and it was even more specialized than MySpace, but the people there were very interested in music, culture, creative business. So, if you wanted to meet someone who could influence others, then Underskog was important at the time. (Mikal Telle, October 2010)

Still, while Underskog represented an important local and national online arena, there is no doubt that the music practitioners' adoption and use of especially MySpace in 2005 and 2006 was part of the start of the emerging global social media and music nexus. As we have seen, the service created potential for different forms of communication and contact among and between users both locally and across the world, and this was soon utilized by music practitioners and MySpace users interested in music. Seen from a user perspective, then, the global social media and music nexus provided a new online arena for these users. However, the development taking place within MySpace soon also caught the attention of the music industry. The next section takes a closer look at the nexus from a corporate perspective.

THE CORPORATE PERSPECTIVE OF THE GLOBAL SOCIAL MEDIA AND MUSIC NEXUS

Global social media soon began to position themselves to capitalize on the rapid rise in the number of users. Music bands and artists and the fans that followed them on MySpace were particularly attractive for such corporate interests. The number of MySpace users who became 'friends' with bands was significant. In 2008, the 10 most popular British MySpace music band profiles had hundreds of thousands of friends (see Table 4.5).

MySpace's creation of a competitor to online media content retailers such as iTunes was one of the early corporate initiatives to monetize the music-interested users. The launch of the MySpace Music service in the US also underlines News Corp's preoccupation with copyright and intellectual property within the online environment (see Figure 4.5). The launch of MySpace Music was made possible through collaboration with major music companies Sony, Universal, Time Warner, and EMI. As we shall see, the

Table 4.5   MySpace's Most Popular Musical Acts

Music Acts	Friends
Gorillaz	682,875
Bullet for My Valentine	596,885
Amy Winehouse	542,268
Coldplay	525,110
Lily Allen	462,159
MIA	399,858
Oasis	353,484
Imogen Heap	351,484

(*Data source:* Michaels, 2008.)

collaboration between global social media and the largest music players also characterizes the relationship between these services and music.

MySpace Music offered streamed music for free within the MySpace universe and the opportunity to purchase downloads of music through the online retailer Amazon.com (Gibson, 2008). Chris DeWolfe, Co-founder of MySpace, underlines the link between the major music companies and MySpace Music:

> We have the three biggest music companies in the world signed on with us. We're in the process of talking to the fourth. We're also working with all the indie music consortiums, so by the time we launch [this summer], it should be a very high percentage in the United States (. . .). Our main goal is to have all the music in the world on MySpace. (DeWolfe, quoted in Locke, 2008)

Still, the involvement of the music majors in online ventures was not new. In 2003 Apple had launched iTunes and "was able to convince all the majors to provide their music to the iTunes service" (Wikström, 2009: 101). However, by 2009 there existed more than 500 digital music services selling music (Wikström, 2009: 101). Several of these are niche services. One of the numerous legal digital music outlets is Beatport. The service was launched in 2004 and has reportedly become the "recognized leader in electronic dance music downloads for DJs and club music enthusiasts" and is referred to as "the most relevant online source of electronic music in the world" (Mansfield, 2009). Still, iTunes is the dominant commercial online outlet for digital music. In 2008, iTunes had more than 70 percent of the "global legal online music market" (Wikström, 2009: 102). Even so, by 2009 MySpace Music had become popular and was one of the most visited online music services in the US (see Table 4.6).

MySpace Music was only one of the ways in which the music industry attempted to adjust to digitization and the challenges posed by the online

Table 4.6   Top US Music Services on the Web (in unique visitors, December 2009)

1.	Vevo	35.4 million
2.	MySpace Music	33.1 million
3.	AOL Music	29.0 million
4.	Warner Music	23.3 million
5.	MTV Networks Music	17.6 million
6.	Yahoo! Music	16.4 million
7.	Jango Music Network	9.6 million
8.	ToneFuse Music Network	8.3 million
9.	MSN Music	6.6 million
10.	Rhapsody	6.5 million

(*Data source*: Schonfeld, 2010.)

environment. In the mid-2000s, there were two key challenges for the music industry—both linked to the digitization process. The first challenge was to figure out how it is possible to hinder "customers from simply reproducing infinite copies of digital files of music." The second challenge was to find "a method of payment that consumers feel happy with" (Hesmondhalgh, 2007: 253). The aim of the MySpace Music service, then, was to tackle these challenges by creating a 'one-stop' commercial multimedia environment for both the music business and the users, according to Chris DeWolfe:

> From a business perspective, we're allowing both the artists and the labels to capture all of the different revenue streams. From a user perspective (. . .) it's really a frictionless environment. (. . .) [Say] I want to go onto my favorite artist's site that may be Flowrida; I go onto the Flowrida site and I can listen to any song I want. (. . .) Then I can also look at a list of cities that he's going to be in and I can see he's coming to my city; I can buy a ticket directly from that site, and you know what? I'm going to want to download 10 of his songs to my iPod, I can do that directly from the site. And I may want to buy a T-shirt with his picture on it. I'll be able to do that directly from his site. (DeWolfe, quoted in Locke, 2008)

However, while MySpace Music aimed to serve as an online retail platform for music labels, the service was initially criticized for only including music from the four partnering major music companies. There are thousands of bands signed to small independent music labels that are not included in the MySpace Music service, not to mention the millions of unsigned music practitioners with a MySpace profile. Although these practitioners have played a vital part in developing MySpace into a global online site for music, it was argued at the time that major music players seemed to be reaping the commercial benefits of MySpace Music.

Just as with MySpace, Facebook soon became preoccupied with positioning its service within the global social media and music nexus. Facebook developed audio and visual features attractive to music practitioners and supporting the artist/fans relationship, as well as creating corporate links with the music industry. Facebook Pages was introduced as an additional service with features aiming to also appeal to music artists:

> If you are a public figure, we highly recommend you create a Page on Facebook in addition to your personal profile. You should continue to use your personal profile to connect with your family, friends and the people who are important to you and use your Page as a public profile to connect with your fans, supporters and followers. (Facebook, 2010b)

On the Facebook Pages, users can include photos, blogs, events, videos: "You can add video clips of just about anything including behind the scenes content, your latest music video or record videos direct to your fans (. . .) Be sure to create events for your upcoming tour, fundraisers or athletic events" (Facebook, 2010b). However, many artists use their ordinary personal Facebook profile. By late 2010, as happened in the mid-2000s with MySpace, music fans are able to link up with artists using Facebook and the most popular bands have also large followings on facebook. Over a million Facebook users have clicked 'like' on Lily Allen's Facebook profile. Close to 1.3 million Facebook users 'like' Arctic Monkeys' Facebook site, and more than 24 million Facebook users 'like' Lady Gaga's Facebook profile.

Facebook chose a different corporate strategy to MySpace, by collaborating with Spotify, an existing music streaming service. Still, this venture also involved the major music companies. Spotify was launched in October 2008 by two Swedish entrepreneurs. At the start the service announced music rights arrangements with Sony BMG Music, Universal Music, Warner Music, EMI, and Merlin. However, according to *Computer Sweden*, a Swedish language publication covering the computer industry, the links with the major music companies were even more intimate. At the time of the launch, these five major music companies were shareholders of Spotify, having reportedly bought 18 percent of the company for €8,800 in total (Jerräng, 2009). Therefore, when Facebook and Spotify agreed to link up, this also meant that the global music players were let into the global social media service. Spotify users who also use Facebook can share their favorite lists of music and songs among their Facebook friends (Barnett, 2009a). However, Spotify CEO Daniel Ek pointed out:

> Spotify is not a social network. Companies like MySpace and Facebook already do a good job of that. However, we do think that music is the most powerful social object on earth and people enjoy sharing music with each other (. . .) We are still building the Spotify platform at the

moment and over the coming weeks and months you will see more features added to the service. (Ek, quoted in Barnett, 2009a)

Similarly, YouTube and the music industry majors collaborate. Vevo, an online music video service, was launched officially in December 2009 in the US. Vevo was launched with partners Universal Music Group, Sony Music Entertainment, as well as the Abu Dhabi Media Company with participation from EMI, and YouTube as an important distribution platform (Evan, 2010). The Vevo service 'syndicates' music videos to other web services such as YouTube. Through YouTube, then, Vevo has a worldwide presence (Smith, 2010). The corporate arm of Vevo is "to help advertisers and content owners (including labels, artists, and music publishers) capitalize on music videos, and to help Google (YouTube's owner) offload some of the cost associated with administering rights to them" (Rosoff, 2009). Just as on MySpace, it is possible to embed YouTube videos on Facebook. It is also possible for users of services like Facebook, MySpace, and Twitter to embed and share Vevo videos on the users' profiles and among their friends.

SoundCloud is among the numerous online services that have emerged and been adopted also in connection with global social media by music practitioners. Launched in 2007, the aim, according to co-founder Alexander Ljung, was to develop a service similar to Flickr (the online site for hosting users' pictures) for musicians and their music. The service has more than 1.5 million users. One popular feature is that users can add "comments to the music, in either freestanding fashion or keyed to specific moments on the time grid, allowing for pinpoint analysis or, in the case of a longer DJ set, to ID specific songs as they appear in the mix." Just as with YouTube, a SoundCloud player can be incorporated on a Facebook profile as well as blogs (Matos, 2010).

As with YouTube, MySpace, and Facebook, the link between Twitter and music has become significant. Already in 2007, in a news piece titled *Twitter: Is Brevity The Next Big Thing?* the magazine *Newsweek* described how the use of Twitter was 'discovered' at South By Southwest (SXSW) in 2007—one of the largest annual music and film conventions in the US:

> Things reached a tipping point last month at the South by Southwest conference in Austin, Texas. The Twitter people cleverly placed two 60-inch plasma screens in the conference hallways, exclusively streaming Twitter messages. Hundreds of conference-goers kept tabs on each other via constant twitters. Panelists and speakers mentioned the service, and the bloggers in attendance touted it. Soon everyone was buzzing and posting about this new thing that was sort of instant messaging and sort of blogging and maybe even a bit of sending a stream of telegrams. (Levy, 2007)

In the wake of this enthusiastic news report, the relationship between Twitter and music began to develope. As with MySpace and YouTube, stories about the 'magic' of Twitter appeared. *The Guardian,* the British newspaper, published the piece "Twitter Power: How Social Networking is Revolutionising the Music" that also described the opportunities provided by Twitter:

> More artists are using social networking sites to bypass the traditional media. This weekend, rapper Kanye West took to Twitter to tell his side of the MTV Video Music awards' controversy where he grabbed the microphone from country music sweetheart Taylor Swift and announced that his friend Beyoncé should have won. (...) On Saturday he apologised, saying as a result of the debacle he had to cancel his tour with Lady Gaga and lost employees. He wrote: "Man I love Twitter . . . I've always been at the mercy of the press but no more . . . The media tried to demonise me." (Topping, 2010)

While Kayne West is a major international music artist, representatives from the independent part of the music industry also express their excitement over the potential of Twitter. David Emery, at Beggars Group, one of the largest independent groups of record labels (i.e., 4AD, Matador, and XL Recordings), points out how "word of mouth has always been incredibly important to us and now it's easier than ever to get the word out there." This is much due to the arrival of services like Twitter, Emery argues: "Twitter is great for artists interacting directly with fans, like MIA, who has millions of followers and will do things like make a video on her phone and post it on Twitter. That is so much more powerful than traditional marketing. But Facebook is a powerful method of direct marketing. It's less personal, but fans don't seem to mind that." (Emery, quoted in Topping, 2010). As happened with both MySpace and Facebook, the artist/fans relationship on Twitter has developed fast. By late 2010, Lady Gaga had more than 7 million Twitter users as 'followers.' Lily Allen had more than 2.5 million Twitter users as followers. Launched in 2009, the service Twiturm allows artists and bands to post music and share track lists of music. The owner of a Twitter profile may decide if listeners are allowed to download the different music tracks (Twiturm, 2009). It is also possible to use Twiturm to connect Twitter to one's Facebook profile. Furthermore, it is possible to embed a music player on the Facebook profile, so visitors can listen to the music without having to visit another site. As with the other global social media, 'how-to' books, such as *Twitter Power 2.0: How to Dominate Your Market One Tweet at a Time* (Comm, 2010), have been published. Similarly to MySpace, Facebook, and YouTube, then, the power and significance of Twitter in relation to music is promoted.

Although iTunes dominates the sales of digital music, the service's involvement within the social media environment has been limited. In a response to the strengthened link between global social media and music, in 2010 iTunes launched Ping—a "music-centric social network" in the US, Europe, and parts of Asia. Ping is integrated in iTunes and cannot be used outside the music outlet (Mediati, 2010), but the service is available on iPhone and iPod. Once a profile is created, one may see the music friends and other people listen to, and follow artists and see where they are playing (Apple, 2010). As such, iTunes' strategy mirrors MySpace Music's original aim of becoming a 'one-stop' destination for music.

The construction of MySpace Music, Spotify's collaboration with Facebook, and YouTube's involvement with Vevo show how the influence of the traditional major music companies extends within the global social media environment. We have also seen how, in the mid-2000s, influence became an issue among music practitioners using MySpace. Certain popular and much-visited MySpace profiles acted as nodes of influence, as the inclusion of a profile in their Top lists directed attention to these profiles. The take-up of global social media in the mid-2000s, then, has had an impact in the music practitioners' work in several ways. The next section explores in further detail in what way the use of MySpace changed their practice.

BEFORE AND AFTER MYSPACE

All the music practitioners interviewed were active prior to taking up MySpace. In this section, they reflect on their work before and after MySpace. A key change in their music practice relates to the difference between aspects of the online and offline in their music practice. Just as with the introduction of media and communications technologies and forms throughout history such as the telephone, MySpace and the digitization of media content and communication have also altered music practitioners' relationship with the physical 'real world.'

The Virtual and Real World

The online environment and MySpace open up for more efficient distribution of information and communication compared to the real world, according to DJ and organizer and promoter of the club Straedet, Vegard Moberg Nilsen:

> The difference is very simple. On MySpace you get information on-screen, and before the digital marketing approach it was (information on) paper. It (the physical distribution of paper flyers) is a very inconvenient way of distributing information, and it costs money and it costs time. We used MySpace (in the following way): You have a lot of friends, and then you go to their profile and deliver the digital flyer on their profile. Previously we walked around town with the flyer in our jacket pockets, and when we met someone we knew, and wanted to come to the event, we gave him a flyer—physically. It is the same that happens (when using MySpace). (Vegard Moberg Nilsen, February 2009)

However, in contrast to a physical promotional flyer made of paper, the digital flyers posted on a MySpace site had a second purpose. They served as a marker for both the sender (the club Straedet) and the receiver (a MySpace user and 'friend' of the club Straedet):

> (Y)ou also get the effect that other people see the flyer. The flyer (physical paper) you give to a person will be seen by this person, and then (he or she) puts it in the pocket and no one else will see it. (Y)ou get a display (using MySpace). You show it to others and you also send out signals socially when you chose which profiles you are going to post the information (flyer) on. It is very important what people you are associated with, and which artists you post your flyers to. It will also give people an impression of the kind of music that will be played (at the club), and gives people a lot of associations about the event. (Vegard Moberg Nilsen, February 2009)

The difference between the digital and the physical also extends to the use of MySpace in developing a network of people you can draw on—and interact with—to successfully book artists and bands to clubs and concerts. Traditionally it has been necessary to travel physically around the world to get to know managers, booking agents and artists in order to create—or become part of—a network. However, Vegard Moberg Nilsen points out that this changed with MySpace:

> It was very time-consuming and difficult, and involved a lot of hard work before. It would take many, many years to create a network comparable to a network you can create on MySpace over a few months by being active and participating there. Previously you had to physically meet the persons. You had to travel to London, and go to the clubs and go to the record shops (to) talk to people. While on MySpace you are present, but sit in your living room. We did book artists, big artists (prior to MySpace), but it was difficult to organize, and it took many years to create the network, because you had to build it from scratch. MySpace is a network, and you only have to join it, and then you are in the network, and then you can send out messages, and link yourself up to the persons you want. You can do it in a couple of days if you are very active. (Vegard Moberg Nilsen, February 2009)

Despite the ability to connect virtually and create an appealing MySpace profile, a club or music venue must be "trustworthy and solid," according to Moberg Nilsen. The physical real world needs to correspond with the online world. To strengthen the relationship between the two worlds, each time the club Straedet had a "good artist," the digital flyer was posted. In this way, Moberg Nilsen built up references that were displayed on the

MySpace profile. The result is that when "people visited the profile and saw the flyers they wanted to come and perform or play. We received queries from some internationally quite well-known artists who wanted to come to Bergen and play. (. . .) You create an electronic identity with the profile" (Vegard Moberg Nilsen, February 2009).

Similarly, the online environment and the arrival of MySpace have influenced the way music practitioners and fans get relevant information. Websites such as Discogs.com, with detailed discographies of music artists, were previously particularly important. MySpace changed this because there are so many bands and artists that have a presence there, Mikal Telle explains:

> MySpace has in many ways, to a certain extent, taken over the role of going into a shop and discovering new music. (. . .) Now, if you want to discover new bands (that) you might want to book, but also perhaps sign to release records, you use MySpace. It has become *the* encyclopedia. (Mikal Telle, February 2009)

Prior to the internet and MySpace, then, physical magazines and indie record stores were the main sources of information about music. DJ Arno, the East London-based DJ, also shares this view:

> I think MySpace, as a music portal, had a dramatic impact on my work as a DJ. Before using digital media, I used to discover new music by spending time in record shops. MySpace and the digital media revolution gave me the opportunity to discover many more music producers, as it allowed to bypass traditional music industry filters (record companies, record shops). I found it very exciting at the beginning, as it gave me access to so much more music. But, very quickly, the mainstream caught up. I found it more challenging to come up with great music that no one had heard before. Since the music I was playing was often free and readily available to all online. Although not so much (through) MySpace, but rather more through blogs that surfaced slightly later. Suddenly, one did not have to spend time and money in record shops to be a DJ. (DJ Arno, 2010)

This indicates a certain shift in the relationship between the offline and online in connection to music practice. Similarly, DJ Arno's East London colleague, DJ and club promoter, DJ Fonteyn, draws attention to particularly the relationship between dance/electronic music shops and the process of digitization of dance/electronic music:

> Digital media in general has seen the end of physical formats for DJing. So, I mean a lot of the shops that you would hope to put flyers in they are not there anymore because nobody buys records anymore. So, it's

all had an effect, and quite a rapid one, over the space of about four or five years. I can't tell you the last time I have been to a record shop. (2000s). (DJ Fonteyn, March 2010)

Digitization and MySpace then contributed to the altering of the role of the offline—or 'real world'—for music practitioners. However, it was not only users of MySpace who had access to bands' MySpace profiles, but also general internet users. When making internet searches of bands, using for example Google, their MySpace profiles would often appear among the search results.

While the internet was important for bands and musicians prior to MySpace, a MySpace profile provided something that a traditional website did not. It is part of the MySpace universe, made up of such user profiles that are linked together, Ketil Mosnes argues:

> The internet was important for music practitioners (before MySpace), but then the activity was centered on individual home pages (of bands). There was no forum where you could put your home page. It was just lying there, and then it was up to you to attract attention to the website. There were not many ways of doing it (other) than putting the web address in as many places as possible, on flyers, on record sleeves, and music demos. (Ketil Mosnes, February 2009)

So, a MySpace profile may have some of the same information as a band's traditional website, but "the big difference is that it (the MySpace profile) exists in an environment in which the users already are" (Ketil Mosnes, February 2009). Being linked within a network of other MySpace profiles makes a profile connected in a different way than the more static and stand-alone traditional website. The enhanced accessibility is the most important difference after the arrival of the internet and MySpace, according to Ketil Mosnes. He points out that if you hear of a new band and become curious, then you just visit the band's MySpace profile and listen to four or five tracks and watch their videos: "The exposure is completely different. The accessibility and exposure have been increased with many 100 percent." (Ketil Mosnes, February 2009).

This accessibility also makes it easier to be contacted by people, as any internet user can search and find artists and bands either through MySpace's own search engine, or by using the Yahoo! or Google search engines. Lars Jacob Tynes Pedersen points out how his band, The Work, has been contacted through MySpace by journalists from Sweden, Los Angeles and other parts of the world who have searched and found their profile on MySpace. In addition, record companies have contacted The Work. The result of such contact is that the band is starting to do remixes and write tracks for the US-based Atlantic Records:

It has not materialized properly yet, but it is probably the most important single contact we have made. It happened through MySpace. Someone at Atlantic in New York found us through the MySpace profile. Similarly, record labels that have contacted us regarding the possible release of our album have almost without exceptions (done it via MySpace). Most of the things that happened to us as a band derive in one way or the other directly from MySpace. And, one may say that if MySpace had not existed, then our music would probably been a different place where something similar could have happened, but if I was to say in a few words what has been important for us so far, even though it is still limited, then MySpace is definitely a key word. (Lars Jacob Tynes Pedersen, March 2009)

The artist Skatebård also emphasizes how his use of MySpace influenced his music practice. Prior to his presence on MySpace, it was difficult for people to contact him. All inquiries would go to his record company and not to him. To some extent then, MySpace, circumvented the traditional relationship between artists and representatives of the music industry, as Skatebård points out:

Fan mail and enquiries regarding possible performances used to go directly to my record company. Now such communication comes directly to me. There was no way to contact me previously. If people had bought my record, then maybe they noticed the record company's email address (on it), and that was it. Booking agents, people who ask me to do a remix, or want to make a music video. There are different enquires via the internal MySpace message system, a kind of email system. This is a feature I use very much (Skatebård, March, 2009).

Similarly, Bjørn Torske, the Bergen-based DJ and producer, has been contacted via MySpace, although to a lesser extent:

Yes, I have come in contact with people through MySpace and have also been contacted directly via the MySpace email system (since starting using it in 2006). For example, there was a guy in Taiwan who was interested in what I was doing. But I think it is only in two instances that the MySpace contact has resulted in a meeting. One time some people in Slovenia that I think had heard my records prior to MySpace, but still got in touch via MySpace and this led to a booking. (. . .) The other time, some people running a club in Offenbach, in Germany got in touch via MySpace, and I have now played there several times. (Bjørn Torske, September 2010)

Torske's colleague Mikal Telle points out how he now has instant access to music and information and this has consequences for his music practice: "MySpace is this instant (communication device). You do not have time to wait. You sit in your office (and think) 'Shall we book this band? Ok, let's check them on MySpace. Ok. Cool. Yes, let's book them.' Efficiency. (However,) the expectations of efficiency have increased after MySpace" (2009). The accessibility and presence of music on MySpace is important when searching for new bands and artists. If you like one band or artist, you look at their friends' (MySpace profile) to see if they make music, and if so, what kind of music. Mikal Telle, record label manager, manager and booking agent, uses this approach when searching for new artists and scenes on MySpace:

> You look at the friends he (an artist) has on his Top list, and usually you will find artists or record labels here, (. . .) people they are a fan of, and in this way you discover. You go from profile to profile to profile and discover bands very fast. I think this is very important; the fact that you can go in and get the bands' recommendations and not just the recommendations of retailers and shops. That is very good. I have done this a lot; finding whole new music scenes round across the world by going from MySpace to MySpace to MySpace (profile) by following the links of friends. (Telle, February 2009)

While Ketil Mosnes, former member of Datarock, points out that MySpace is only one of the factors in Datarock's ability to reach and build an audience, the service has been of considerable importance to the band:

> It might have happened, but on a much smaller scale. Then we would have used our home web page more actively. We might have received some fan emails because we had an info-email address, but definitely not on the same scale. Not even close to it, I think. Some of these big commercial successes that have taken place in England such as Lily Allen and Arctic Monkeys have often been described as bands that are MySpace phenomena (. . .). That it started there, and that MySpace created them. I do not know the extent to which this is correct, but it is to go too far by saying that MySpace has created Datarock's status, because there are so many other aspects. But it (MySpace) has clearly been a relatively important part, I would say. It has not been decisive, but it has been an important part. The perhaps most decisive for Datarock has been Fredrik's (the current single Datarock member) extreme work rate, but both he and the management have used MySpace as an important tool. (Ketil Mosnes, February 2009)

We have seen now, during the last decade, a global social media and music nexus has emerged as a consequence of the wider changes in the media and communications industry. MySpace helped music practitioners to establish an online presence. Gradually, as more and more people and music practitioners adopted the service, they applied numerous strategies for communicating with other bands and artists, as well as reaching MySpace users that became their 'friends' or they simply targeted MySpace users as potential fans. These strategies could be utilized both locally and internationally. However, the major media players quickly spotted the commercial potential of these social media services and created alliances and launched joint ventures, amongst others with the major music companies. The creation of MySpace Music, Spotify's collaboration with Facebook, and the music majors' Vevo music video player supported by YouTube, all show the significant role of music within the global social media milieu. These online services have become part of the media conglomerates' and the music industry's efforts to secure their position and profit from the digital environment. Still, from a user perspective, MySpace in the mid-2000s became a tool for music practitioners who incorporated the online service in their music practice.

5 Social Media and Music Practice
Connectedness or Closed Circuit?

By late 2010, electronic music practitioners had been active within the global social media environment for around five years. They first adopted MySpace around 2005 and then other global services such as Facebook and Twitter. Looking at the users' perspective, this chapter examines how electronic music practitioners use these services to communicate and connect with members of music scenes locally and internationally. To what extent does this facilitate transnational communication, interaction, and 'transnational connections?' Hannerz argues that, in contrast to 'the old "global" over the "local"', it is this global criss-crossing and interconnection that characterizes current world society (Hannerz, 1996: 6). Similarly, the concept of 'cosmopolitan fluidity' may be relevant here as it relates to the ability to exist in the global and local—geographically close and distant—at the same time: "Such cosmopolitanism involves comprehending the specificity of one's local context, to connect to other locally specific contexts" (Urry, 2003: 137). Do social media encourage music practitioners to work and operate in such a way? This chapter explores the nature of contact the electronic music practitioners have with other individuals who share music interests and other music scenes—through the use of global social media—both within and outside their geographical area.

By 2010, the global social media environment had developed significantly. Facebook and Twitter had become popular also among the music practitioners studied, while MySpace's position had changed and its relevance diminished for them. This development is also reflected in other user studies involving MySpace (boyd, 2008), as well as the wider macrotrends within this environment (see Chapter 3). However, the electronic music practitioners focus on three reasons for reducing their use of MySpace. Firstly, there was too much information distributed, referred to by some as spam. Secondly, there was a lack of usability caused by technological problems. This became even more apparent as Facebook appeared as an alternative social media. Thirdly, the general shift and movement of users—not just music practitioners—from MySpace to Facebook made it more relevant for the music practitioners to use Facebook to reach fans and friends. This chapter maps this development, from the perspective of these music practitioners. It starts by scrutinizing the role of MySpace within the global social media and music nexus as online facilitator for the connecting of music scenes, before it lost its appeal among the music practitioners who adopted competing services.

GLOBAL SOCIAL MEDIA AND MUSIC SCENES

The issue of virtual communication has been on the research agenda for decades (Benedikt, 1991; Turkle, 1995; see also Chapter 2). As within other spheres in society, the relationship between the global and local has increasingly also become an issue in relation to virtual communication (Hampton and Wellman, 2003). The rapid adoption and maturing of the internet and subsequent arrival of global social media has accentuated this issue. The potential for such contact has increased significantly (Papacharissi, 2009: 201). As the previous chapter showed, this is certainly the case with electronic music practitioners. Soon after adopting MySpace, they used the global social media as a device to communicate both locally and with people geographically distant. This chapter, then, continues the exploration of how global social media, in particular MySpace at first, was used to connect with fellow practitioners and members of music scenes. Vegard Moberg Nilsen, DJ and club organizer and promoter, reflects on his experience with MySpace in this regard:

> Yes, it is very fascinating because you choose which part (of MySpace) you want (to operate in). You have all kinds of hyper, hyper commercial players, and also very, very big players, Madonna, and Coldplay. They have a significant presence, but when I was (using MySpace), this did not concern me. What was interesting for me was these clubs in London, a few clubs in Oslo. There was something (clubs) in Copenhagen, and people who made music. You created your own universe where you are comfortable, and very interested in, and then it is pretty uninteresting that there exists many, many millions of other profiles that have nothing to do with what you are doing. You make a personal version of what you like, and that you are very interested in. You get a lot of information from it, and you can send out a lot of information. So, you have many 'cells' within (MySpace) that are very, very closely linked together. (Vegard Moberg Nilsen, February 2009)

Such connected 'cells' based around special interest relate to wider developments observed within the media industry. Cable and satellite television channels pioneered the addressing of niche audiences, but the internet now facilitates increasing opportunities for providing 'customized content' also for traditional media (Freedman, 2006: 280). MySpace, then, certainly exemplifies the differences of the online environment from traditional media, but there are similarities as well. As with global cable and satellite channels, both MySpace and Facebook launched ambitious programs to localize their operations and structures (see Chapter 3). Their global ambitions, in terms of brand and presence, can only be realized through successful localization of their operations and structures. As such, they cater for national and linguistic segments of internet users. The localization process of global social media has been far quicker than for the global television channels, but a key difference between these global media outlets is that, in contrast to the cable and satellite television viewer, the user of global social media is able to communicate with other users based on personal preferences and interests. As Vegard Moberg Nilsen points out, MySpace enabled him to locate and connect with clubs in Oslo and London as well as international music producers. The ability to communicate with people with similar tastes and interests brings us to the issue of being part of a music scene. Mikal Telle, artist manager and record company owner, explains:

> I notice that I can still very much live on the Tellé-name, because I have released records. People know that I have not released whole albums with Röyksopp, or Annie's whole album, but they know and remember that (it was my) label that released the 'cred-singles' first. And, for example, when the phone called now (during this interview), it was someone who had been in touch with a record label in England called Deadly. It is a label that releases the first vinyl record of various artists. And, the fact that he contacts me (means) that we are part of the same scene. So, then we know each other without really knowing each other. In a way, you communicate through vinyl records. On MySpace, it is like (when you discover that); "Okay, we share 'friends'!" It is like when you read fanzines (paper). Hardcore music and punk rock music has been a lot more community-based, and linking up through mail-order catalogues, and fanzines and lists of records is very, very important. But that is exactly what it is like (on MySpace). Now you go onto MySpace; "Okay, this band or this artist recommends these 'friends.'" (Mikal Telle, February 2009)

According to Mikal Telle, then, the experience and position he developed prior to social media is brought into the social media environment. This is valuable when contacting and communicating with fellow music practitioners, familiar, or unfamiliar, but part of a 'scene' (i.e., music scene). *Cambridge Advanced Learner's Dictionary* provides a general definition of a scene as "a particular area of activity and all the people or things connected with it" (2010). Within music, the term 'music scene' was originally used in "journalistic and everyday contexts" but is more and more used by scholars "to designate the contexts in which clusters of producers, musicians, and fans collectively share their common musical tastes and collectively distinguish themselves from others" (Bennett and Peterson, 2004: 1). The two definitions' use of the words 'connected' and 'collectively share' resonate with Mikal Telle's reflection on the role of fanzines in creating connections between music fans and scenes. Fanzines are a form of newsletter that in addition to music may, for example, cover genres such as science fiction and comics but are produced by fans "who seek to share their opinions about a particular kind of music, musicians, or social concerns of common interest." Each edition of a fanzine is only printed in a couple of hundred copies, and they usually run for only a small number of editions (Bennett and Peterson, 2004: 12). The point is that music fanzines, then, represent 'an independent voice' compared to the foremost magazines and newspapers on "so-called alternative popular and contemporary music" (Hodgkinson, 2004: 225). Mikal elaborates, comparing such music fanzines with the opportunities that arose with the arrival of MySpace:

> It is something that I have never really understood, and that is that people do not understand the value of having an interest for a scene—because, if you do, then it is just to jump into it, then you become part of it. Then it is much easier to get contacts. And, it surprises me—Norwegian bands that do not think like that: "If you like 'this' kind of rock, why not just mingle with (other people who like) that kind of rock?" So, previously through fanzines, then through MySpace, you automatically become part of it (a specific scene). (Mikal Telle, February 2009)

This points to an important aspect of the communication between members of various music scenes. These individuals make qualitative evaluations of the music and the music practitioners' activities. The members of scenes decide to what extent other music practitioners belong to a scene, but also potential fans or people interested in music can make evaluations and decide if they want to become part of such milieus. Historically, fanzines have been a key medium for such evaluations, but gradually MySpace also took on a such a role. Vegard Moberg Nilsen points to MySpace as a facilitator for people who share interests:

> I would claim that the big (MySpace) universe only exists in theory, because there is no one who is interested in it. Of course, it exists, but it is almost not a universe. It only exists, and then you have a lot of small cells within it, and the big universe is so big and so fragmented that there is no one who is interested in it, because it contains so many different things. I think that there are very few who are preoccupied with everything that is there. It is very uninteresting. (. . .) It (MySpace) is enormous, and I am inside a micro-part of MySpace. (Vegard Moberg Nilsen, February 2009)

The idea of connecting with a music scene through MySpace, then, differs somewhat from the view that "on most social networking sites, users are not looking to meet new people or to network, but rather to sustain contact with their existing group of friends and acquaintances" (Papacharissi, 2009: 201 ref. to boyd and Ellison, 2007). Instead, as we also saw in the previous chapter, the electronic music practitioners use global social media also to connect with unknown people—although according to shared interests, and by looking at a band's or artist's MySpace profile prior to getting in touch. As pointed out in relation to the role of fanzines, such communication between music practitioners is not new within music. But the electronic musicians' use of global social media certainly exemplifies Hannerz's early reflections on 'transnational connections.' Such connections affect different spheres of social life, including music: "It seems, rather, that in the present phase of globalization, one characteristic is the proliferation of kinds of ties that can be transnational; ties to kin, friends, colleagues, business associates, and others" (Hannerz, 1996: 89). MySpace facilitated such cross-national and cross-border contact as the service made it easier to get in touch with fellow practitioners, according to Mikal Telle:

> It is actually quite interesting because the barriers to get in contact with quite big artists are quite small. And, a lot of MySpace pages are run by managers or record companies—the artists are never themselves on them, but I know that Annie (is). I guess that many fans would never believe that she answered and ran her own MySpace profile, but she does so. (. . .) So, the chances are quite big that if you go on to MySpace and email someone, that it is actually the band that answers. Unfortunately, due to MySpace's problems with spam, and problems with updating, then I am not that good at checking my messages on MySpace. I only do it every other week but on Facebook then I check my emails every day (. . .). But we have booked several (bands and artists) through MySpace, and then move to email correspondence, and telephone correspondence. (Mikal Telle, February 2009)

Here, Mikal Telle also draws attention to the difference between MySpace and Facebook, and how the take-up and use of the latter has increased. The second half of this chapter will return to this issue and explore how the Bergen-based electronic music practitioners' use of global social media had developed toward the end of 2010. Returning to MySpace, Telle points out how the service helped make it possible to create various forms of connections between users:

> Yes, because if you contact them, then they can very easily check out who you are as well, by visiting your (MySpace) profile, and see who and what you are. So then it is important to be representable. Now our profile is a bit outdated, so we have to try to update it, but it is a very good way to get in touch with people. The barriers for contacting

people are quite low. One does not necessarily have to have met (in person) each other previously. (Mikal Telle, February 2009)

Skatebård also points out the increased opportunities for getting in contact with fellow practitioners and music scenes, and the possible outcome of this communication:

> Offers to play (DJ or live), remixes, videos, plain boasting, boasting both ways, just because you want to boast about the ones you like, or perhaps with 'ulterior motives'—thinking that it may lead to some form of collaboration or something. (. . .) One may contact everyone—from the smallest to the biggest artists directly. But it is not certain that the biggest artists operate their own MySpace pages themselves. They do not have time to do it. (Skatebård, October 2010)

Despite not using MySpace much, Bergen-based Röyksopp made use of the service to connect with an artist who ended up featuring on their album *Junior* released in 2009: "It should be mentioned that we have made use of MySpace in a way. Lykke Li, a Swedish artist, who we collaborated with on our record, *Junior*, established herself as an artist using MySpace. That is where she started" (Svein Berge, December 2010). Lykke Li's presence on MySpace was very convenient for the duo: "When someone made us aware of Lykke Li, we did not have to write a letter, but we just visited her MySpace profile to hear her sing. You just clicked 'Play' on one of the tracks and then you could very quickly hear that this was something interesting for us" (Torbjørn Brundtland, December 2010). Svein Berge emphasizes how MySpace exemplifies the wider impact of digitization and the online environment on their music practice: "Again, you notice that the distance and time is much shorter in all parts of the music-making process. Both in relation to the distribution of music, to move files when making music, get hold of software. Things move faster, and the distances are shorter. There is less traveling and waiting. Things do not happen in '14 days' but 'now,' It is immediate," (Svein Berge, December 2010). The example of Röyksopp and Lykke Li shows how MySpace helped facilitate access to information about shared music interests and preferences that led to professional collaboration.

While Bjørn Torske started using MySpace in the mid-2000s, he has not used MySpace as much as some of his colleagues. Although the contact through MySpace has, as with Röyksopp, led to benefits for his music practice such as DJ bookings and contact with music scenes in Europe, Torske points out that the site has limited use for his music practice:

> I would consider (the contact on MySpace) as superficial. I present myself as an artist, and what I write there is only related to my music practice. I do not blog on MySpace and do not write about myself (as a person). That is not of interest to me. But that is a natural thing to do

if you are in contact with people, and then you become familiar. It is not the case that I get to know people on MySpace. It is called friends, but in reality it is only potential contacts. Because one does not have contact with all the people you have on your list of friends. If I were to keep in touch with all my 2,000+ friends on MySpace, then I would not have had time to do anything else. (Bjørn Torske, September 2010)

In contrast to Bjørn Torske, who only is preoccupied with this artist persona on MySpace, Lars Jacob Tynes Pedersen, producer, DJ, and club promoter, points out how initial professional contact may develop further:

It is definitely a potential for developing something more. I am thinking about the local contact (here in Bergen) that develops into friendship, but then there are those who are more business-oriented. But, then you have examples of (contact) that goes from one thing to another thing. One example is the Swedish artist, Krazy Fiesta, who did a remix of one of our tracks on the record Powerblytt Myths that we did. (Krazy Fiesta) came to Bergen and played and we met later in other circumstances. I consider him a friend today. This has also happened to Skatebård (becoming a friend of Krazy Fiesta). (Lars Jacob Tynes Pedersen, March 2009)

So, as Lars Jacob Tynes Pedersen sums up, "Sometimes then it is purely business, but other times there is a potential for something more." MySpace, then, facilitates the possibility for music artists to present themselves to others, and this may lead to further online communication, but also offline contact:

(O)ne thing that MySpace facilitates is that people use it to communicate something about who they are. It creates a potential to visit any (MySpace) profile, and say: "Is this person, or this band, or this record company, or this club night, like me?" There is definitely a potential there to build more trust that can lead to doing something together. Those kinds of considerations you can make based on a MySpace profile, but you cannot do it based on a Gmail account, for example. So, there is a powerful aspect of signaling who you are (within MySpace) that I think affects the interaction to a very large extent. (Lars Jacob Tynes Pedersen, March 2009)

This again exemplifies how people make qualitative assessments of music and music practitioners. One may orient oneself and make decisions based on information and cues available on MySpace profiles since they contain relevant audio, visual, and textual information. As such, it is easier to find and contact individuals with shared music interests. Furthermore, there is a range of different ways and combinations of ways members of MySpace use the service. While some present and promote their music to numerous members to attract attention and build a fan base, others make contact with fellow music practitioners one-to-one often for business purposes. Also, as we have seen, in some cases online contact may lead to offline contact and meetings.

The electronic musicians' use of global social media connects with both Straw's (1991) and Hannerz's (1996) early reflections on the relationships between the local and international and transnational. Within the global social media and music nexus, contact may occur between people who are geographically close and distant. Prior to the emrgence of the internet. Straw argues that "the manner in which musical practices within a scene tie themselves to processes of historical change occurring within a larger international musical culture will also be a significant basis of the way in which such forms are positioned within that scene at the local level" (Straw, 1991: 373). Frith draws attention to a key point in Straw's (1991) essay on music scenes—highly relevant to this book's context—by pointing out how "music pathways can be global (and virtual) as well as local (and communal)" (2004). The international expansion of electronic music, partly made possible through low-cost technology that required conventional skills of neither writing nor reading music, is certainly a good example of these dimensions of music scenes. On a national level, Hesmondhalgh points out how "the success of dance music in one regard seems clear: it has been the basis of a significant *decentralization* of British subcultural music production" (1998: 236). Such decentralization can also be observed internationally. Furthermore, the European dance music scene, an umbrella for numerous subgenres, is characterized by 'flows of affinities' that stretch geographically—across borders– but in which "centers of production shift from country to country (Belgium to Italy to Germany to the Netherlands) as well as from genre to genre" (Laing, 1997: 130). This form of 'network,' Laing notes, should be seen in contrast to the 'geographical hierarchy' that reflects the power of established music organizations and the major cities of cultural production such as New York, Los Angeles, and London. However, the dance music networks and major record companies may connect as the former "attempt to insert themselves at the level of distribution of recordings and to exercise control over the direction of the musical flow" (Laing, 1997: 131). This development has increased as the popularity, and thereby the commercial value, of electronic music forms also increased. Still, the notions of 'decentralization' and 'network' help explain why electronic music practitioners in Bergen, a small city on the west coast of Norway, have become part of international music scenes. The networks of music scenes prior to the emergence of global social media and the role these online services have come to play in developing and maintaining such contact resonate with Hannerz's notion of 'transnational connections.' Bennett and Peterson's classifications of three 'general types of scenes' address these developments, also in relation to the internet:

The first, local scene, corresponds most closely with the original notion of a scene clustered around a specific geographic focus. The second, translocal scene, refers to widely scattered local scenes drawn into regular communication around a distinctive form of music and lifestyle. The third, virtual scene, is a newly emergent formation in which people scattered across great physical spaces create the sense of scene via fanzines and, increasingly, through the internet. (Bennett and Peterson, 2004: 6)

The attempt to differentiate between forms of scenes is valuable—particularly as it explicitly takes into account the role of the online environment. Still, these differentiations were made at a time when global social media had yet to emerge. The electronic music practitioners, helped by these services, form combinations of such local, translocal, and virtual scenes. As we have seen, while MySpace facilitated contact with the local scene leading to the physical meeting at, for example, clubs in Bergen, it also opened up opportunities for cross-national communication between music practitioners as well as music fans.

MySpace, then, has been used to initiate and cultivate contact on a range of levels: with known or unknown people with shared musical interests either geographically close or distant, and physically and virtually. As such, the service helped enhance the electronic practitioners' ability to become part of a variety of music scenes and enabled other people to contact them. The way these music practitioners are part of music scenes or a 'micro part of MySpace' or 'cells' within MySpace (Vegard Moberg Nilsen, February 2009) connects not only with Bennett and Peterson's typology of three kinds of scenes, but also with Hampton and Wellman's (2002) reflections on 'community' and 'virtual community':

The creation of a whole new type of community, the 'virtual community,' has done much to highlight the geographic dispersion of social ties. Yet the study of virtual communities has largely maintained the traditional framing of 'community' as something that is physically bounded, but by geographies of bits and bytes rather than by streets and alleyways. Online relationships are treated as entities in themselves as if existing social networks and existing means of communication did not exist. (Hampton and Wellman, 2002: 346)

This resonates with the studied music practitioners' use of MySpace. They make use of "multiple methods of communication in maintaining ties with community members" (Hampton and Wellman, 2002: 346). Still, one should qualify the use of the term 'community.' In this case, "communities of shared interests" (Wellman et al, 2003), seems more precise as these members are part of music scenes, with shared musical interests, but may be based geographically close and far away. This is clearly the case with Skatebård:

Usually it is sufficient with the contact you have on the internet. It is written messages, an oral language. Emails are often more informal than letters, but still polite. But, it is not developing a friendship or anything (like that); it is only: "Nice meeting you man!" And, sometimes you meet some of the people you have been in a lot of contact with on MySpace. You meet them eventually, or you start by meeting them for real. (Skatebård, March 2009)

Skatebård elaborates, "It is often people who are far away that it is difficult to meet them face to face" (March 2009). Lars Jacob Tynes Pedersen, producer and DJ, also reflects on the relationship between face-to-face contact and virtual contact:

I think that for some purposes then face-to-face communication is very important. In other incidences, then it might be just as appropriate to not have face-to-face contact. It depends on what the goal is, what you want to achieve. I have always thought that I would like to meet the person: either a fan in Tokyo or it is a DJ in London that plays our records in clubs, or it is a label in England that would like to release a record by us, or Atlantic Records that we work with. I feel that if I had met them personally, then the relations would have been stronger. And thereby the conditions for collaboration could also have been improved. MySpace, and all the other online communications services, Skype, with video, can maybe add something, but at the end of the day, there is a limit to what you can get out of online communication. (Lars Jacob Tynes Pedersen, March 2009)

Similarly, Vegard Moberg Nilsen, DJ and club organizer and promoter, reflects on the relationship between talking on the telephone and online communication:

I think it is easy to be concrete and direct (via MySpace). You have a much larger opportunity to work systematically and send out queries. You make a list of priorities of artists you like. Then you send out a message through the internal message system (on MySpace) to everyone (on the list), and then you get an answer from some. To do the same physically, or to call everyone, is very difficult and complicated. If you call a management and want to book someone, and then call another management, then you cannot shop around in the same way because it is much more binding with a telephone call. You have a much greater opportunity to check out alternatives—to send out a message to a lot of different people and then see what happens. It is a very different way of working—it is a lot more efficient. (Vegard Moberg Nilsen, February 2009)

MySpace has certainly had a role in the practice of electronic music practitioners. The service has been used to initiate and cultivate contact with either familiar or unfamiliar people locally or far away with common music interests. As such, the service has helped enhance the electronic practitioners' ability to develop and maintain links with music scenes. However, one should not forget that these music practitioners have several other ways of communicating with fellow practitioners. We see how they employ and compare the use of both online and offline means of communication. Still, it is clear that MySpace provided a new online space that these practitioners utilized. However, since 2005 the global social media environment has matured and changed (see Chapters 3 and 4), and it is now dominated by the fast-expanding global social media service Facebook. The next part of the chapter examines the electronic music practitioners' use of global social media in late 2010. It gives insight into how the uses of social media have developed, and also why the uses of MySpace have changed.

THE USE OF GLOBAL SOCIAL MEDIA BY 2010

Friendster, in 2002, revolutionized the early social media environment by facilitated connection of personal profiles into networks (Angwin, 2009). In the following years a global social media landscape emerged. However, during these formative years, 2005–2010, this landscape is characterized by change and unpredictability. After News Corp acquired MySpace in 2005, the service expanded internationally and gained tens of millions of users. MySpace initially had more users than Facebook, both in the US and internationally. But, as Facebook became available to the wider public in 2006, its popularity grew. In the same year, Google acquired YouTube, and Twitter was launched publicly. By April 2008, Facebook had reportedly gained more users internationally than MySpace. Facebook's expansion continued at an astonishing rate. By the end of 2010, Facebook had reportedly been adopted by over 500 million users. In this period, YouTube and Twitter have also expanded internationally through localization and have experienced increased use and adoption (see Chapter 3). So, MySpace was very important from the mid-2000s, but the internationally expanding Facebook, as well as Twitter, was becoming a popular social media—for the electronic music practitioners as well. This part of the chapter examines the electronic music practitioners' engagement with this environment in 2010. As such, it examines how the development of and shifts within this environment observed from a corporate perspective correspond with the music practitioners' experience, seen from a user perspective, in the five seminal years of the global social media and music relationship.

While MySpace provided a new online space, the electronic practitioners soon began to adopt the other emerging global social media services as well. In fact, by late 2010 the global social media arena was considered the central component in Datarock's music practice:

> I think I do not exaggerate when I say that (social media) are the most important. The social media form the spine (of our music practice) in a way. But, a spine without arms cannot play the guitar. But, it is like that. Since MySpace emerged, then I think social media have been, yes, the spine in the system, actually. So, therefore, I think it is good that more of them have arrived. (Fredrik Saroea, October 2010)

Datarock now uses both Facebook and Twitter on a daily basis: "I do not know how often we post things, but we spend a lot of time on it." Facebook and Twitter, then, are the key global social media, but these are then linked to MySpace, according to Fredrik Saroea:

> We do still use our MySpace (to some extent), because on Facebook there are less opportunities to place (and store) media content. One of the things we do now—and have done in the last few years—is to copy press stories about Datarock and place them on the blog on our MySpace profile. So, instead of linking directly to the newspaper website (where the story appeared) then we post a link on our Facebook profile to the MySpace blog. Instead of generating traffic to other sites, then, we generate traffic to ourselves via Facebook. The same goes for videos. Instead of linking directly to YouTube, we incorporate the video on our MySpace blog, and then we post a link on our Facebook profile. When people click on the link on Facebook profile they arrive at our MySpace profile. And, when they have arrived there, they might check out some of our music, and find out where we are playing. (Fredrik Saroea, 2010)

While MySpace was commonly used by many of the electronic music practitioners to promote club nights and concerts, Facebook is now the key global social media in the promotion of music events: "As far as I know, there are not better ways, and have never existed any better ways of promoting concerts than through social media, and specifically Facebook" (Fredrik Saroea, October 2010). A band or venue creates an 'event page' on Facebook, and users may click 'Attending.' All the Friends of the users can then see that he or she will attend the concert. This shows in practice how Facebook allows users to personalize their profiles (see Chapter 3) and signal their interests and social activities:

> Suddenly, then, all your Friends do the same, and then these people talk and communicate about them going. I remember when we played in Singapore, then I think there were 1,700 people (that had clicked) attending. And when I played at Vegard Moberg Nilsen's club (Electric

Café) here in Bergen, then there were 250 that had clicked 'Attending' on the Facebook event page for this gig, and there were exactly 250 sold tickets that night. So, social media are a super-efficient way of promoting concerts. (Fredrik Saroea, October 2010)

MySpace did not have such opportunities for creating 'event pages' and it was far more cumbersome to promote a music event. When distributing flyers to other MySpace users, one had to visit each MySpace profile and place the flyer on it. Still, Facebook's and Twitter's limited opportunities to store media content, videos, and music mean that MySpace is now used as a homepage or platform for the band's music and videos, as well as tour information. Datarock is now working on developing an advanced web homepage for the band that Fredrik Saroea claims will make MySpace obsolete for the group. However, the site will also incorporate social media such as Facebook and Twitter (Fredrik Saroea, October, 2010).

The influential club Straedet in Bergen ran from 2006 to around mid-2008. Vegard Moberg Nilsen, the club organizer and DJ, started using MySpace in the mid-2000s and was using MySpace to promote the Stra-edet until it closed. However, he started using Facebook in 2007 and used the two services in parallel for a while. MySpace was then used as a library and webpage for promotional flyers for Straedet and some music: "When booking people to play at the club, it was good to have a link to MySpace. However, now (by late 2010—in relation to Moberg Nilsen's current club, Electric Café, started in mid-2010 in Bergen) I only use Facebook, and link to the club's Facebook group. The active use of MySpace faded and Facebook took over before Straedet closed, because it was much easier to communicate with people using Facebook" (Vegard Moberg Nilsen, December 2010). All the interviewees in this study have played at this club during the second half of 2010. Moberg Nilsen, then, uses only Facebook to promote the club: "We had thought about Twitter, but I think it is important to focus our efforts. I think if we used both Facebook and Twitter, it would have been less activity on both services. But I have never considered MySpace. I have not even thought about it" (Vegard Moberg Nilsen, December 2010).

The use of these services has also changed for the artist Annie. As with Fredrik Saroea (Datarock), Annie now uses mostly Facebook and Twitter:

I use MySpace a lot less than previously. I log on perhaps twice a week. Facebook I log onto a least two times a day, if not three, and Twitter once daily. Twitter is useful. Recently I received from a fan an article about me and two other artists in *Spin* magazine. And, then it is easy to post that link, and then fans and others can follow me then. And I got very, very many responses. I get around 60–70 responses from fans daily who follow, and write things, and perhaps find different links. If someone has written about me in Thailand, then they will send it.

And then I often post it on Facebook, or forward it on Twitter. (Annie, November 2010)

Similar to Annie, Vegard Moberg Nilsen, and Fredrik Saroea, Skatebård's use of global social media has also changed significantly:

> (My use of social media) has changed a lot. I am more active today when it comes to updating (on social media). One-line updates, mostly on Facebook. I use Facebook Page, a kind of fan page that I created myself on Facebook. There is not much happening on my MySpace profile at the moment. I rarely log on and check it. It is much easier to use other media if I want to contact someone. Still, festivals and others who book artists (festivals and clubs) will write it on their MySpace profile instead of on their home page. MySpace is still a place where one can easily check three or four tracks by a band one has not heard yet. I think people still do that, but that is not 'social.' But YouTube is (still) a popular place for fans to check out bands. It is perhaps easier to search on YouTube (than MySpace). (Skatebård, October 2010)

Skatebård uses Twitter once a week, but only to announce when something is happening: "That I have a gig. I do not Twitter if I have made a cheese sandwich." In addition, Skatebård has a homepage, skatebard.no, that is linked to skatebard.blogspot.com. This homepage was launched in early 2010: "The Blogspot site works as my homepage—a kind of 'umbrella' web page. On the Blogspot page I have links to Twitter, Facebook, iTunes, and YouTube, and my record company. There are seven to eight links there" (Skatebård, October 2010). Still, in Skatebård's opinion, MySpace is still important:

> One must have a MySpace profile, but I have written at the top of mine that I do not update my profile very often any more. I ask people to check my Twitter and Facebook profile. On the front of my MySpace, I have embedded players and shops (that sell music online)—Beatport and a couple of others—MP3 shops. As an artist you get a code—an html code—that you can put on your MySpace (profile), and then there is a box where you can play a minute of each track, and then you can buy them. So, those things are on my MySpace page now, and these shops update automatically. All the music I release can be purchased on Beatport. And, when my music is available on Beatport, the players on my MySpace page is updated automatically. So, everything I release, if it is digitally distributed, will be displayed on these players. (Skatebård, October 2010)

Skatebård's use of MySpace, then, has changed significantly, and in late 2010, this is the message that greets visitors on his MySpace profile:

> I don't update this myspace very much anymore . . . you should rather go to http://skatebard.blogspot.com/ !And check my links from there, first and foremostly I will update Twitter and my Facebook page.Thank you.

Just as both Skatebård and Datarock are now doing, Röyksopp has long used a stand-alone website as an online platform. In contrast to the other studied artists who adopted MySpace in the mid-2000s, the website royksopp.com has been the band's main online presence. Still, by late 2010, the website had links to all global social media: "Visit us on: Facebook, YouTube, Twitter and MySpace." The band's global social media profiles are not run by the band members themselves, but their management DEF Ltd in London. These profiles are all updated, and more than 200,000 Facebook users have linked up with the band's Facebook profile. Röyksopp's Facebook profile also displays three bands or artists that Röyksopp 'likes': Lykke Li, Fever Ray, and Robyn. Similarly to the advantages experienced by artists and DJs when placed on Annie's MySpace profile's 'Top 8 Friends list' in the mid-2000s, it is certainly advantageous to be placed on Röyksopp's much-visited Facebook profile.

Mikal Telle, the Bergen-based manager, DJ and club organizer, and record label manager, points out how, by late 2010, "There is almost too many things happening, so you just have to dare not being on top of it all. But you have to check out most of it" (Mikal Telle, October 2010). Telle now uses Facebook and Twitter for communication: "But MySpace is still quite convenient for checking out biographies, list of tour dates, information about record companies and booking agencies. It is the interaction between MySpace users that has ended." So the relevance of MySpace has changed significantly:

> The only important reason for using MySpace is so you can check and make sure you have a long list of tour dates and that you have updated your tracks, so that people very quickly can check out. If I post a message (on Twitter or Facebook) saying: "Check out The New Wine" (a new rock band Telle is managing), then people can very quickly find out: "Ok, good tracks, tour dates—okay, exciting!" (Mikal Telle, October 2010)

And, like Skatebård, Telle points out the possibilities now for creating homepages can threaten MySpace further:

> (MySpace) still (works as) a homepage, but I think it can change fast, because it is becoming quite easy to create a homepage. My homepage is houseoftelle.com, without Blogspot or WordPress, but it is a WordPress site. So, as more and more people can easily design their own website (using Blogspot or WordPress), and then put their own domain

name on top of it, then this can soon take over from MySpace. Because at the end of the day, you want traffic directed to your own website. (Mikal Telle, October 2010)

To discover new music, "I visit MySpace or blogs or SoundCloud or Facebook. Facebook has started to include features for musicians and artists, so at the moment we're in a period of transition I think" Telle elaborates. MySpace was key for the electronic music practitioners to connect with other scenes. Mikal Telle still uses social media to connect with scenes, but now blogs are important. However, he points out:

> You do not find them (artist blogs) automatically (on blogs), like you did on MySpace. On MySpace everyone had 20 or 8 friends (on the front page), and then you clicked on them and then you just created the networks (you saw who other artists were linked up to, and then you could link to them). On most blogs it is not like that, but still most of them have links to their favorite blogs, so in a way you can still do that. (Mikal Telle, October 2010)

As Mikal Telle and Skatebård suggested, DJ Fonteyn, the East London-based DJ and club organizer, claimed (in early 2010) that MySpace was still relevant for music practitioners, but mostly as a webpage or site for music and video content and not for communication:

> MySpace is now a good way for bands and artists to maintain a presence online that they can adapt at a quite short notice. But I personally have not used MySpace in a year and a half, two years, for my purposes to promote and build up an audience for my club events. The main source of communication on MySpace was the bulletin boards, and now the bulletin boards are almost solely record companies or companies sending out very generic mailouts. It is very, very little personal interaction on the bulletin boards at all. (DJ Fonteyn, March 2010)

Also for Bjørn Torske, the Bergen-based international DJ and music artist and producer, the relationship with MySpace has changed: "I have almost stopped using MySpace. I sometimes log on to check and see." However, as Torske points out, he has not institutionalized the use of these media as many people have done:

> If one has the time and enjoys spending time on this, then perhaps there is something to gain from it. I have simply not familiarized myself very much with these media. If I want to contact someone, then I send them an email. It is mostly th(e) way it works. I have perhaps not been good at using MySpace to get in touch with people even though people have

contacted me via MySpace. I have simply not the time to do it. (Bjørn Torske, September 2010)

Still, as with Röyksopp, Torske's business associates—in this case the Norway-based record company Smalltown Supersound that releases much of his music internationally—utilize global social media to promote his records: "I have a record company that does those things. They are on Facebook and Twitter, and there they are hammering it out. They are very good at that" (Bjørn Torske, September 2010).

The formative years, 2005–2010, of the global social media environment and the emergence of a global social media and music nexus are characterized by not only rapid technological change and rate of adoption of these services, but also unpredictable shifts in loyalties among the users of them. By late 2010, the situation for MySpace was very different from in the mid-2000s. The electronic music practitioners were early adopters of the service, and they point to reasons why their relationship with MySpace has deteriorated. This is elaborated in the next section.

THE DECLINE OF MYSPACE

MySpace's diminished importance for the electronic music practitioners reflects other user studies involving MySpace (for example, boyd, 2008) and the general political, technological, and economic development of the global social media environment (see Chapter 3). The electronic music practitioners focus on three reasons for MySpace's decline. First, too much information was distributed within the MySpace universe. Second, there were technological problems and a lack of usability. Third, there was a general shift and movement of users from MySpace to Facebook.

Fredrik Saroea, currently the sole member of Datarock, now uses Facebook and Twitter actively, and MySpace only as a platform for media content. He points out how MySpace has become inferior as a tool for communication:

> Now, the people who are using MySpace actively are almost completely 'backwards.' If you go and check your messages (internal emails within the MySpace network) on MySpace now, then there is a lot of bullshit. And, the same with comments (comments from other users on the front of one's MySpace profile). It is just nonsense. It is extremely rare that someone post photos or nice messages. (. . .) So, the very nice communication among people that existed within MySpace previously is practically nonexistent now. Then a young person could write us and ask, "How do you play that tune?" And we answered such queries.

So, even if we were quite active in maintaining the communicational aspect of MySpace, now it seems as if MySpace has disappeared from people's lifestyle. No one needs it anymore. It is much more efficient to use Facebook and Twitter. (Fredrik Saroea, October 2010)

In addition to the enormous amount of information or 'spam,' the decline of MySpace as a tool for music practitioners can also be explained by technological problems, according to Fredrik Saroea:

MySpace's music players are very bad. No one can bother to, for example, edit their playlists (of tracks). If you try to create a new list of the tracks and then press 'Update,' then they end up being wrong. And, if you want the first track to start automatically, and you write 'Autoplay,' it does not happen. Suddenly you think the player is playing, and then you click on a new track and then suddenly two tracks are playing at the same time. So what made MySpace so big—music—has been completely screwed up. And, as many people say, it seems as if the owners have simply neglected it and just let it all go to hell. (Fredrik Saroea, October 2010)

Similarly, Annie points out, "I actually use MySpace very little now, but only because far less people read me than previously. MySpace is okay for presenting new tracks." As with Fredrik Saroea, Annie points to the positive role MySpace had early on: "In some ways I miss MySpace," she elaborates. "Yes, it was much stronger on music. Artists I was interested in often contacted me directly, and said, 'We like your music very much. Perhaps we could write something together, or do a remix or we can have some sort of collaboration?' I found this very appealing with MySpace. On Facebook, it is not so much of that" (Annie, November 2010). While MySpace was more specialized and particularly favored by musicians and fans, Facebook was adopted by a much broader public, and many different user groups:

There was a big focus on music on MySpace. You could write on the MySpace blogs: "I am working on a new track, or I am remixing this or that artist." While with Facebook, it is much easier to be personal—to have more personal style. I think perhaps for that reason, people use it more. It is easier. It is based on persons. It is greater age range among the users—young to older people; 50–60 years old can have Facebook pages, but on MySpace, it was narrower. (Annie, November 2010)

Also, Mikal Telle draws attention to Facebook's wider appeal and points out how Facebook took over much of the communication between users:

MySpace was very music-oriented, and then came Facebook that was not music-related. It was for everyone. And, when everyone participates, then you can reach even more people. You started talking to people. Instead of talking to (only) other bands, you found old classmates. In the beginning, I think they were two different things (MySpace and Facebook), but then Facebook began to see that "okay, there are a lot of our users who are interested in music." So now they try to improve the features for us (music practitioners). (Mikal Telle, October 2010)

Similarly, Vegard Moberg Nilsen, the Bergen-based DJ and club organizer and promoter, points to the differences in users of MySpace and Facebook: "If your band is on MySpace, then you communicate with other bands on MySpace. But, if your band is on Facebook, then you communicate with potential consumers that might buy your music or attend your concerts. MySpace was a pretty good reference point, like a webpage, but the communication and interaction with the consumers was not really there. Now, on Facebook, you can create a fan group to which you can daily pump out tour plans, record releases and information. MySpace was not even close to this" (Vegard, Moberg Nilsen, December 2010). This clearly indicates how Facebook, in contrast to MySpace, was adopted by a much broader and larger segment of internet users. Furthermore, there are substantial differences in technology between the two services. When promoting a club night or concert through MySpace, you had to post flyers by 'clicking' on their MySpace profiles one by one. However, as also pointed out earlier by Fredrik Saroea (Datarock), Facebook allows users to join groups such as Moberg Nilsen's most recent club, the Bergen-based Electric Café. By late 2010, The Facebook group of Electric Café had close to 1,300 members. In contrast to MySpace, it is possible to invite and post a flyer to all these members with just a click. And all the members of the group, as well as your regular Facebook friends, can see if you then decide to click on 'I'm attending' this event:

> You only receive information if someone writes something on your MySpace profile or posts something there. But no one else will receive this information. MySpace might have changed that by now, but when we're using the service, it was not like that. The good thing about Facebook was that you were notified about what other people were doing, what they liked, where they were going to go out, and what kind of music they were listening to. In comparison to MySpace, then, you exchange enormous amounts of information on Facebook. On MySpace, you did not exchange that much information nor communicate with other users in that way. (Vegard Moberg Nilsen, December 2010)

Skatebård also draws attention to the issue of people moving to Facebook, but also the way technical issues and spamming hamper the usability:

> During the last two years everyone (has taken up) Facebook. Facebook is much more tidy (graphics and technology) and it is much

easier to have direct contact with people. MySpace has tried to copy the social features that Facebook came up with, but it is completely unsuccessful—a bad copy. (On MySpace, these functions include) updates on what you are doing, your mood, and things like that, but it is no point in that when you have 6,000 friends on MySpace, and many of these are bogus bands that spam. It is not very interesting. (Skatebård, October 2010)

MySpace's usability and the ability to update the site and post comments on other users proved to be inferior to both Twitter and Facebook:

> MySpace takes a lot of time and work. It is very longwinded to update and post comments. On Facebook, it is more or less just to push a button and say 'go.' On MySpace, it is cumbersome and slow. It can take several hours to wait for the profile to update changes, and then the machine (Skatebård's computer) crashes because there is so much Java and Flash all the time. The computer freezes. It is a lot of hassle. It became so much more easy and still more appealing and tidier with Twitter and Facebook. Of course, it is for this reason they have won (against MySpace). They are very easy to use and very logical. (Skatebård, October 2010)

Also, Bjørn Torske points to the information overload or spamming, or in his words 'information inflation,' within MySpace:

> I have practically stopped using MySpace. Of course, the number of users went down when Facebook came, for a lot of the people who had personal MySpace accounts (in contrast to music accounts) found out that Facebook was more relevant for them to use. Facebook had more chat functions. On MySpace, now, you get what I would almost call spam. Not directly, but it is a lot more mass messages saying, "visit my profile, and listen to my music!" It has become a space for advertisements. (Bjørn Torske, September 2010)

Torbjørn Brundtland, half of duo Röyksopp, points out the problems related to both technology and issues related to spam with MySpace:

> I have used MySpace when people have said to me, "okay, if you want to hear my music then visit my MySpace profile." And I have done so and listened to their music. But this has not appealed much to me mainly due to the sound quality. If I like a track then I want to be able to download it in high quality. I would definitely have used MySpace more if I could visit profiles and download music and then put tracks together and mix them as I want to. There is an option on MySpace to make music downloadable, but very few use it. And, when they use

it, the sound quality of the music is very low. (Torbjørn Brundtland, December 2010)

Furthermore, Brundtland was struck by the amount of information that was being distributed and seemed to clog up the MySpace system:

> I was struck by how little it seemed that people were paying attention on MySpace. In the comments section of MySpace profiles, it was written things like "I have a club there, and there." And people seldom acknowledged the things that were written there. There was not much feedback or two-way communication, as far as I could see. It seemed a bit egotistical. But, I guess it was the way it developed more and more—into a kind of advertising thing. (Torbjørn Brundtland, December 2010)

Overall then, the electronic music practitioners argue that their use of MySpace declined because there was an excess of information and technological problems that reduced the usability of the service. Furthermore, there was a general shift of users from MySpace to Facebook that also affected the music practitioners.

It is clear that MySpace played a central role for these music practitioners in the early years: it was used to instigate contact with other MySpace users on a range of levels, unknown or known, with shared musical interests either geographically close or distant. While the service played a role in facilitating music practitioners' increasing opportunities to connect with music scenes, they also employed other means of communication, both online and offline, in their practice. Still, during these seminal years, the experience of the electronic music practitioners' use of MySpace seems to subscribe to the concepts of 'transnational connections' (Hannerz, 1996) and 'cosmopolitan fluidity' (Urry, 2003). MySpace represents a glocalization device that, similar to the "harbinger of 'glocalization'" (Hampton and Wellman, 2003), has helped the electronic music practitioners to operate and connect with music scenes both locally and internationally. However, the global social media environment is subject to continuous transformation. Both the general growing popularity of Facebook and Twitter and the diminishing role of MySpace are reflected in their practice. Their use of MySpace has declined for several reasons: there was an overload of information within the MySpace universe; MySpace had technological shortcomings that hampered its usability, and the service suffered from the shifting loyalties of global social media users. A wider segment of the world's internet users adopted Facebook, and the service soon outperformed MySpace and became the dominating global social media service. Together with Facebook's opportunities for personalization, the service therefore became a much more efficient vehicle for bands to reach fans and potential consumers, and on its part, Facebook became a more convenient way to signal interests and social activity.

6   The Logic of Social Media
Power, Participation, and Paradox

The relationship between corporate influence and global social media exists on two levels: within the social media environment and the social media entities in relation to the outside environment. This chapter examines the often hidden corporate monetization strategies, in contrast to the visible localization strategies, that both MySpace and Facebook have implemented. As the global social media neither generate income from subscriptions nor charge membership fees, these strategies aim to create profit from the gathering and commercial use of data on their users. By utilizing various forms of surveillance technology, the services aim to create an online milieu in which users and communities are sold to and targeted by advertisers. These efforts are mapped, first from a corporate perspective, and then from the point of view of the music practitioners' awareness of such strategies and their experience of operating within this commercial environment.

While both MySpace and Facebook increase users' opportunities to operate within the global social communications infrastructure, this activity has consequences. As with other electronic and digital 'mobilities systems' (i.e. mobile phones, networked computers) influential in creating the 'mobility turn,' much of the users' activity within these systems are subject to a form of surveillance (Urry, 2007), often for commercial purposes. Some warn against this development: "This new economy of web advertising has spawned a whole new method of audience analysis in the dark art of user metrics—measuring user behaviour and engagements" (Lister et al, 2009: 172). Paradoxically, such surveillance technologies are crucial for many online services to function. Global social media, for example, apply such technology for authentication to recognizing users' passwords and usernames when they log on. However, the global social media's relationship with users and gathering of information on them for commercial purposes needs to be further understood.

This chapter also explores the global social media in relation to the external environment—the very media and communications landscape in which they exist. The previous chapters show how these online entities differ from traditional global television and media outlets in particular because of the users' participation, contribution, and activity. In addition, these services also mix this user-generated content and user activity with traditional media content. Together, this represents challenges for transnational audiovisual policy. This, again, is linked to how corporate strategies to develop global social media reflect more general tendencies as there is strong corporate, political, and user interest in the development of these services. Also, certain political stakeholders have promoted a more deregulated media landscape, eying economic growth within the online sphere. As such, the interests of various parties from different spheres of society are tied to the global social media phenomenon.

DEVELOPING A COMMERCIAL SOCIAL MEDIA ENVIRONMENT

The selling of media audiences to advertisers has been a central activity since print media in the 1920s not only offered "circulation guarantees or willingly submitting to circulation audits, but were actively devising ways to sell themselves to advertisers" (Leiss et al, 2005: 127). Since then, ever more advanced ways of targeting and reaching audiences and making them commercially attractive to advertisers have been developed. The rise of television and print mass media facilitated outreach to large national mass audiences first in the US, then in Europe and across the world. The emergence of cable and satellite television channels throughout the 1980s and 1990s contributed to the transformation of the targeting of the television audience first in the US and then in other world regions. In contrast to mass advertising through national broadcasting, narrowcasting became a vehicle for reaching segments of the television audience. The cable and satellite television channels pioneered the targeting of global or pan-European and pan-regional segments of the national television audiences through localization (Chalaby, 2009).

Narrowcasters used specific television program genres and relied on language localization of the television programming to reach the preferred audience. While Disney Channel attracts the youngest television audience through animation programming, Discovery Channel has adapted and reshaped the factual television genre to attract a male audience aged 25 to 45 years across the world (Mjøs, 2010). Errol Pretorius, director of advertising sales at the News Corp-controlled National Geographic Channel, highlights the logic of narrowcasting: "Don't count the people you talk to, talk to the people who count. I'd rather talk to a thousand people who can afford to buy a new Volvo, than talk to a million people who can't" (Pretorius, quoted in Chalaby, 2002: 201). The arrival of digital satellite in 1996 gave increased opportunity for localization though the introduction of program opt outs, local advertising, and local on-air presentation into the feeds (Brown, 1998). The splitting of video signals allowed for the targeting of large culturally and linguistically diverse regions. In Europe, pan-European television channels could increasingly insert programing and advertising for specific countries, in contrast to the whole European territory. This had consequences for both the media and the advertising industry:

The financial shape of many transnational TV networks improved with the upturn of the pan-European advertising market in the 1990s. The pool of international advertisers expanded as multinationals adjusted their marketing strategy to the challenges and opportunities of globalization. The advertising industry restructured, creating media-buying agencies with specialist knowledge of pan-European television and the network to run transnational advertising campaigns mixing local and global objectives. Cross-border TV stations began to offer flexible local advertising windows that suited the multi-territory needs of advertisers. (Chalaby, 2009: 83)

This approach of addressing a cross-national but targeted audience reflected the way in which, through transnational communication, people are "increasingly being addressed across national boundaries on the basis of their purchasing power" (Thussu, 2000/2006: 79).

However, parallel to the development of the multichannel universe, the internet and the dawn of an online environment were drawing increased attention, particularly for their perceived commercial potential (McStay, 2010). Although the main task for marketers and advertisers remained the same as previously—to get the audience to buy products or services—the online milieu represented something more, marketing people claimed:

The new interactive arsenal would accommodate new ways to separate people into different lists according to lifestyles they expressed in viewing and computer use. One consultant exhorted marketers that "hundreds of thousands of names and addresses are floating on the internet, waiting to be listed, organized, sliced and diced." After all, he pointed out, "the internet is essentially one giant agglomeration of special interests." (Turow, 1997: 175)

While applauded by marketers and advertisers, this development raised major concerns among critical scholars and activists. They feared the consequences of the surveillance of electronic communication taking place on the 'information superhighway' and the internet. Many compared such practice to Bentham's idea of Panopticon (Robins and Webster, 1988; Rheingold, 1993/2000; Turkle, 1995: 246, 247; Elmer, 2004: 29). Robins and Webster's early predictions pointed to a particularly bleak future involving surveillance of the individual:

The cabled electronic grid is a transparent structure in which activities taking place at the periphery—remote working, electronic banking, the consumption of entertainment or information, tele-shopping, communication—are *visible* to the "eye" of the central computer systems that manage the numerous electronic transactions is simultaneously, and integrally, a process of observation, recording, remembering, surveillance. The electronic worker, consumer, or communicator is constantly scanned, and his or her needs/preferences/activities are delivered up as information to the agencies and institutions at the heart of the network. The lives of those on the periphery are subject to constant surveillance and documentation—and, hence, control—from the central observatories of the social Panopticon. (Robins and Webster, 1988: 61, 62)

In 1994, a technological invention was introduced that resembled Robins and Webster's earlier predictions. This was the year that, as Sassen puts it, "business 'discovered' the Net" (1998, 177, quoted in Hesmondhalgh, 2007: 258). A technology called 'cookie' was created in 1994 and introduced in the Netscape internet browser the same year (Schwartz, 2001; Elmer, 2004). This technology enabled the collection of data on parts of the users' online activity. This development signaled the arrival of technologies that some claim have led to a situation where "practically all uses we make of the Web are recorded for market research purposes" (Hesmondhalgh, 2007: 259). Cookies were therefore considered key in commercializing the online environment and in developing an audience that could be sold to for example advertisers. The technology created "a relatively stable platform for interactions" between users and the owners or controllers of a website. This meant that the cookies helped "identifying repeat visitors to their websites" and thereby "fundamentally challenge(d) the ability of users to remain anonymous on the Net" (Elmer, 2004: 118).

Cookies caused significant controversy not least since companies controlling the web browsers Netscape and Microsoft (who owned Internet Explorer) "neglected to make public the use of cookie technology in 1995 and early 1996" (Elmer, 2004: 119). By informing the public about this technology from the outset, one could have avoided some of the criticism at the outset, and the continuing suspicion of the cookies technology (Elmer, 2004: 119). *The New York Times* journalist, Michelle Slatalla, put her unease with this new technology into words when discovering 'cookies' in her computer browser folder that had been sent to her computer:

> Actually, those Cookies were sent without my permission, and since I cannot decode the little aliens, how can I be sure that they are not whooping it up with one another, exploring my hard drive, sending my secrets back to their leader on some distant planet? (Cookie A: "Hey, Moe, get a look at this file. No wonder she calls it a rough draft!" Cookie B: "Yeah, did you notice she's so cheap that she's played solitaire 749 times without paying the shareware fee?")
>
> I know this was not a rational response, given that cookies are not programs that can run amok. They are merely bits of text, a tool created by Netscape in 1994 to enable Web sites to identify repeat

visitors. Sent primarily by the biggest commercial Web sites, cookies get stored on your computer. If you return to the site, your browser will send back the cookie, a gesture roughly equivalent to saying, "Hey, it's me again."

(Slatalla, 1998)

Others voiced far more critical views. Law scholar and activist Lawrence Lessig claimed that the consequences of cookies have been devastating for the privacy of internet users. While the Web was "essentially private" prior to the launch and implementation of cookies, after the arrival of this technology, it has been turned into "a space capable of extraordinary monitoring" (Lessig, quoted in Schwartz, 2001). Similarly, others considered cookies as "one of the most common examples of on-line surveillance" as the technology allowed for the registration of "how users surf the internet, which websites they visit, how long they spend in a particular site, and which links they use" (Molz, 2006: 380). It is difficult to detect the cookies at work, but one of the most noticeable ways in which this technology affects online use is when users try to obstruct them. Often, if users try to block cookies, they will not be able to fully use or even be prevented from accessing websites. The web browser and the cookie have enabled the "automating" of the gathering of information of internet users. If users try to deny the "software's use of cookies," the user may be prevented from using various services and functions. (Elmer, 2004: 112)

A case in hand is the online version of the newspaper *The New York Times* and *Amazon.com,* the giant online retailer. The newspaper's website collects data on customer and user behavior through the use of cookies. If a customer's web browser prevents the use of cookies, he or she is not allowed access to, for example, *The New York Times*' website: "In order to access our website, your web browser must accept cookies from NYTimes.com" (*The New York Times*, 2008). Similarly, Amazon. com does not permit a customer to make purchases from the site under these circumstances:

> If your web browser is set to refuse cookies from our website, you will not be able to complete a purchase or take advantage of essential website features, such as storing items in your Shopping Basket or receiving personalised recommendations. As a result, we strongly encourage you to configure your web browser to accept cookies from our website. (Amazon, 2008)

The role of cookies in the relationship between the users and online services like *Amazon.com* is reminiscent of the earlier predictions of panoptication. The way the technology has been applied has, in Elmer's view, resulted in a "symbiotic, panoptic relationship" (Elmer, 2004: 112). However, this symbiotic relationship is also at the heart of global social media, as cookies make a service like Facebook work. The social media is open about its use of such technology, but just as with *The New York Times* and *Amazon. com*, the disabling or blocking of cookies limits, or may even prevent, the use of Facebook's services:

> Cookie Information. We use "cookies" (small pieces of data we store for an extended period of time on your computer, mobile phone, or other device) to make Facebook easier to use, to make our advertising better, and to protect both you and Facebook. For example, we use them to store your login ID (but never your password) to make it easier for you to login whenever you come back to Facebook. We also use them to confirm that you are logged into Facebook, and to know when you are interacting with Facebook Platform applications and websites, our widgets and Share buttons, and our advertisements. You can remove or block cookies using the settings in your browser, but in some cases that may impact your ability to use Facebook. (Facebook, 2010c).

Cookies therefore play a key part in creating and maintaining a Facebook persona, by linking the Facebook profile with personal usernames and passwords. However, this again provides opportunities for the collection of information and mapping of users' activity when they are logged on. Similar to earlier concerns on information technology and surveillance, global social media is subject to critique: "MySpace is not about creativity, it is about detecting related *activity*. Facebook does not want to link friends to friends, it is in the business of linking people to advertisers and products. Not content, but connections and profiled actions are the new commodities" (Van Dijck and Nieborg, 2009: 866). The next part of the chapter examines such claims that the key motive of the owners of global social media is to turn these entities into commercial and profitable environments by capitalizing on users.

GLOBAL SOCIAL MEDIA AND ADVERTISING

Prior to News Corp's acquisition, the number of unique visitors to MySpace grew dramatically. In January 2005, MySpace had 5.8 million unique visitors, and by May the same year, the site attracted 15.6 million unique visitors (Angwin, 2009: 140). To set up a social media service such as YouTube, or take control of a service like MySpace and develop it further, requires major investments. This can only be justified if the owner of the IP address can "prove the site or platform will attract the right kind of audience and attention" (Lister et al, 2009: 172). The approximately 100 million videos viewed daily on YouTube were a key reason for Google's acquisition of the video-sharing site (Wasko and Erickson, 2009), but in the case of MySpace, it was not only the large numbers of users that caught the conglomerates' attention. MySpace's ability to attract specifically young people proved attractive for investors. MySpace's young users, many aged between 16 and 24, were very attractive to advertisers (Cohn, 2005; Siklos, 2005; Naughton, 2006; La Monica, 2009). MySpace's popularity among young people and potential as a vehicle for advertising were of great interest to News Corp, but as pointed out, also the Viacom-owned MTV Network that was developing a digital strategy. MTV saw MySpace as an attractive online asset, but eventually lost out to News Corp (Angwin, 2009).

Throughout the second half of the 2000s, both MySpace and Facebook have attempted to turn themselves into profit-generating entities by launching a range of monetization initiatives either on their own or in collaboration with online industry giants such as Google and Microsoft. The social media services were, some argue, "probably the most hyped online advertising and marketing vehicle in 2007" (McStay, 2010: 61). While these services can be used as conventional advertising-carrying channels, the commercial worth of social media such as MySpace lies in the fact that these services can be utilized "as market research platforms," according to Spurgeon, who points out that "many accounts of the early history of MySpace suggest that it was established as a new kind of advertising medium: one where consumers were conceived as advertisers, and where advertisers would be invited into the quasi-private worlds of young consumers" (2008: 110). Facebook, too, may easily be described in such a way. The owners of web communities, such as global social media, have increasingly come to engage in a process of attracting, recruiting, and keeping users, while at the same time attempting to capitalize on them:

> Community management has become the starting point for web marketing—web media invite the user to join, to create a profile, to post blogs or their announcements, to make links, to invite other friends and so on. This is not because the advertising and media industries just want us all to play nice and have lots of warm friendships. It is because they are seeking, in a crowded, transient marketplace characterised by a nomadic audience to create brand engagement. (Lister et al, 2009: 172, 173)

The potential and prospect of the idea of 'community management' motivated major media and communications conglomerates to enter the social media environment. This created unease and skepticism from a user perspective, but also uncertainty from the corporate perspective. "Underpinning anxieties about News Corporation's acquisition of MySpace were concerns that it would stifle the vibrant social network site and cause its nascent innovation culture to stagnate. The concern for MySpace participants was over the burden of exit costs they might face if changed terms and conditions of involvement created disincentives and obstacles to participation" (Spurgeon, 2008: 110). News Corp's acquisition of MySpace in 2005, then, also represented uncertainty for the media conglomerate. While News Corp had high hopes and ambitious plans for MySpace, it did not have any experience with owning and running a globally expanding social media: "The business concern was whether the marketing potential of the site would be fully realized" (Spurgeon, 2008: 110).

Since then, the efforts of the social media giants' strategies have represented a move toward increased observation of media users and much more customized and individualized targeted marketing practices. Shortly after acquiring MySpace, News Corp made a deal with Google for advertising linked to searches and also started developing other systems for gathering data on its users for corporate purposes. As Facebook's popularity increased, its efforts to create systems to utilize user information for commercial purposes also intensified.

The Commercial Environments of MySpace and Facebook

At the time of the MySpace acquisition, News Corp claimed that MySpace "served more than 8 percent of all advertisements on the internet," and this was "putting it in the company of web giants Yahoo!, Google, and AOL" (News Corporation, 2005). The official size of MySpace's revenue from advertising is not publicly available, but a year after News Corporation acquired MySpace the conglomerate's internet operations generated only a small part of the company's total profit and revenues. While News Corporation earned a total of around $3.6 billion and had $25.6 billion in revenues in 2006, the company's internet division reportedly created revenues of around $185 million in the first half of 2006 (Kafka, 2007). Without mentioning any figures, News Corporation's Annual Report for 2006 claimed that "revenues from MySpace alone have nearly doubled every four months over the past year" (2006: 6). In early 2007, Murdoch claimed that MySpace's "advertising had gone from basically nothing to about $25 million a month" (Murdoch, quoted in La Monica, 2009). The media ratings company Nielsen suggested that Facebook's advertising revenue for 2008 was $300 million, and MySpace $1 billion (Nielsen Online, 2009).

While it is difficult to get financial information on MySpace, the size of the deal between Google and MySpace was widely reported in the news media. Google guaranteed to pay a minimum of $900 million to Fox Interactive for the exclusive right to operate the search and keyword advertising on MySpace and other Fox Interactive online companies from 2007 to 2010. The News Corporation-owned Fox Sports already had a similar arrangement with Microsoft's MSN (Doran, 2006; La Monica, 2009). As pointed out in News Corporation's annual report for 2006, the sum Google agreed to pay was actually higher than the amount News Corporation had paid for MySpace:

Earlier this summer, after the fiscal year-end, we announced a landmark deal with Google to provide search functionality to most of our internet sites—most importantly MySpace. Google will also become the exclusive text-based advertising provider and has the right of first refusal on all remnant display advertising. With at least $900 million committed to us over four years, this agreement more than pays for the MySpace acquisition. More importantly, it allies us with one of the great companies of the digital age, while signifying our ability to monetize our traffic in ways that make sense for our audience. (News Corporation, 2006: 6)

While a big part of MySpace's revenues came from the deal with Google, MySpace also embarked on developing its own advertising targeting systems and techniques. However, only a year after MySpace's acquisition by News Corporation, in 2006, some began to raise critical voices:

By now, everyone knows what MySpace is—or at least, they think they do. The generally held assumption is that MySpace is a social networking site: "a place for friends," as their slogan puts it. In reality, MySpace is the next generation of marketing, advertising and promotion, exquisitely disguised as social networking. Simply put, MySpace.com is Spam 2.0. (Lapinski, 2006)

The profiles of MySpace users include a range of information about users, including bands and artists, and this information is believed to be sought after by advertisers. Also the mainstream press such as *The New York Times* drew attention to this corporate/user duality: "Members of the booming social network website treat their individual profile pages as a creative canvas for personal expression. (. . .) The social networking companies see those pages as a lush target for advertisers—if only they could customize their ads" (Stone, 2007b).

Fox Interactive Media, the part of News Corporation controlling MySpace, strongly believed that scanning, gathering, and processing the information the users provide on their profile were key for developing a model for generating advertising revenue. Adam Bain, EVP at Fox Interactive Media, explained optimistically: "For users, MySpace is a platform for public self-expression. For advertisers, it's now a platform for understanding user behavior" (Kaplan, 2007). Peter Levinsohn, president of Fox Interactive Media, claimed, "We are blessed with a phenomenal amount of information about the likes, dislikes and life's passions of our users" (Levinsohn, quoted in Stone, 2007b).

The information was used to develop the new targeting technique called HyperTargeting. Fox Interactive Media's 'monetization technology group' created computer algorithms to search through MySpace profiles. The first phase of this project is called 'interest-based targeting.' The computer algorithms group each MySpace user in one of ten categories according to main interests, such as sports, fashion, finance, video games, autos, and health. During the second phase of the targeting project, these ten categories are split further. Hundreds of subcategories are created as sports enthusiasts are divided into basketball, college football, and skiing. In the same way, film enthusiasts are divided into film genres (Stone, 2007b). Chris DeWolfe, co-founder and chief executive of MySpace, explained:

> We now have probably 250 or 300 people just in our technology monetization group who are working on algorithms that identify enthusiasts in different buckets. We have over 1,000 enthusiast categories that we can sell to our advertisers. For example we could sell to soccer moms or horror-movie enthusiasts. (DeWolfe, quoted in Bartiromo, 2008)

In this way, HyperTargeting represented a further move toward surveillance of users and individualized marketing.

HyperTargeting, it was claimed, allowed brand advertisers to 'microtarget' users with advertisements. The MySpace Selfserve or MyAds service represented a further way of exploiting users' information, as the MySpace users themselves could purchase advertising to target their fellow users: "This expanded MyAds platform will allow anyone to create an account, choose from among 1,100 niche categories, upload/choose creatives and start an ad campaign, targeting the 76 million US MySpace users. (. . .) This is a display ad system, unlike Google's text-based ad system (at least on its own site)." The new MyAds service was reportedly allowing the targeting of users according to age, sex, geographical location, combining it with user-interest categories including specific keywords within each category (Ali, 2008). MySpace presented this new advertising service as follows:

MySpace Advertising for Any Size Business

With MySpace's exclusive targeting you can advertise to over 80 million U.S. users or pinpoint a niche group based on their hobbies, interests, age, gender and location.

- How It Works
  - Create an ad using a free template or upload your own ad.
  - Send people who click on your ad to your website or MySpace profile.
  - Choose who sees your ad by gender, age, location, hobbies and interests.
  - Select a date range to show your ad.
  - Enter a daily budget limit for the ad. This can be changed at any time.
  - Monitor the ad performance with free reports.
  - Open up to 100 different ad campaigns in one account.

- Exclusive MySpace Targeting
  Nowhere else can you target a pay per click banner ad to people based on their MySpace profile interests.

- Targeting Option
  Location, age and gender.
  Show your ads to people interested in sports, fashion, yoga, gospel music, politics, TV shows, and over 1,100 more interests.

  (MySpace, 2009)

Through MySpace's advertising platform MyAds, the aim was to allow users to buy and run advertising campaigns on their own and target MySpace users locally. According to MySpace's promotion, it was possible to "show ads to women 18–38 who love shopping in your city" or "show ads to wine lovers living near your store" (MySpace, 2009). However, despite the increased scanning and segmenting of users for commercial purposes, MySpace executives claim that HyperTargeting is far less controversial than 'behavioral' advertising. MySpace pointed out that it does not track people's movements on the web and does not send users advertisements according to their online activity or behavior (Allison and Garrahan, 2007).

Facebook decided to take a different approach when attempting to turn itself into a commercial environment. The Beacon program was launched by Facebook in November 2007 and aimed to map Facebook users' actions on websites outside Facebook that had paid to be part of the Beacon program. Beacon registered when a Facebook user made a purchase from an online retailer participating in the program. *The New York Times* published an example of how a purchase at the website Fandango that sells movie tickets in the US was registered and forwarded to a Facebook friend of the purchaser.

The Beacon initiative met fierce criticism for distributing details about the activity of members without their permission. MoveOn.org Civic Action organized a protest, and more than 50,000 members of Facebook opposed the practice of distributing this information without peoples' full consent. Facebook later changed the Beacon system and no longer distributes information about purchases and websites visited without the user's agreement (Story and Stone, 2007). In response to the reactions, Facebook's founder, Mark Zuckerberg, wrote on his Facebook blog:

> About a month ago, we released a new feature called Beacon to try to help people share information with their friends about things they do on the web. We've made a lot of mistakes building this feature, but we've made even more with how we've handled them. We simply did a bad job with this release, and I apologize for it. While I am disappointed with our mistakes, we appreciate all the feedback we have

received from our users. I'd like to discuss what we have learned and how we have improved Beacon.

When we first thought of Beacon, our goal was to build a simple product to let people share information across sites with their friends. It had to be lightweight so it wouldn't get in people's way as they browsed the web, but also clear enough so people would be able to easily control what they shared. We were excited about Beacon because we believe a lot of information people want to share isn't on Facebook, and if we found the right balance, Beacon would give people an easy and controlled way to share more of that information with their friends.

But we missed the right balance. At first we tried to make it very lightweight so people wouldn't have to touch it for it to work. The problem with our initial approach of making it an opt-out system instead of opt-in was that if someone forgot to decline to share something, Beacon still went ahead and shared it with their friends. It took us too long after people started contacting us to change the product so that users had to explicitly approve what they wanted to share. Instead of acting quickly, we took too long to decide on the right solution. I'm not proud of the way we've handled this situation and I know we can do better. (Zuckerberg, 2007)

The use of the word 'balance' shows what is at stake: the search for monetization strategies that work and can be accepted by the users. However, clashes between users and the corporate are happening regularly. To maintain credibility among particularly its users, Facebook attempted to put to rest rumors of new features that were thought to violate privacy:

Debunking Rumors about Advertising and Photos
Barry Schnitt 24. November 2009 kl. 11:42

UPDATE on Tuesday, Nov. 24: This rumor about Facebook using your photos in ads without your consent is spreading again. The rumor was not true earlier this year and it is not true now. For more information on Facebook's advertising policies and how we use photos, please take a look at the blog post below.

Published on Friday, July 24
In the past couple of days, a rumor has begun spreading that claims we have changed our policies for third-party advertisers and the use of your photos. These rumors are false, and we have made no such change in our advertising policies.

If you see a Wall post or receive a message with the following language or something similar, it is this false rumor:

FACEBOOK has agreed to let third party advertisers use your posted pictures WITHOUT your permission.

The advertisements that started these rumors were not from Facebook but placed within applications by third parties. Those ads violated our policies by misusing profile photos, and we already required the removal of those deceptive ads from third-party applications before this rumor began spreading.

We are as concerned as many of you are about any potential threat to your experience on Facebook and the protection of your privacy. That's why we prohibit ads on Facebook Platform that cause a bad user experience, are misleading, or otherwise violate our policies. Along with removing ads, we've recently prohibited two entire advertising networks from providing services to applications on Facebook Platform because they were not compliant with our policies and failed to correct their practices.

We're committed to remaining vigilant in enforcing our policies to prevent bad ads from appearing on Facebook—whether served by us or a third party. But we also need your help. If you ever see a misleading ad or believe it violates our policies, report it to us.

If it's one of our ads, you can simply click the thumbs-down icon that appears above or below the ad to report it. If the ad is from a third-party application, click the "Report" link at the bottom of the page to report it to the developer and us.

How We Use Photos

We've run advertisements from our own advertising system for more than a year that let your friends know if you have a direct connection with a product or service, in the same way that your friends learn through your News Feed if you're connected with another friend or an organization's Facebook Page.

These social ads always require that you and your friends have taken an express action to indicate your connections with the product or service and that no data be shared with the third party.

Barry, manager of policy communications at Facebook, likes checking the facts.

(Schnitt, 2009)

Despite the reassurances from the owners of global social media, the study of the corporate/user duality is of major importance. Hundreds of millions of internet users are adopting these services and incorporate them into their everyday social life. A recurring theme is how these services gather and use information on their users for commercial purposes. As the global social media does not charge membership fees, their monetization strategies rely on the involvement of various third parties, i.e., advertisers. In 2010, *The Wall Street Journal* reported that both Facebook and MySpace, along with several other social media, had distributed information "to advertising companies that could be used to find consumers' names and other personal details, despite promises they don't share such information without consent" (Steel and Vascellaro, 2010). According to general practice, advertisers often get access to the "address of the page from which a user clicked on an ad," but this information does not make it possible to trace the internet user. In the case of several social media sites, the information and addresses "typically include user names that could direct advertisers back to a profile page full of personal information. In some cases, user names are people's real names." This matter is of great concern in relation to Facebook, *The Wall Street Journal* argued, as "the company has been pushing users to make more of their personal information public and the site requires users to use their actual names when registering on the site." Facebook acknowledged that the service had been sending such data to advertising companies: "We were recently made aware of one case where if a user takes a specific route on the site, advertisers may see that they clicked on their own profile and then clicked on an ad (. . .)," a Facebook representative commented. Facebook claimed that the service had made changes and now operates in line with the common online advertising standards (Steel and Vascellaro, 2010). Studying MySpace's and Facebook's attempts to monetize their services, then, give insight into their commercial strategies and, in a wider sense, the escalating commercialization of the internet and the contoversies this leads to. The next section explores the electronic music practitioners' reflections on some of these developments.

THE ELECTRONIC MUSIC PRACTITIONERS

Global social media have implemented major initiatives to capitalize on the user activity within these services. While critics worry about the corporate influence, marketers and advertisers are preoccupied with the commercial potential. How do some of the Bergen-based music practitioners experience this development? The reflections on this issue by electronic music practitioners provide a snapshot of thoughts and views on operating within this landscape. There is an awareness of the corporate among these music practitioners. However, perhaps surprisingly, those interviewed do not consider this a problem:

> Even if I have, shall we say, political objections to many sides of business, then I do not see any areas of conflict for me as a musician or me

as involved in a record label—I do not see any contradictions between running that kind of artistic activity, that we do, and using MySpace as a vehicle for this dissemination or distribution. Absolutely not. There are several classic idealistic arguments that I do not buy in relation to this. I do not have any illusions and accept the "unholy" alliance. (Lars Jacob Tynes Pedersen, March 2009)

Tynes Pedersen, then, has a pragmatic view on the use of these commercial services: "When it comes to people like us who run a record label and activities like that, then we are just as much business people like Rupert Murdoch" (Lars Jacob Tynes Pedersen, March 2009). This view is shared by several of those interviewed including Fredrik Saroea of Datarock: "It has never bothered me. But I do think that perhaps there is a devil lurking behind it all, and that something may happen sometime" (Fredrik Saroea, October 2010). Fellow artist Annie shares this pragmatic view:

I have not paid much attention to it, even if you often noticed various advertisements. Personally it does irritate me quite a bit. There is a lot of rubbish. But, still, one is exposed to so much advertising in general that you do get used to it. This means that when you are inside the little box (your Facebook profile), then you do not think much about it. (. . .) And, at the same time, my music is being promoted via Facebook, so in a way I am also advertising, and take part in this. So, I am skeptical, but do not think much about it, even though I perhaps should. (Annie, November 2010)

Skatebård emphasizes how he has taught himself to not pay attention to advertising:

I have become very good at ignoring all advertising when online. I have become very good at distinguishing between actual content and advertising. And I notice that everything has 'become' Google. The Google search engine, Gmail, YouTube, and blogspot.com are all (owned) by Google, and usually the advertising is very direct. But they are not blinking and are very small. If I had been a bit less trained (it would have been harder). Because, if I get an email where (one of the words in it) is 'music studio,' then, due to the search-based advertising, then an advertising saying: 'Do you need new microphones?' suddenly appears. (Skatebård, October 2010)

Similarly to Annie, Bjørn Torske argues that you do not pay much attention to the corporate initiatives of global social media:

Regardless of who owns and administers MySpace as a brand, it has not affected my music practice. MySpace is not Spotify. With Spotify you are more conscious about it being a company that has made the music service. You do not think in that way when you use MySpace, because you are operating in your own little 'garden,' your own little box where, although you are a user, have freedom to engage, design your own profile. So, you have more control, and then the issue of brand becomes less important or significant. (Bjørn Torske, September 2010)

Still, Torske, who has yet to institutionalize global social media in his personal music practice, acknowledges the services' power to make changes but does not see this as limiting the users' opportunities:

MySpace has of course the opportunity to regulate your profile. You sign a user agreement when you create an account and profile, but still, there is this element of 'own will' in this system, so it does not actually mean so much. One chooses how one should use it, and how much you want to use it, and how much music one wants to place on the profile. It does not cost anything to use MySpace, even though I think if you pay, then you get even more 'freedom,' more space, but that I do not have much experience with. (Bjørn Torske, September 2010)

Mikal Telle also has a pragmatic approach to the use of these services:

I do not think much about it. No, not really. You do think about it when you get inappropriate advertising. Let's say that you have a blog, and the agreement with the provider of the blog is that they may place advertisements on your site. Then sometimes you might think that: 'This is a stupid advertisement' to have on your blog, but in general I do not think about it. Instead, I think: 'How can I commercially benefit from the 2000 friends I have on Facebook'—now I am a bit cynical. But, no, I have not thought much about it. Perhaps I should? (Mikal Telle, October 2010)

Instead, Telle points out that his main objection to these services is not the commercial aspect, but the time spent using them:

It is actually someone who builds a (communication) structure that you (do not) have to pay to use. You pay by giving away too much information about yourself, or that people can place advertisements on your page. I have a few friends who do not want to be on Facebook. I understand that, but I would rather say that the main reason for not using it is that it steals my time more than anything else. I am not that paranoid. (Mikal Telle, October 2010)

Torbjørn Brundtland, half of the duo Röyksopp, has not adopted global social media in his personal music practice but draws attention to the influence Facebook has due to its global reach and size:

I feel sometimes that people do not have a choice. It is has become a bit like a technologic imperative: That you have to be on Facebook. And, I think that is a bit sad. I would have liked it (if there) was more of a variety of different social media, and more competition between them, and more choices (for the user). Hopefully that will happen in the future. Now it feels like a monopoly you are entering and that makes me feel a bit uneasy. It is not based on any rational fear. It is just that it doesn't feel quite right. There should have been more choices. (Torbjørn Brundtland, December 2010)

These reflections only give some indication of the users' experience of the corporatization of this environment, but give insight into some of their tactics and pragmatic approach when operating within this landscape. Still, the next section shows how the activity within the expanding social media creates potential for struggles also between the global social media and the outside environment.

GLOBAL SOCIAL MEDIA AND AUDIOVISUAL REGULATIONS[1]

The global social media environment is a contested space as the interests of many stakeholders converge within these services. However, there is also potential for disagreement and a struggle for influence between the global social media and the media and communications landscape in which they exist and engage. The mixing of user-generated content and communication and traditional media content represents a challenge for transnational audiovisual policies' attempts to regulate a transforming media and communications landscape. The study of the pioneering overseas expansion of MySpace seen in relation to EU's audiovisual regulation in the second half of 2010 also gives insight into how the global social media can represent a media form that may prove difficult to regulate. In a wider perspective, the challenges posed by global social media are linked to corporate and political motives of economic rewards and growth generated within the online sphere. This, together with technological factors such as digitization and cross-media distribution, poses challenges for media regulation.

The changes in the media and communications sector, and the increasing role of the internet as a site for distribution of audiovisual media content, meant that such online activity could come to be included in the European Commission's new audiovisual directive of 2007. However, member states and industry representatives, as well as parts of the press, strongly

---

1. This part of the chapter has been previously published in Mjøs, O. J. (2010) News Corporation's MySpace and the digital challenges to audiovisual regulations. In J. Gripsrud & H. Moe (Eds.), *The Digital Public Sphere: Challenges for Media Policy*. Gothenburg: Nordicom.

emphasized the potential for economic growth in the online environment. Some of these stakeholders, therefore, argued fiercely against any regulation that they feared could slow down or hinder economic development within the internet sector. In the mid-2000s, at the time of the public debate leading up to the new audiovisual directive, MySpace had been launched in the US and was also growing rapidly overseas (see Chapter 3).

As pointed out earlier, in Europe MySpace was receiving increased attention. This was partly due to the extensive news coverage in 2005 of News Corp's acquisition. At the same time, the UK mainstream press in particular reported about music bands and artists suddenly becoming popular and reaching the top of the official national music charts through the use of MySpace. MySpace was portrayed as a motor for growth and promotion within the music sector, as bands and fans flocked to the network. In the UK, MySpace was presented as key to the continuing success of major artists such as Madonna and also the rapid rise in popularity of unknown music artists and bands (see Chapter 4; Cieslak, 2006; Buskirk, 2007). Internet users across the world became familiar with the social media phenomenon, and millions began to adopt these services. These developments, together with the story of Google that had already shown how it was possible to generate revenue and profit after the dotcom crash, supported the notion of social media as internet-based entities with major financial and business potential.

The debate prior to the finalization of the European Commission's new audiovisual directive took place around the same time as News Corporation decided to buy MySpace. As part of the process to develop the new directive, both European commercial and public media and communications stakeholders were invited to submit written observations and to express their views on the 'Television Without Frontiers Directive Issues Papers' to the European Commission. The US-originated search engine giant Yahoo!, one of the world's major internet-based companies, was among the companies commenting on parts of these papers in 2005. Yahoo! Europe argued fiercely against regulating audiovisual content on the internet: "We are not convinced of the need for an extension of the current TVWF Directive to cover any element of the online sector." Yahoo! Europe pointed to how major changes within the European audiovisual sector had given rise to a plethora of television channels, and thereby increased the choice for viewers:

> In the 1980s barriers to entry into the AV broadcast market were extremely high. This resulted in only a handful of channels in each Member State enjoying very high, passive, audiences and arguably having an impact on citizens' thinking. The environment today bears no resemblance to that of the 1980s, with a multitude of satellite, cable, analogue, and digital terrestrial channels. The control the consumer exerts, like his/her sophistication in the consumption of AV content, has increased just as the impact of any particular programme

or channel has decreased. The trend is continuing apace. (Yahoo! Europe, 2005)

Within the online environment, the 'choice' for 'consumers' is even greater, according to Yahoo!:

> The online environment is still more fragmented, with literally millions of content-based websites and applications, from numerous countries, to choose from. There is no concern over spectrum and barriers to entry are extremely low. The consumer uses numerous tools and services to control what s/he views (and often interacts with) online. The 1980s broadcasting regulation simply does not fit this new and very different environment. (Yahoo! Europe, 2005)

In today's media and communications landscape, Yahoo! continued, "deregulation, not increased sector-specific regulation, is the way to ensure the economic health of the EU AV industry, while ensuring an adequate level of protection for citizens" (Yahoo! Europe, 2005). Also within the political environment, the possible consequences of the new European regulations were debated. Similar to Yahoo!, UK media authorities, representing perhaps the most influential member state (in terms of facilitating commercial pan-European media activity for more than two decades), also pointed out the importance of fostering and harnessing the financial potential of the online environment.

The European Commission's directives provide a minimum of media regulation, and member states can choose to implement stricter regulation. While the UK has traditionally interpreted the directive liberally, other countries such as France have taken a more strict approach (Brown, 1998; Chalaby, 2002). The former British media authority, ITC, granted permission to transmit from the UK for a symbolic fee of £250 and practiced a liberal approach to the regulation of programming, sponsorship and advertising on satellite television channels operating throughout the European Union (Chalaby, 2002). The wish to strengthen London's position in the European media market is seen as one explanation for the loose regulation of satellite television channels transmitting non-European programming (Syvertsen, 2001). This has contributed to making the UK, and in particular London, a bridgehead for expanding US-originating media companies and, in particular, American pan-European cable and satellite television operators transmitting from the UK.

Most pan-European television channels transmit from the UK and a key reason "is the relaxed regulatory (and commercial) regime" (Tunstall and Machin 1999: 72). The majority of programming transmitted by such pan-European television channels should be 'European works,' audiovisual productions of European origin, according to the Television Without Frontiers Directive. However, the directive allowed for flexibility by including the words 'where practicable.' The UK has practiced this flexibility liberally by taking a lax position in regards to the quota requirements to the benefit of, amongst others, American-originated, pan-European television channels with major non-European program archives (Tunstall and Machin, 1999).

In line with the historically British pro-market position, Shaun Woodward, the British Broadcasting Minister, argued against any further EU regulation of audiovisual content in the online environment—and particularly not content on sites such as MySpace:

> It's common sense. If it looks like a TV programme and sounds like one then it probably is. A programme transmitted by a broadcaster over the net could be covered by extending existing legislation. But video clips uploaded by someone are not television. YouTube and MySpace should not be regulated (Woodward, quoted in Sherwin, 2006)

Woodward emphasized that British national law already protects minors in relation to media, and his main concern was possible new regulations hampering the commercial potential of the internet: "The real risk is we drive out the next MySpace because of the cost of complying with unnecessary regulations," Woodward pointed out. "These businesses can easily operate outside the EU" (Woodward, quoted in Sherwin, 2006).

The European Commission's Audiovisual Media Services Directive (AMSD) entered into force on 19 December 2007, and replaced the Television Without Frontiers Directive. The AMSD aims to address the 'new media realities.' It not only covers traditional television broadcasting, but also includes on-demand services such as films and news. Traditional television is categorized as a 'linear' service because the broadcaster decides when programming is scheduled and transmitted. On-demand is referred to as a 'non-linear' service, as the user or viewer chooses when to watch the programming offered:

> For the purposes of this Directive, the definition of an audiovisual media service should cover only audiovisual media services, whether television broadcasting or on-demand, which are mass media, that is, which are intended for reception by, and which could have a clear impact on, a significant proportion of the general public. Its scope should be limited to services as defined by the Treaty and therefore should cover any form of economic activity, including that of public service enterprises, but should not cover activities which are primarily non-economic and which are not in competition with television broadcasting, such as private websites and services consisting of the provision or distribution of audiovisual content generated by private users for the purposes of sharing and exchange within communities of interest. (European Commission, 2007)

Services that are not primarily distributors of audiovisual content, such as private email communication and electronic versions of newspapers and magazines, are not covered by the directive: "Examples include websites that contain audiovisual elements only in an ancillary manner, such as animated graphical elements, short advertising spots or information related to a product or non-audiovisual service" (European Commission, 2007). The European Commission's new audiovisual directive thereby distinguishes between 'non-linear' and 'linear' audiovisual services, but these two categories do not include private communication or user-generated media content online. However, since the directive of 2007, News Corporation has stepped up its efforts to develop MySpace into an even more advanced media and communications service. The service began to offer both 'non-linear' and 'linear' audiovisual content, as well as user-generated media content and communication.

MYSPACE: A MULTIMEDIA SYNERGY DEVICE

After News Corporation acquired MySpace, the social media service attempted to develop into a synergy device—a vehicle for the distribution of both corporate and user-generated audiovisual content and communication. This development has mainly taken place in the US but signals what the European media and communications landscape might expect. As we shall see, this development raises the question further of how MySpace and other social media should be regulated and complicates the categorizations that the European Commission's new Audiovisual Media Services Directive attempts to address.

Synergy has become a common strategy for all large media enterprises as they attempt to use the internet to harness the possible benefits of cross-platform distribution of their various operations (Thussu, 2006). The (former) MySpace CEO and co-founder, Chris DeWolfe, also emphasized the potential for synergy between News Corporation's media content and MySpace: "I really thought that we would fit well with a media company. We'd have access to content, we'd have access to unlimited capital, and we'd have access to international markets" (DeWolfe, quoted in Maney, 2009). Furthermore, DeWolfe claimed, "So they [News Corp] allowed us to stay in our own silo and grow and find synergy—or whatever word you want to use—within the other groups in News Corp" (DeWolfe, quoted in Maney, 2009). "There is a fair amount of synergy. When people think of News Corp they may think of Fox Channel and Fox News first," said DeWolfe. "So there is a lot of crossover and potential for interesting promotions" (DeWolfe, quoted in La Monica, 2009). While such proclamations might be considered public relations messages, MySpace has been central in News Corporation's attempts to distribute media content online.

MySpace's early forays into legal online distribution of television content started soon after News Corporation took control. The offering included online downloads of episodes of the television series *24*, produced by News Corporation-owned Fox Entertainment (Becker, 2006):

As we focus on growing revenues, we are also intent on improving the user experience for our 120 million-plus users worldwide. MySpace's offerings have expanded more in the past three months than in the previous four years since its creation. We've added streaming video, special comedy clips, free classified ads and instant messaging. In a major deal with Burger King, we made available on MySpace episodes of hit shows like *24*. MySpace is a major driver of traffic to the so-called "Internet 2.0" sites—picture-hosting sites like Photobucket and video repositories like YouTube. There is no reason why we can't replicate that functionality and retain that traffic—and its attendant revenue. (News Corporation, 2006: 6)

At the time, MySpace was considered a multimedia synergy device with enormous potential. Also episodes of other Fox-produced television shows such as *Prison Break* and *Bones* were made available on MySpace and on the websites of News Corporation-owned local television stations in the US after they been had aired on traditional television. Similar to the MySpace management, Ross Levinsohn, president of Fox Interactive Media, the News Corporation arm that controls MySpace, claimed that "leveraging this unique opportunity with our sister company Fox enables us to experiment and innovate and deliver some of the most compelling video experiences online to consumers" (*USA Today*, 2006). A number of changes were made to facilitate the distribution of audiovisual content. In 2007, MySpace re-launched its video-sharing service and called it MySpaceTV (Stone, 2007a). MySpaceTV was later renamed MySpace Video—an umbrella for MySpace's video offerings.

While YouTube has been embroiled in copyright issues over its distribution of unlicensed film and television programming, MySpace claims to take a different approach: "Video could have been that big win, we could have been YouTube. But since we were owned by News Corporation that has a great respect for intellectual property, we couldn't have been YouTube" (Anderson, co-founder of MySpace, quoted in Gibson, 2008). The media conglomerate Viacom, owner of the cable and satellite television channels MTV and Comedy Central, sued YouTube for making video segments of the television series *South Park* and other television programs available without permission. Viacom argued that 160,000 program segments had been viewed 1.5 billion times and demanded $1 billion in compensation from YouTube (Ahrens, 2007). As part of the ongoing dispute between the two media giants, the owner of YouTube, Google, was in 2008 ordered to give Viacom the records that list which users watched which videos on YouTube. According to *The New York Times*, Viacom could then use this information to help decide to what extent YouTube's popularity has been achieved through the distribution and use of 'copyrighted clips' (Helft, 2008). Despite News Corporation's and MySpace's stance against copyright infringement, it is common for users of MySpace to also incorporate—or embed—music videos and other video clips on their user profiles from YouTube. YouTube made it easy to embed its videos on other websites, such as MySpace, and this helped increase the use of YouTube videos, which in turn helped raise the financial value of the video service—bought by Google in 2006 for $1.65 billion (Stone, 2007a; Stross, 2008: 116; see also chapter 3 and 4).

Only a year after Google purchased YouTube, News Corporation and the media conglomerate NBC Universal launched an internet video-distribution network in the US. The advertising-supported portal claimed to offer 'thousands of hours' of streamed television programming and movies, as well as content from the television programming libraries of the two companies. The joint-venture online portal was named Hulu.com, and News Corporation has a 45 percent equity interest in the company. The initial distribution partners were AOL, MSN, Yahoo!, and MySpace, and the media content was made available for free, but with advertising (News Corporation, 2007, 2009: 23).

MySpace also has a central role in the distribution of video content from Hulu. The same year as Hulu was launched, media content from the web site was being showcased in the new portal MySpace PrimeTime within MySpaceTV (Nicole, 2007). The relationship between Hulu and MySpace developed further as users were allowed to view Hulu content either on their own MySpace profiles or on the separate MySpace PrimeTime site—part of the MySpace Video initiative. This means that MySpace users could search and watch the whole Hulu video database as well as MySpace's own video content without leaving the MySpace service (Albanesius, 2008). The media content is available either from a MySpace Video Player or in the form of embedded online video services such as YouTube.

Hulu has expanded rapidly in the US. When it started, NBC and Fox were the main providers of video content, with only around 90 show titles. By 2009, the site had 130 providers contributing more than 11,000 titles to internet users in the US (Errol, 2009). Similarly, large traditional media companies, such as CBS and ABC, that own or control television and film programming, also distributed their media content on dedicated online outlets. CBS's internet video sites CBS Innertube and TV.com offered CBS television programming with embedded ads, and ABC.com distributed ABC television programming (Pomerantz, 2008). By late 2010, Google Sites, which includes YouTube, dominated the online viewing of video, but also both Facebook and News Corporation had a major presence among the ten most used online video services in the US (see Table 6.1). Facebook did not feature on this list in 2009 but has in one year become the third most used site for online video viewing. Internet users could watch videos on News Corporation-controlled websites such as Hulu or its wholly owned Fox Interactive Media outlets such as MySpace. Together these entities made News Corporation one of the most popular online providers of video content (see Table 6.1).

Table 6.1   Top US Online Video Properties by Videos Viewed September 2010; Total US—Home/Work/University Locations

Property	Total Unique Viewers (000)	Viewing Sessions (000)	Minutes per Viewer
Total internet: total audience	174,685	5,254,794	863.7
Google sites	144,166	1,904,315	260.4
Yahoo! sites	54,356	239,154	31.5
Facebook.com	52,174	202,813	18.5
Microsoft sites	45,490	282,449	40.6
Fox Interactive Media	43,851	240,037	18.3
VEVO	43,650	208,442	73.3
Viacom Digital	33,570	72,095	46.7
NBC Universal	29,961	62,315	16.5
Hulu	29,890	145,070	162.6
Turner Network	27,195	91,836	25.4

(Data source: comScore Video Metrix, 2010.)

By 2009, Hulu was only available legally in the US. Outside the US, various online services offer Hulu unofficially and illegally. However, just like the American cable and satellite television channels throughout the 1980s and 1990s and MySpace in 2006 and later Facebook, Hulu is reportedly planning to expand outside the American market—and the UK is also seen as the natural first market (Barnett, 2009a). However, launching Hulu in the UK is complicated due to copyright issues on programming, and raises regulatory issues. Would an online European Hulu service be regulated as 'non-linear' on-demand service? The British newspaper *Daily Telegraph* reported that Hulu considered launching in the UK with 3,000 hours of American-originated programming content, as well as content from the British national broadcasters BBC, ITV, and Channel 4 (Barnett, 2009b). However, Hulu's plans for a launch in the UK were later abandoned as the negotiations with British television broadcasters did not lead to any media content deals. One of the British national players, ITV, decided to focus on developing its ITV Player online service instead of distributing its media content to third parties, according to the *Daily Telegraph* (Barnett, 2010). Still, due to Hulu's success in the US, it would be no surprise if the online film and television service establishes itself in the UK and Europe at a later stage. If the UK version of Hulu is distributed from the UK and across Europe, will the British media authorities also, in the case of Hulu, allow for flexibility—favoring an American-originated, online, 'non-linear,' on-demand service perhaps lacking European media content? Furthermore, if MySpace is not regulated by the European Commission's new audiovisual directive, how will a European Hulu service embedded in MySpace be regulated?

Global social media make up a contested online space. This becomes clear when examining the corporate and user perspectives within the social media environment, and also the global social media entities in relation to the outside environment. New issues of corporate influence make the services different from traditional media. While there is nothing new in the selling of media audiences and users, it is the sophistication of the mapping of the self-disclosure and user participation and behavior that take place within a corporate online environment that make them stand out. At the same time, the users—in this case music practitioners—show an awareness and experience of the corporate strategies, but their reflections indicate the use of conscious tactics when navigating and a generally pragmatic approach to this environment. Furthermore, as soon as News Corporation acquired MySpace, the company attempted to introduce News Corporation-owned media content online. The aim was to develop MySpace into a commercial multimedia giant and synergy device. The case of MySpace exemplifies, and may signal, what the European media and communications landscape might expect. This raises the question of how MySpace or Facebook should be regulated and complicates and challenges the categorizations that the European Commission's new Audiovisual Media Services Directive attempts to address.

7 New Spaces of Global Mobility
Re-evaluating Media Globalization

Global social media have become the site for the converging interests of media conglomerates, the world's largest computer software company and the major music companies, along with the hundreds of millions of internet users who have adopted them. As such, the development of these services throughout the seminal period 2005–2010, is at the heart of the transformation taking place within the media and communications sector. The exploration of the components of the global media and music nexus, both from a corporate and a user perspective, gives insight into these transformations and thereby the characteristics of the processes associated with media globalization. It reveals how this nexus embodies a corporate/user duality. On the one hand, the historical, political, and economic examination gives insight into the corporate perspective—the tendencies and factors central in the development of the global social media environment. On the other hand, these services facilitate opportunities for user activity. These opportunities are being utilized by the group of electronic music practitioners in this study. This duality is what facilitates a new space for global mobility. In contrast to traditional audiovisual spaces, this space enhances the potential of the global social media users' opportunities to operate, and communicate, within the media and communications infrastructure. These corporate services have come to play a role in allowing music practitioners to connect with music scenes, fans, and other practitioners locally and internationally. At the same time, this duality also facilitates extensive possibilities for commercial and corporate activity within these services, i.e., monetization strategies.

This final chapter discusses first how this development has theoretical consequences as it challenges, in particular, some political economic perspectives on international communication and media globalization. The chapter then suggests how we may theoretically describe this development of new spaces for global mobility. Incorporating the theoretical mobilities framework into the field of media and communications helps us achieve a more nuanced understanding of the way media globalization unfolds and evolves.

We study the processes of media globalization taking place within the media and communications' sphere by answering the following questions:

how is this situation created, and to what extent and in what way are the opportunities for global mediation and communication utilized? In practice, we explore how the phenomenon of media globalization develops by examining the central economic, political, and technological processes creating a cross-national and increasingly global media and communications infrastructure and, at the same time, by studying the characteristics of specific activity within it (Tomlinson, 1999; Mjøs, 2010). This allows us to examine and understand the development and functions of the components of the global social media and music nexus. By applying both a corporate and a user perspective to our study, we are able to trace the political and economic factors underpinning the expansion of global social media milieu and, at the same time, aspects of what is taking place within this environment. As we place the global social media and music nexus within the historical theoretical tradition of internationalization and globalization of media, we see the extent to which this nexus represents transformation and continuity with the past.

Much of our knowledge of how the relationship between media and globalization evolves and what it leads to is based on studies of the film and television industries—traditional audiovisual media. The increase in cross-national distribution of US-produced films and television programming and the international expansion of media firms gave rise to discourses on the power relations and consequences of this development. This discourse on internationalization and media was characterized by concepts such as 'cultural imperialism' (Schiller, 1969; Dorfman and Mattelart, 1975), 'media imperialism' (Boyd-Barrett, 1977), and 'cultural synchronization' (Hamelink, 1983). Since the 1990s, US-originated traditional media players have also been central in the discourse on the relationship between globalization and media (Schiller, 1998). The uneven power relations within the international media sector, not least as seen in the US' position as dominating media exporter, also show how the concept of 'media imperialism' remains central (Boyd-Barrett, 1998). However, some scholars question the validity of such concepts and arguments of power and domination. Some point out that globalization is multi-directional, not a one-way flow (Tomlinson, 1991). This is certainly the case within today's audiovisual industry. Although the US continues to dominate the world's television market, national and regional players increasingly produce television, music, and other media products for home markets or initiate new distribution flows from the south to the north, or between neighboring territories both in the south and north (Thussu, 2000/2006, 2005, 2007a; Hafez, 2007; Hesmondhalgh, 2007; Straubhaar, 2007).

The development of the global social media and music nexus clearly resonates with the worries of the critical political economy tradition. Traditional media conglomerates such as News Corporation and Time Warner, along with the computer software giant Microsoft, soon considered the emerging global social media as a phenomenon that could help them reach media audiences and potential customers online. As such, these media companies used social media to extend influence into the online environment. There are further suggestions of how influence within the traditional media sector also extends to the social media milieu when we scrutinize the components of the global social media and music nexus. The new owners of these services created alliances and launched joint ventures among others with the major music companies. Some of these players were already linked as cross-ownership and collaborations connect the traditional media and music industry. The creation of MySpace Music, Spotify's collaboration with Facebook, and the music majors' Vevo online music video player supported by YouTube all show how the influence of the music industry exists within social media. The traditional music industry entered the global social media environment attempting to profit from the millions of users of these services. As such, we see how media conglomerates and music industry giants collaborate within this nexus.

Furthermore, to expand globally and appeal to local audiences and compete with smaller social media services, MySpace and Facebook launched ambitious localization strategies. These strategies were intended to anchor the services among media users across the world and thereby create more stable conditions for corporate activity. First MySpace, closely followed by Facebook, could soon compete with national social media entities. The localization of Facebook and Twitter is unprecedented—in effect turning these global entities into a local or national social media service. This has paved the way for Facebook to outperform MySpace and compete with smaller services around the world. So, from a corporate perspective, there is no doubt that the corporatization of global social media connects with earlier observations of dominating and influential US operators and the uneven relations within the international and global media sphere.

Still, the user perspective applied throughout the book allows us to see how these services offer a new space for the users not previously provided by traditional audiovisual media. It is true that television audiences can choose television programming from a rapidly growing number of television channels, and the traditional audiovisual space has increasingly come to include a greater diversity. This is particularly evident in the factual television genre. The docu-soaps and reality TV formats have been welcomed for providing a space for 'ordinary' people's lives. The popular factual television form, 'lifestyle programs,' for example, plays an important role as it "represents a greater attention paid to the stuff of everyday lives and a broader definition of what 'cultural broadcasting' might consist of" (Brunsdon, 2004: 88, 89). On a global level, the factual broadcaster, the Discovery Channel, provides factual entertainment programming that portrays the everyday life of people previously rarely represented in factual television (Mjøs, 2010a).

Despite these changes within traditional audiovisual content, such spaces still offer very limited opportunities for the individual media users' actual participation and input. The way media globalization has evolved—characterized also by the logics of the maturing internet and the emergence of the global social media environment—has created new spaces where also electronic music practitioners operate within the global communications infrastructure in an unprecedented way.

One should, however, be careful not to overestimate this development. The general widespread adoption of global social media services taking place, not only among youth and music practitioners, but among all age groups, also resonates with some of the most optimistic or even utopian views. Some consider new media and the internet as having a central place in peoples' lives because it "fulfils the personalization of our needs in a way that past media could never achieve" (Marshall, 2004: 26). Such celebratory accounts emphasize how:

> The user subjectivity of new media with this production ethos is a massive and unparalleled challenge to the traditions of media use that have been in place for most of the previous century. The reception/consumption ethos and dichotomy of the twentieth century has given way to a production ethos of users. In some ways, new media has heralded a transformation of contemporary culture through a democratization of cultural expression. (Marshall, 2004: 27)

Such beliefs have certainly been fueled by the immense preoccupation in both the Internet industry and among practitioners and scholars with the potential significance and implications of the behavior of new media users. The widespread adoption of the industry term 'Web 2.0' as *the* buzzword that described the rise of the creative user or consumer (Web 2.0 Conference, 2004; O'Reilly, 2005), but also many "other derivative '2.0' concepts" appeared for corporate purposes (Bruns, 2008: 4). One should therefore be careful not to blindly accept the "myth of mass democratization as a direct effect of technological change" (Burgess and Green, 2009: 20). Within the music industry, the idea of "democratization of cultural production" is clearly related to the assumption that "raw talent combined with digital distribution can convert to legitimate success and media fame" (Burgess and Green, 2009: 21).

Critical scholars within the field of international communication and global media studies have also raised concerns about the distribution of power within new media, including the online environment, and questioned the actual influence of the users. On a general level, Mansell calls for the examination of "What dominant principles, values and perceptions of power are being embedded in our technologically-mediated interactions?" And, furthermore, Mansell asks, "How is technological innovation in the new media field being structured; by whom and for whom is it being negotiated?" (Mansell, 2004: 103). Wasko also expresses concern specifically in relation to global social media and its users: "Clearly, one of the most worrisome aspects of YouTube's monetization strategies is the commodification of labor. This issue arises most acutely when we consider how advertisers and media companies exploit users for profit" (Wasko and Erickson, 2009: 383). And, Boyd-Barrett, who originally coined the term "media imperialism," points explicitly to how the theoretical concept continues to be relevant when explaining the US' dominant role in information and communication technologies (ICT). The term "media imperialism" originally aimed to explain the American presence and power in the television market, but this focus "may have distracted attention from the emergence of microprocessor-based computer networking technologies" and the "influence these have exerted on US economic and foreign policies" (Boyd-Barrett, 2006: 21).

While global social media and the online environment increase the potential for mobility for media users, this activity takes place within a contested corporate environment. Therefore, as the previous chapters show, the application of the corporate and user perspective uncovers and maps the role of the various components of the global social media and music nexus. As such, the approach resonates with the call for studies that take into account both macro and micro perspectives (Morley, 1991) and combine the study of the political economy of the media and the study of reception and thereby utilize both perspectives rather than debating which approach is the most fruitful (Curran and Morley, 2006).

The large traditional US television and media entities, for decades at the center of studies on power relations in international and global media sector production, incorporate gate-keeping policies in their media content and services and distribute similar media products and service offerings globally, all in line with a defined brand (Chalaby, 2002; Urry, 2003; Mjøs, 2010a). Although the major media players, and music companies, were quick to view the millions of users congregating within these services, among them music practitioners and fans, as a potentially attractive audience for advertising and other corporate initiatives, global social media differ from traditional media forms. These entities exist within the global social media environment that is a more unpredictable landscape compared to the traditional television and film sectors. Users of global social media do not pay any fees to join MySpace, YouTube, Facebook, or Twitter, and users of these services are free to start and stop using them at any time. There are numerous competing social media, and the short history of these services shows how they may experience a rapid increase in the number of users, but then lose their popularity, signaling a certain vulnerability. MySpace, once considered the most popular website in the US (Angwin, 2009), is struggling. In contrast, YouTube and Facebook have continued to expand—the latter attracting more than 500 million users across the world (Facebook, 2010).

In the mid-2000s, MySpace had a central role for these electronic music practitioners. MySpace was used to initiate and cultivate contact on a range of levels, either with people they already knew or perhaps had not met in person or those who were unknown, but with a shared interest in music. As such, the service played a role in allowing music practitioners to connect with music scenes locally and internationally. However, as we have seen, during these five formative years the global social media environment has been subject to major shifts and changes. The expansion of Facebook and Twitter, and their subsequent popularity, is also reflected in the electronic music practitioners' practice. While certain gate-keeping functions may place limits on expression, the potential influence of these services makes them different from the traditional global media. The experience of the electronic music practitioners certainly relates to the concepts of 'transnational connections' (Hannerz, 1996), and 'cosmopolitan fluidity' (Urry, 2003). Furthermore, the global social media represent globalization devices that, similar to Netville's role as a 'harbinger of "glocalization"' (Hampton and Wellman, 2003: 306), have helped the electronic music practitioners to operate and connect with scenes on both a local and global level. Still, we need to keep in mind that in response to a volatile internet environment and the sudden shifts in user take-up and use, global social media attempt to create a predictable commercial environment through localization strategies, and through alliances with the music industry, as well the monetization of the users.

Placing the global social media and music nexus within the 'mobilities' framework helps us to theoretically articulate the logic and characteristics of these online entities and the user-activity taking place within them. According to the theoretical 'mobilities' framework, social science fails to address the emerging practices of mobility in social and cultural life. The significance of "issues of movement", in its various forms, are increasingly characterizing our civilization:

> From SARS to train crashes, from airport expansion controversies to SMS (short message service) texting on the move, from congestion charging to global terrorism, from obesity caused by "fast food" to oil wars in the Middle East, issues of "mobility" are centre stage. (Sheller and Urry, 2006: 208).

This "mobility turn" also contributes to theory development. It affects social science by merging key aspects of transport research and social science research: "putting social relations into travel and connecting different forms of transport with complex patterns of social experience conducted through communications at-a-distance." (2006: 208) As a consequence a "new paradigm" within the social sciences appears to be emerging; the "new mobilities" paradigm. This theoretical framework confronts social science research claiming that the discipline has traditionally been 'a-mobile' (2006: 208). The 'mobility turn' in society is linked to the emergence of 'mobility systems' throughout the twentieth century. These systems include national telephone systems, low-cost air travel, mobile phones, and networked computers. And these systems facilitate numerous forms of mobility in society such as physical or virtual travel and movement or, as pointed out, "social experience conducted through communications at-a-distance" (Sheller and Urry, 2006: 206; Urry, 2007). Global social media is the result of the development of systems like the internet so MySpace, Facebook, and YouTube are therefore part of this 'mobility turn.' These cross-national social media facilitate enhanced potential for communicative and virtual mobility (Elliott and Urry, 2010: ix) for individual media users within the global media and communications landscape. The adoption and utilization of these services by hundreds of millions of internet–users stand in contrast to developments within the traditional media sector in the second half of the twentieth century, which have been the focus of much of the research on the internationalization and globalization of media. The mobilities' paradigm introduces two metaphors of systems that help to place this development in a wider practical and theoretical perspective. 'Global networks' and 'global fluids' describe systems central in shaping and creating increased interconnectedness and interdependence of the world society. They also characterize the developments of the media and communications landscape, and thereby how media globalization unfolds and develops.

'Global networks' are global commercial, public, or non-profit networks or organizations, characterized by their predictable aims, a common brand, and how the actions of the employees or participants of the globally network are coordinated. Examples of globally integrated networks are Greenpeace, MasterCard, and McDonalds: "These companies have produced enormously effective networks with few 'failings'" (Urry, 2000: 37; 2003) Transnational corporations (TNCs) have been at the heart of media and communications research since the 1960s. TNCs have increasingly exploited political, economic, and technological factors to form global networks within the media sector such as Walt Disney Company's worldwide operations, the Hollywood film and television industry, and global television distribution operations such as CNN, MTV, and the Discovery Channel.

'Global fluids' are unpredictable powerful global systems such as world money, environmental and health hazards, and the internet—the 'iconic' global fluid—and its users are key actors in the development of it. The global fluids are characterized by waves or fluid systems consisting of people, objects, images, and risks whose development, movement, and consequences are far less predictable than the global networks (Urry, 2003, 2005). The emergence of the internet and development of MySpace and Facebook therefore introduce to the global media and communications landscape a logic characterized by significantly less control, non-linearity, and a much larger degree of unpredictability. Together the two systems 'global networks' and 'global fluids' coexist and overlap across the world. This theoretical approach certainly typifies the characteristics of the findings of the previous chapters—the various components of the corporate/ user duality existing within the global social media and music nexus.

The world's major media and communications companies' moves into the global social media environment exemplify the challenges they are facing from digitization and the internet. They consider social media as key to their online expansion both in the US and internationally. In particular, News Corporation's acquisition of MySpace played a role in reviving the confidence in the commercial potential of the internet in the wake of the dotcom crash a few years earlier. News Corporation's acquisition and global expansion of the social media service was an early attempt to extend the conglomerate's influence online.

Global social media, then, are entities with characteristics of 'global networks,' but at the same time, they embody—and exist within—the logics of the 'global fluid,' the internet. The intersecting and intertwining of the two systems is what creates the peculiar nature of global social media, which sets them apart from traditional 'global networks.' The corporate and user perspectives reveal both the extent of the users' ability to communicate and operate within the global social media and music nexus, and the corporate influence within and between the global-local and macro-micro connections within this nexus. The characteristics of these relationships shape the nature of the virtual mobility. But, these relationships can only be understood by examining their key components. These components are the corporate development of global social media, the process of localization and personalization of these services, the widespread take-up and the various uses of these services, the efforts to monetize them, and the relation between global social media and media policy and external corporate interests.

In recent years, Facebook and Twitter in particular have utilized new technology and exploited the opportunities the online environment provides. The result is an unparalleled rapid and detailed localization across the world. Facebook and Twitter revolutionized localization by recruiting thousands of users across the world to participate in translating the services. Facebook is now available in minority languages never before catered to by global media. The involvement of users and its localization strategy that offers an extensive rage of languages is part of the explanation for Facebook's success, as the service shows an unprecedented ability to connect with local conditions and contexts. However, MySpace played a pioneering role in the global social media and music relationship. And the relationship between MySpace and music fans and artists, and specifically the electronic music practitioners, shows how the service was key in increasing possibilities for communication between users both locally and across national borders. As numerous users began to flock to MySpace and later Facebook, we also see how the service has developed to cater for music practitioners and interested individuals. Furthermore, we also see how the corporatization of these services takes place, as also the music industry—fronted by the music majors—considers the users as potential consumers of music.

The change in MySpace's position is a spectacular example of the volatility in this online environment. The service's role diminished substantially due to the wider macro trends within this environment (see Chapter 4), as well as developments taking place on the micro level. The electronic music practitioners focus on three reasons for reducing their use of MySpace. Firstly, there was too much information distributed among the users, or as some would call it, spam. Secondly, there was a lack of usability that complicated the communication among users, mostly due to technological problems. This became even more visible as Facebook appeared as an alternative. Thirdly, the general shift and movement of users—not just music practitioners—from MySpace to Facebook made it more relevant to use Facebook to reach fans and friends. The uncertainty of the online environment is further underlined by News Corporation's early efforts to develop and stabilize MySpace as a commercial global multimedia synergy device by introducing corporate traditional media content.

Furthermore, MySpace and Facebook's major monetizing strategies make these services different from other media. Global social media exploit the information provided by the users and, in some cases, map their activity within this milieu in new ways. This represents possible challenges for the privacy of social media users and has caused controversies, forcing Facebook officials to respond and react. At the same time, the studied music practitioners show an awareness and experience of the corporate strategies, but their reflections indicate the use of conscious tactics when navigating and a generally pragmatic approach to this environment as they do not consider them as obstructing their activity.

Together the corporate and user perspectives draw out the characteristics of the components of the global social media and music nexus, and this explains how new spaces of virtual mobility are created within this nexus and also highlights the limits and possibilities for users within it. This shows the significance of connecting the theoretical mobilities framework to these recent transformations in the media and communications sector. There is a need to further interpret what these developments lead to:

> As mobile connectivity and disconnection begins to occur in new ways across a wide range of cyber-devices and integrated places, so we need better theorization and research, especially to examine the interdependencies between changes in physical movement and in electronic communications, and especially in their increasing convergence, including both mobile communications and new forms of "virtual" and "imaginative" mobility. (Hannam, Sheller, and Urry, 2006)

The music practitioners' experience of virtual mobility and their awareness of the existence of power within these spaces, then, connect with wider concerns in relation to mobility in society. Referring to Massey's concept of 'power geometry' (1993), Morley draws attention to the fact that some people are more mobile than others, by asking, "who moves and who doesn't, who has control of their movements and who doesn't?":

> As soon as we pose that question, we see that whether in terms of access to physical transport (possession of a car, for instance) or to communications systems (the ability to pay for a cable television subscription or to rent time on the internet), access is heavily structured by class, by gender, by ethnicity and a whole range of other social factors. The idea that "we" somehow all experience the same form of postmodern nomadology then appears little more than a cruel nonsense. (Morley, 2000: 196)

Although written long before the arrival of global social media, Massey's notion of "the power geometry of time-space compression" relates to the characteristics of virtual mobility within this online space. It reminds us that whether we talk about physical or virtual movement and mobility, people "are placed in very distinct ways in relation to these flows and interconnections." It is not just a matter of who moves and who does not move, Massey argues, but we need to recognize that "some people are more in charge of it than others; some initiate flows and movement, others don't" (Massey, 1993: 62). This point is also emphasized by mobilities scholars who argue, "There are new places and technologies that enhance the mobility of some peoples and places even as they also heighten the immobility of others" (Hannam et al, 2006: 3). The corporatization of global social media, represented by the investments and acquisitions of media conglomerates and the following expansion of these services, along with the surveillance of users for commercial purposes, shows how this is a contested online space. At the same time, much-visited and popular global social media user profiles act as nodes of influence that can direct users' attention and user traffic to other profiles. It certainly reminds us that also within these services some individuals have more influence than others.

By incorporating the theoretical mobilities framework within the historical discourse on international communication and media and globalization, the significance of the rise of global social media becomes clearer. This helps develop a more accurate articulation of media globalization that takes into account the possibilities and limits within this new space for global mobility.

Appendix

Discographies of the Interviewed Electronic Music Practitioners

Annie

Albums

2004	Anniemal	679 Recordings
2009	Don't stop	Totally, Smalltown Supersound

Singles and EPs

1999	The Greatest Hit (TELLÉ 003)	Tellé
2002	I Will Get On	Tellé
2003	Untitled	Not On Label
2004	Chewing Gum	679 Recordings
2004	My Heartbeat	679 Recordings
2004	Annie	679 Recordings
2005	The Wedding	Studio !K7
2005	Always Too Late	679 Recordings
2005	Me Plus One	Big Beat
2008	I Know UR Girlfriend Hates Me	Island Records
2008	Two Of Hearts	Island Records
2009	Anthonio	Pleasure Masters
2009	Songs Remind Me of You	Smalltown Supersound

Bjørn Torske

Albums

1998	Nedi Myra	Ferox Records
2001	Trøbbel (TELLÉ 012)	Tellé
2002	Nedi Myra (TELLÉ 013)	Tellé
2008	Feil Knapp	Smalltown Supersounds
2010	Kokning	Smalltown Supersounds

Singles and EPs

1999	Expresso/Railtrack	Ferox Records
1999	Sexy Disco	Svek
1999	Tore/Torske—Battlestar XB-7/Jeg Vil Være Søppelmann	Svek
2000	Aerosoles	Svek
2000	Disco Members (TELLÉ 006)	Tellé

Continued

Continued

2001	Hard Trafikk (TELLÉ 011)	Tellé
2006	Bjørn Torske & Crystal Bois—As'besto	Sex Tags Mania
2006	Ny Lugg (Kort Bak/Lang På Siden)	Smalltown Supersound
2007	Kokt Kveite	Smalltown Supersound
2008	Kan Jeg Slippe?	Sex Tags Mania

Datarock

Albums

| 2005 | Datarock | Young Aspiring Professionals |
| 2009 | Red | Young Aspiring Professionals |

Singles and EPs

2002	Datarock/Stockhouse—Split EP	Éllet Records
2002	Demo/Greatest Hits	Kaptein Kaliber Records
2003	Computer Camp Love (ÉL 011)	Éllet Records
2006	Fa-Fa-Fa	Young Aspiring Professionals
2006	Bulldozer	Young Aspiring Professionals
2007	I Used to Dance With My Daddy	Nettwerk
2007	Datarock / New Violators—Princess (Morgan Z Remix) / Tonight Becomes Tomorrow	Nettwerk
2007	See What I Care	Young Aspiring Professionals
2008	Princess	Nettwerk, Young Aspiring Professionals
2009	Give it UP	Young Aspiring Professionals
2009	The Pretender	Nettwerk
2009	True Stories	Nettwerk

Fredrik Saroea

Singles and EPs

| 2002 | I Will Always Remember You (TELLÉ 018) | Tellé Records |
| 2003 | Ganguro Girl | Ketil |

Fredrik Saroea and the Fredrik Saroeas

Singles and EPs

| 2003 | Charmonix et Paris (ÉL 010) | Éllet Records |

Krisp

Singles & EPs

| 1996 | Footnotes | Love OD Communications |

Continued

Continued

2001	Farlige Fiffus (12fot0102)	Footnotes Records

Röyksopp

Albums

2001	Melody A.M	Wall of Sound
2005	The Understanding	Labels
2005	The Understanding / Melody A.M	EMI Music (France)
2009	Junior	EMI Music (France)
2010	Senior	MB3 Records

Singles and EPs

1999	So Easy (TELLÉ 002)	Tellé
2001	Poor Leno	Labels
2001	Eple (TELLÉ 009)	Tellé/Wall of Sound
2002	Remind Me	Wall of Sound
2003	Sparks	Wall of Sound
2005	What Else Is There?	Virgin Music (France), Labels, Wall of Sound
2005	Only This Moment	Wall of Sound, Virgin Music, Labels
2005	49 Percent	Virign Music (France), Labels, Wall Of Sound
2006	Röyksopp Night Out (Live EP)	Virgin Music (France), Labels
2006	Beautiful Day Without You	PIAS/Wall of Sound
2009	The Girl And The Robot	Wall of Sound
2009	This Must Be It	Wall of Sound
2009	Happy Up Here	Wall of Sound
2010	The Drug	Wall of Sound
2011	Forsaken Cowboy	Wall of Sound
2011	Dandy Warhols, The / Röyksopp—We Used To Be Friends / Eple	Popular Music

Skatebård

Albums

2002	Skateboarding Was A Crime (in 1989)	Tellektro
2006	Midnight Magic	Digitalo Enterprises
2008	Cosmos	Digitalo Enterprises

Continued

Continued

Singles and EPs

2003	Garlic / Den	Not On Label
2003	Future	Keys Of Life
2004	Sky City	Keys Of Life
2005	Conga	Sex Tags Mania
2006	June Nights South Of Siena	Sex Tags Mania
2006	Flashes In The Night	Digitalo Enterprises
2006	Love Attack	Digitalo Enterprises
2007	Marimba/Pagans	Supersoul Recordings
2007	Vuelo EP	Radius Recordings
2008	Kosmo	Digitalo Enterprises
2009	Sgnelkab	Digitalo Enterprises
2010	Way Out/Why Not?	Totally/Sex Tags UFO
2010	The Starwatcher EP	Luna Flicks

The Work

Singles and EPs

2006	Givin' It Up/Just Talk (POWPOW001)	Powerblytt Records
2007	Don't You Know/Take My Love (POWPOW002)	Powerblytt Records

Torske-Mundal Explosion / Erot

Singles & EPs

1998	In Disco/Song For Annie (TELLÉ 001)	Tellé

Various

Albums

2000	Samleplate (TELLÉ 007)	Tellé
2004	Tellé Sampler 01 | Spring 2004 (TELLÉSAMPLER 01)	Tellé

Singles & EPs

2008	Powerblytt Myths Volume 1 (POWPOW003)	Powerblytt Records

(*Source:* www.discogs.com)

Bibliography

Ahrens, F. (2007) Viacom sues YouTube over copyright. *Washington Post*, 14 March. http://www.washingtonpost.com/wp-dyn/content/article/2007/03/13/AR2007031300595.html (accessed 21 July 2011).

Albanesius, C. (2008) MySpace goes 'Primetime' with embedded Hulu video. http://www.pcmag.com/article2/0,2817,2334598,00.asp (accessed 8 April 2009).

Ali, R. (2008) MySpace expands self-serve MyAds display ad service. 12 October. http://www.forbes.com/2008/10/12/myspace-ads-beta-tech-cx_pco_1012paidcontent.html (accessed 7 April 2009).

Allison, K., & Garrahan, M. (2007) Mining a rich vein of user information. *Financial Times*, 5 November.

Allison, K., & Van Duyn, A. (2007) Facebook considers non-English sites. 30 September. http://us.ft.com/ftgateway/superpage.ft?news_id=fto093020071816325975&page=1 (accessed 5 March 2010).

Amazon (2008) http://www.amazon.co.uk (accessed 17 September 2008).

Andrews, R. (2010) 2009 music sales shed $1 billion, while US downloads stagnant. http://www.guardian.co.uk/media/pda/2010/apr/29/digitalmusic-research (accessed 14 October 2010).

Angwin, J. (2009) *Stealing MySpace: The Battle to Control the Most Popular Website in America*. New York: Random House.

Apple (2010) Ping. http://www.apple.com/itunes/ping/ (accessed 5 December 2010).

Arango, T. (2010) In retrospect: how the AOL-Time Warner merger went so wrong. *The New York Times*, 11 January. http://www.nytimes.com/2010/01/11/business/media/11merger.html (accessed 26 October 2010).

Arango, T. T. (2009) U.S. media see a path to India in China's snub. *The New York Times*, 3 May. http://www.nytimes.com/2009/05/04/business/media/04media.html (accessed 4 May 2009).

Arrington, M. (2005a) Profile—YouTube. 8 August. http://techcrunch.com/2005/08/08/profile-youtube/ (accessed 4 May 2010).

Arrington, M. (2005b) Comparing the Flickrs of video. 6 November. http://techcrunch.com/2005/11/06/the-flickrs-of-video/ (accessed 5 May 2010).

Arrington, M. (2008) Facebook taps users to create translated versions of site. Spanish, French and German available. 21 January. http://techcrunch.com/2008/01/21/facebook-taps-users-to-create-translated-versions-of-site/ (accessed 5 Mar 2010).

Arrington, M. (2009a) Social networking: will Facebook overtake MySpace in the U.S. In 2009? 13 January. http://www.techcrunch.com/2009/01/13/social-networking-will-facebook-overtake-myspace-in-the-us-in-2009/ (accessed 13 January 2009).

Arrington, M. (2009b) Facebook now nearly twice the size of MySpace worldwide. 22 January. http://www.techcrunch.com/2009/01/22/facebook-now-nearly-twice-the-size-of-myspace-worldwide/ (accessed 22 January 2009).

Arrington, M. (2010) MySpace expands Twitter syncing to six new countries. 22 September. http://techcrunch.com/2009/09/22/myspace-expands-twitter-syncing-to-six-new-countries/ (accessed 19 October 2010).

Arsenault, A. H., & Castells, M. (2008) The structure and dynamics of global multi-media business networks. *International Journal of Communication*, 2, 707–748. http://ijoc.org/ojs/index.php/ijoc/article/view/298/189 (accessed 11 July 2009).

Arthur, C., & Kiss, J. (2009) MySpace and Bebo are running out of friends. 11 June. http://www.guardian.co.uk/technology/2009/jun/11/myspace-bebo-social-networking (accessed 20 July 2011).

Baker, B. (2006) *MySpace Music Marketing: How to Promote & Sell Your Music on the World's Biggest Networking Web Site*. St. Louis, MO: Spotlight.

Barboza, D. (2007) Murdoch is taking MySpace to China. *The New York Times*, 27 April. http://www.nytimes.com/2007/04/27/business/worldbusiness/27myspace.html (accessed 9 April 2009).

Barnett, E. (2009a) Spotify to launch Facebook app and music sharing service. *The Daily Telegraph*. http://www.telegraph.co.uk/technology/news/5331275/Spotify-to-launch-Facebook-app-and-music-sharing-service.html (accessed 11 October 2010).

Barnett, E. (2009b) Hulu set for September UK launch. 20 May. www.telegraph.co.uk/scienceandtechnology/technology/5356527/Hulu-set-for-September-UK-launch.html (accessed 4 June 2009).

Barnett, E. (2010) Hulu 'abandons UK plans' after broadcaster talks collapse. 27 April. http://www.telegraph.co.uk/technology/news/7639763/Hulu-abandons-UK-plans-after-broadcaster-talks-collapse.html (accessed 20 July 2011).

Barrett, M. (2007). It's WHAT'S NEXT. Paper presented at the Accenture Global Leadership Conference, 11 April.

Bartiromo, M. (2008) Facetime with Chris DeWolfe. 2 June. http://www.businessweek.com/magazine/content/08_22/b4086025019774.htm (accessed 21 May 2011).

BBC (2001) Murdoch's brief love affair with the web. 5 January. http://news.bbc.co.uk/2/hi/business/1102560.stm (accessed 11 July 2009).

BBC (2005) News Corp in $580m internet buy. 19 July. http://news.bbc.co.uk/2/hi/business/4695495.stm) (accessed, 24 October, 2011).

Becker, A. (2006) 24 finds a space on MySpace. *Broadcasting & Cable*, 15 May. http://www.broadcastingcable.com/article/104183–24_Finds_a_Space_on_MySpace.php (accessed 8 April 2009).

Bell, D. (2007) Introduction. In D. Bell & B. M. Kennedy (Eds.), *The Cybercultures Reader* (pp. 1–9). London: Routledge.

Belzman, J. (2006) Bands, fans sing new tune on MySpace. 13 February. http://www.msnbc.msn.com/id/11114166/ (accessed 13 April 2009).

Benedikt, M. (1991) Cyberspace: Some Proposals. In M. Benedikt (Ed.), *Cyberspace: First Steps* (pp. 119–224). Cambridge, MA and London: MIT Press.

Bennett, A., & Peterson, R. A. (2004) *Music Scenes: Local, Translocal and Virtual*. Nashville, TN: Vanderbilt University Press.

Blackshaw, P., Bruce, M., Higginson, M., & Nagaranja, K. (2010). *Asia Pacific Social Media Trends: Global Perspectives and Local Realities*. 10 July: NM Incite—A Nielsen/McKinsey Company.

Blevins, J. L. (2004) Battle of the online brands: Disney loses internet portal war. *Television New Media*, 5, 247.

Boston Globe. (2005) Viacom's MTV buys Neopets for $160m. 21 June. http://www.boston.com/business/technology/articles/2005/06/21/viacoms_mtv_buys_neopets_for_160m/ (accessed 17 July 2011).

boyd, d. (2004) Friendster and Publicly Articulated Social Networks. Paper presented at the Conference on Human Factors and Computing Systems (CHI 2004) Vienna: ACM, 24–29 April.

boyd, d., & Heer, J. (2006) Profiles as conversation: networked identity performance on Friendster. In *Proceedings of the Hawai'i International Conference on System Sciences* (HICSS-39), Persistent Conversation Track, Kauai, HI: IEEE Computer Society. 4–7 January.

boyd, d. m. (2008) *Taken Out of Context American Teen Sociality in Networked Publics*. University of California, Berkeley.

boyd, d. m., & Ellison, N. B. (2007) Social network sites: definition, history, and scholarship. *Journal of Computer-Mediated Communication*, 13, 1. http://jcmc.indiana.edu/vol13/issue1/boyd.ellison.html (accessed 3 April 2009).

Boyd-Barrett, O. (1977) Media imperialism: towards an international framework for an analysis of media systems. In J. Curran, M. Gurevitch, & J. Woollacott (Eds.), *Mass Communication and Society* (pp. 116–135). London: Edward Arnold.

Boyd-Barrett, O. (1998) Media imperialism reformulated. In D. K. Thussu (Ed.), *Electronic Empires: Global Media and Local Resistance* (pp. 157–176). London: Arnold.

Boyd-Barrett, O. (2006) Cyberspace, globalization and empire. *Global Media and Communication*, 2, 1: 21–41.

Brown, D. (1998) *Revenue trends and projections in European Pay-TV*. London: FT Media and Telecoms.

Bruno, A. (2005) MySpace is the (online) place. *Billboard*, 2 July, 117: 14.

Bruns, A. (2008) *Blogs, Wikipedia, Second Life, and Beyond: From Production to Produsage*. New York: Peter Lang.

Brunsdon, C. (2004) Life-styling Britain: the 8–9 slot on British television. In L. Spigel & J. Olsson (Eds.), *Television after TV: Essays on a Medium in Transition*. Durham: Duke University Press.

Burgess, J., & Green, J. (2009) *YouTube: Online Video and Participatory Culture*. Cambridge, UK: Polity.

Butow, E. and M. Bellomo (2008) *Amp Your MySpace: Essential Tools for Giving Your Profi le an Extreme Makeover*. New York: McGraw-Hill.

Caesar, E. (2007) How Kate Nash rose to become the new queen of MySpace. *The Independent*, August 16. http://www.independent.co.uk/student/student-life/music-film/how-kate-nash-rose-to-become-the-new-queen-of-myspace-460737.html (accessed 21 April 2009).

Cambridge Advanced Learner's Dictionary Online. (2010) http://dictionary.cambridge.org/ (accessed 16 September 2010).

Castells, M. (2004) Informationalism models of the network society: a theoretical blueprint. In M. Castells (Ed.), *The Network Society: A Cross-cultural Perspective*. Cheltenham: Edward Elgar.

Castells, M. (2009) *Communication Power*. Oxford: Oxford University Press.

Chalaby, J. K. (2002) Transnational television in Europe—the role of pan-European channels. *European Journal of Communication*, 17, 2: 183–203.

Chalaby, J. K. (2005) The quiet invention of a new medium: twenty years of transnational television in Europe. In J. K. Chalaby (Ed.), *Transnational Television Worldwide: Towards a New Media Order* (pp. 43–65). London: I.B. Tauris.

Chalaby, J. K. (2009) *Transnational Television in Europe: Reconfiguring Global Communications Networks*. London: I.B. Tauris.

Cieslak, M. (2006) Rise of the web's social network. *BBC News*, 30 September. http://news.bbc.co.uk/go/pr/fr/-/2/hi/programmes/click_online/5391258.stm (accessed 13 April 2009).

Clash Music (2009). Ungdomskulen's Bergen: A hometown lowdown from its musical residents. *Clash Music, 2010*. http://www.clashmusic.com/feature/ungdomskulen-s-bergen (accessed, 24 October, 2011).

Clickz (2005) Stats—Web Worldwide. http://www.clickz.com/stats/web_world-wide (accessed 3 April 2009).

Cohn, D. (2005) Bands embrace social networking. *Wired*, 18 May. http://www.wired.com/culture/lifestyle/news/2005/05/67545 (accessed 2 October 2008).

Collins, R. (1990) *Satellite Television in Western Europe*. London: John Libbey.

ComScore (2009) Number of Hulu Video Viewers Increases 42 percent in February, according to comScore Video Metrix. 24 March. http://www.comscore.com/Press_Events/Press_Releases/2009/3/Hulu_Video_Viewing_Increases_in_February (accessed 23 March 2011).

ComScore (2010) ComScore releases September 2010 U.S. online video rankings. http://www.comscore.com/Press_Events/Press_Releases/2010/10/com-Score_Releases_September_2010_U.S._Online_Video_Rankings (accessed 10 November 2010).

Comm, J. (2010) *Twitter Power 2.0: How to Dominate Your Market One Tweet at a Time*. Hoboken, NJ: John Wiley.

Credit Suisse (2007) Implications of Microsoft's Facebook investment for MySpace. Equity Research. Movies & Entertainment.

Croteau, D., & Hoynes, W. (2006) *The Business of Media: Corporate Media and the Public Interest*. Thousand Oaks, CA: Pine Forge Press.

Curran, J. (2002) *Media and Power*. Abingdon, UK: Routledge.

Curran, J., & Morley, D. (2006) Introduction. In J. Curran & D. Morley (Eds.), *Media and Cultural Theory* (pp. 1–13). London: Routledge.

Curran, J., & Seaton, J. (2010) *Power Without Responsibility* (7th ed.). Abingdon, UK: Routledge.

Davis, J. (2010) Architecture of the personal interactive homepage: constructing the self through MySpace. *New Media & Society*, 12, 7: 1103–1119.

De Moragas Spa, M., & Lopez, B. (2000) Decentralization process and proximate television. In G. Wang, J. Servaes, & A. Goonasekera (Eds.), *The New Communications Landscape. Demystifying Media Globalization*. London: Routledge.

De Sola Pool, I. (1977) When cultures clash: the changing flow of television. *Journal of Communication*, 27, 2: 139–149.

Deleon, N. (2009) Chinese social networks `virtually' out-earn Facebook and MySpace: a market analysis. 5 April. http://www.techcrunch.com/2009/04/05/chinese-social-networks-virtually-out-earn-facebook-and-myspace-a-market-analysis/ (accessed 9 April 2009).

Dey, I. (1993) *Qualitative Data Analysis: A User-Friendly Guide for Social Scientists*. London: Routledge.

Discovery (2004) Job description "Reversioning Specialist." *Careers@Discovery*. http://secured.Kenexa.com/discoveryv4/newhr/jobdesc.asp?ID=1723 (accessed 2 November 2004).

Disney (2010) The Walt Disney Company to acquire leading game developer Playdom. 27 July. http://corporate.disney.go.com/news/corporate/2010/2010_0727_playdom.html (accessed 22 October 2010).

Doran, J. (2006) Google and News Corp link up in $900m MySpace deal. *The Times*, 8 August. http://business.timesonline.co.uk/tol/business/industry_sectors/media/article602302.ece (accessed 29 March 2009).

Dorfman, A., & Mattelart, A. (1975) *How to Read Donald Duck: Imperialist Ideology in the Disney Comic*. New York: International General.

Editors of Bottletree Books LLC (2006) *MySpace Maxed Out: Explode Your Popularity, Buzz Your Band, and Secure Your Privacy on MySpace*. Bottletree Books.

Elliott, A., & Urry, J. (2010) *Mobile Lives*. London: Routledge.

Ellison, N. B., Steinfield, C., & Lampe, C. (2007) The benefits of Facebook "friends": Social capital and college students' use of online social network sites. *Journal of Computer-Mediated Communication*, 12, 4: Article 1.

Elmer, G. (2004) *Profiling Machines: Mapping the Personal Information Economy*. Cambridge, MA: MIT Press.

Errity, S. (2007) YouTube.ie—coming to a PC near you. *ENN*, 19 June. http://enn.ie/article/47869.html (accessed 2 November 2010).

Errol, P. L. (2009) Hulu. *Review*, Spring 2009. http://www.pcmag.com/article2/0,2817,2344265,00.asp (accessed 8 April 2009).

European Commission (1984) Television without Frontiers. Green Paper on the Establishment of the Common Market for Broadcasting, especially by Satellite and Cable. 14 June. Introduction; Parts One, Two and Three, 47. 84(300). http://aei.pitt.edu/archive/00001151/01/TV_frontiers_gp_pt_1_3.pdf (accessed 5 May 2005).

European Commission (2007) Directive 2007/65/EC of the European Parliament and of the Council of 11 December 2007 amending Council Directive 89/552/EEC on the coordination of certain provisions laid down by law, regulation or administrative action in Member States concerning the pursuit of television broadcasting activities Text with EEA relevance. *Official Journal L 332*, 18 December. http://eur-lex.europa.eu/LexUriServ/LexUriServ.do?uri=OJ:L:2007:332:0027:01:EN:HTML (accessed 4 June 2009).

Evan (2009) VEVO launches as #1 Music Network in the US. 13 January. http://blog.vevo.com/vevo-launches-as-1-music-network-in-the-us/ (accessed 30 November 2010).

Facebook (2008a) Facebook releases site in Spanish; German and French to follow. 7 February. http://www.facebook.com/press/releases.php?p=16446 (accessed 8 November 2010).

Facebook (2008b) Facebook to establish international headquarters in Dublin, Ireland. 2 October. http://www.facebook.com/press/releases.php?p=59042 (accessed 1 November 2010).

Facebook (2008c) Facebook releases site in German. 3 March. http://www.facebook.com/press/releases.php?p=20727 (accessed 8 November 2010).

Facebook (2010a) Press Room. http://www.facebook.com/press/info.php?statistics (accessed 30 May 2010).

Facebook (2010b) Build your presence on Facebook: get started in 5 easy steps. http://www.facebook.com/note.php?note_id=68842278095 (accessed 3 December 2010).

Facebook (2010c) Facebook's privacy policy. http://www.facebook.com/policy.php (accessed 20 April 2010).

Facebook (2010d) http://wiki.developers.facebook.com/index.php/Internationalization (accessed 5 March 2010).

Facebook Careers (2010) http://www.facebook.com/careers/department.php?dept=tokyo (accessed 31 October 2010).

Flew, T. (2007) *Undestanding Global Media*. New York: Palgrave.

Flynn, B. (1992) Small is profitable? TBI Niche Channels. *Television Business International*.

Forrest, E. (2005) Welcome to MySpace: it's fun and it's sexy, but it's highly addictive. *The Guardian*, 11 December. http://www.guardian.co.uk/technology/2005/dec/11/news.observerfocus (accessed 8 April 2009).

Fortt, J. (2007) Nielsen: Facebook growth outpaces MySpace. 15 November. http://tech.fortune.cnn.com/2007/11/15/nielsen-facebook-growth-outpaces-myspace/ (accessed 20 July 2011).

Freedman, D. (2006) Internet transformations: "old" media resilience in the "new media" revolution. In J. Curran & D. Morley (Eds.), *Media and Cultural Theory* (pp. 275–290). London: Routledge.

Frith, S. (2004) Introduction. In S. Frith (Ed.), *Popular Music*, Volume 4, *Music and Identity* (pp. 1–5). Abingdon, UK: Routledge.

Garrahan, M. (2009) The rise and fall of MySpace. 4 December. http://www.ft.com/cms/s/2/fd9ffd9c-dee5–11de-adff-00144feab49a.html (accessed 4 March 2010).

Gibson, O. (2006) Music TV? That's so last century. *The Guardian*, 28 July. http://www.guardian.co.uk/media/2006/jul/28/broadcasting.arts (accessed 6 May 2009).

Gibson, O. (2008) 200 million friends and counting. *The Guardian*. www.guardian.co.uk/media/2008/jun/23/myspace.tomanderson/print (accessed 23 June 2008).

Global Information Technology Report (2010–2011) http://www.weforum.org/issues/global-information-technology (accessed 20 July 2011).

Goggin, G. (2006) *Cell Phone Culture: Mobile Technology in Everyday Life*. London: Routledge.

Google (2006) Google to acquire YouTube for $1.65 billion in stock. 9 October. http://www.google.com/press/pressrel/google_youtube.html.

Google (2009) Investor relations. http://investor.google.com/fin_data2003.html (accessed 5 April 2009).

Grossman, L. (2006) You—Yes, You—Are TIME's Person of the Year. *Time Magazine*, 25 December. http://www.time.com/time/magazine/article/0,9171,1570810,00.html (accessed 20 July 2011).

Grunwald, D. (2010) Lost in translation? Twitter language crowdsourcing project. 26 January. http://blog.gts-translation.com/2010/01/26/lost-in-translation-twitter-language-crowdsourcing-project/ (accessed 31 October 2010).

Guribye, F. (2007) Facebook-farsotten. *Norsk medietidskrift*, 4, 363–377.

Hafez, K. (2007) *The Myth of Media Globalization*. Cambridge: Polity Press.

Ham, A., Roddis, M., & Lundgren, K. (2008) *Lonely Planet Norway*. London: Lonely Planet Publications.

Hamelink, C. J. (1983) *Cultural Autonomy in Global Communications*. New York: Longman.

Hampton, K., & Wellman, B. (2003) Neighboring in Netville: how the internet supports community and social capital in a wired suburb. *City & Community*, 2, 4: 277–311.

Hampton, K. N., & Wellman, B. (2002) The not so global village. In C. A. Haythornthwaite & B. Wellman (Eds.), *The Internet in Everyday Life* (pp. 345–371). Oxford: Blackwell.

Hann, M. (2009) First sight: Casiokids. 13 March. http://www.guardian.co.uk/music/2009/mar/13/casiokids-norwegian-electro-pop (accessed 18 July 2011).

Hannam, K., Sheller, M., & Urry, J. (2006) Editorial: Mobilities, immobilities and moorings. *Mobilities*, 1, 1: 1–22.

Hannerz, U. (1996) *Transnational Connections: Culture, People, Places*. London: Routledge.

Hartley, J. (2002) *Communication, Cultural and Media Studies: The Key Concepts* (3rd ed.). London: Routledge.

Haythornthwaite, C. (2005) Social networks and internet connectivity effects. *Information, Communication and Society*, 8, 2: 125–147.

Haythornthwaite, C., & Wellman, B. (2002) The internet in everyday life: an introduction. In B. Wellman & C. Haythornthwaite (Eds.), *The Internet in Everyday Life* (pp. 3–41). Malden, MA: Blackwell.

Helft, M. (2008) Google told to turn over user data of YouTube. 4 July. http://www.nytimes.com/2008/07/04/technology/04youtube.html (accessed 22 March 2011).

Hesmondhalgh, D. (1998) The British dance music industry: a case study of independent cultural production. *The British Journal of Sociology*, 49, 2: 234–251.

Hesmondhalgh, D. (2007) *The Cultural Industries*. Los Angeles: Sage.

Hesmondhalgh, D. (2009) The digitalisation of music. In A. C. Pratt & P. Jeffcut (Eds.), *Creativity and Innovation in the Cultural Economy*. Abingdon; New York: Routledge.

Hodgkinson, J. A. (2004) The fanzine discourse over post rock. In A. Bennett & R. A. Peterson (Eds.), *Music Scenes: Local, Translocal and Virtual* (pp. 221–253). Nashville: Vanderbilt University Press.

Howe, J. (2005) The hit factory. *Wired*, 13 November. http://www.wired.com/wired/archive/13.11/myspace.html?pg=4&topic=myspace&topic_set=) (accessed 24 October, 2011).

Howe, J. (2006) The rise of crowdsourcing. *Wired*, June. 14(6).http://www.wired.com/wired/archive/14.06/crowds.html (accessed 1 November 2010).

Howe, J. (2009) *Crowdsourcing: Why the Power of the Crowd is Driving the Future of Business*. New York: Crown.

Hunt, A. (1999) Stockmarkets: a crash to come? BBC News, 30 December. http://news.bbc.co.uk/2/hi/business/582792.stm (accessed 23 October 2010).

IFPI (2010) IFPI publishes recording industry in numbers 2010. http://www.ifpi.org/content/section_news/20100428.html (accessed 30 September 2010).

Internet World Stats (2010) http://www.internetworldstats.com/top20.htm (accessed 22 July 2011).

Jenkins, H. (2006) *Convergence Culture: Where Old and New Media Collide*. New York: New York University Press.

Jerräng, M. (2009) Documents reveal major labels own part of Spotify. 8 July. http://computersweden.idg.se/2.2683/1.240046/documents-reveal-major-labels-own-part-of-spotify (accessed 11 October 2010).

Jobs.climber.com (2010) http://jobs.climber.com/jobs/Media-Publishing/Los-Angeles-CA-USA/Localization-Manager-MySpace-/5457165/Careers?source=simplyjobs&bid=5457165&cid=Localization-Manager-MySpace- (accessed 31 October 2010).

Jobs.climber.com (2010) http://jobs.climber.com/jobs/Media-Publishing/Los-Angeles-CA-USA/Localization-Coordinator-MySpace-/6052596/Careers?source=simplyjobs&bid=6052596&cid=Localization-Coordinator-MySpace- (accessed 31 October 2010).

Joshi, S. (2008) YouTube now has an Indian incarnation. 8 May. http://www.hindu.com/2008/05/08/stories/2008050857242200.htm (accessed 5 May 2010).

Kafka, P. (2007) Murdoch 2.0. 24 January. http://www.forbes.com/2007/01/24/murdoch-myspace-tribune-tech-media-cz_pk_0126murdoch.html (accessed 5 April 2009).

Kalliongis, N. (2008) *MySpace Music Profit Monster: Proven Online Marketing Strategies for Getting More Fans Fast*. First MTV Press.

Kan, M. (2010) Google CEO: China's internet censorship will fail in time. *Computerworld*, 4 November. http://www.computerworld.com/s/article/9194860/Google_CEO_China_s_Internet_censorship_will_fail_in_time (accessed 22 March 2011).

Kaplan, D. (2007) MySpace ramps up ad targeting initiatives. 4 November. http://paidcontent.org/article/419-myspace-ramps-up-ad-targeting-initiatives/ (accessed 22 July 2011).

Katz, Y. (2005) *Media Policy for the 21st Century in the United States and Western Europe*. Cresskill, NJ: Hampton Press.

Kincaid, J. (2009) MySpace struggles in Korea, shuts down regional office. Techcrunch, 5 February. http://www.techcrunch.com/2009/02/05/myspace-struggles-in-korea-shuts-down-regional-office/ (accessed 6 April 2009).

Kirkpatrick, D. (2007) As Facebook takes off, MySpace strikes back. 19 September. http://money.cnn.com/2007/09/18/technology/myspace_strikes.fortune/index.htm?postversion=2007091906 (accessed 22 March 2011).

Kiss, J. (2010) Facebook hack day: Zuckerberg talks up merits of personalization. *The Guardian*, 21 June. http://www.guardian.co.uk/technology/pda/2010/jun/21/facebook-zuckerberg-personalising-the-internet (accessed 11 October 2010).

Kollock, P., & Smith, M. A. (1999) Communities in cyberspace. In M. A. Smith & P. Kollock (Eds.), *Communities in Cyberspace* (pp. 3–25). London; New York: Routledge.

Kraidy, M. (2005) *Hybridity, or the Cultural Logic of Globalization*. Philadelphia: Temple University Press.

Kramer, S. D. (2008) News Corp. Working on music 'Hulu' for MySpace. http://www.paidcontent.org/entry/419-draft-news-corp-working-on-music-hulu-for-myspace/ (accessed 13 February 2009).

Krasilovsky, M. W., Shemel, S., & Gross, J. M. (2003) *This Business of Music: The Definitive Guide to the Music Industry*. New York: Billboard Books.

Kutchinsky, S. (2007). Datarock are lunatics who occasionally border on genius. Your life will be greyer. . . . *BBC Review*. http://www.bbc.co.uk/music/reviews/j3jw (accessed 24 October, 2011).

Laing, D. (1997) Rock anxieties and new music networks. In A. McRobbie (Ed.), *Back to Reality: Social Experience and Cultural Studies* (pp. 116–132). Manchester, UK: Manchester University Press.

La Monica, P. R. (2009) *Inside Rupert's Brain*. London: Penguin.

Lapinski, T. (2006) MySpace: The business of Spam 2.0. Exhaustive edition. 11 September. http://gawker.com/valleywag/tech/myspace/myspace-the-business-of-spam-20-exhaustive-edition-199924.php (accessed 20 July 2011).

Lastufka, A., & Dean, M. W. (2008) *YouTube: An Insider's Guide to Climbing the Charts*: O'Reilly Media.

Lathrop, T. (2007) *This Business of Global Music Marketing*. New York: Billboard Books.

Le Monde (2008) Réseaux sociaux: des audiences différentes selon les continents. 14 January. http://www.lemonde.fr/web/infog/0,47-0@2-651865,54-999097@51-999297,0.html (accessed 1 October 2008).

Leiss, W., Kline, S., Jhally, S., & Botterill, J. (2005) *Social Communication in Advertising Consumption in the Mediated Marketplace* (3rd ed.). New York: Routledge.

Levine, R. (2006a) MySpace growth faces cultural hurdles. *New York Times*, 6 November.

Levine, R. (2006b) MySpace aims for a global audience, and finds some stiff competition. *New York Times*, 7 November. http://www.nytimes.com/2006/11/07/technology/07myspace.html (accessed 5 April 2006).

Levy, F. (2008) *15 Minutes of Fame: Becoming a Star in the YouTube Revolution*. Indianapolis, IN: Alpha Books.

Levy, S. (2007) Twitter: is brevity the next big thing? *Newsweek*, 30 April. http://www.newsweek.com/2007/04/29/twitter-is-brevity-the-next-big-thing.html (accessed 19 October 2010).

Libert, B. and Spector, J. (2010a) *Crowdsourcing Customer Service: How May We Help We?* Upper Saddle River, NJ: FT Press.

Libert, B. and Spector, J. (2010b) *Crowdsourcing Your Sales: Let Customers Sell Themselves (and Others)*. Upper Saddle River, NJ: FT Press.

Libert, B. Spector, J. (2010c); *Crowdsourcing Your Brand: How to Tap Customer Desire*. Upper Saddle River, NJ: FT Press.

Lister, M., Dovey, J., Giddins, S., Grant, I., & Kelly, K. (2009) *New Media: A Critical Introduction* (2nd ed.). London: Routledge.

Locke, L. (2008) MySpace Music sees major money in free tunes. *Wired*, 17 April.

Lyons, D. (2009) Old media strikes back. *Newsweek*, 2 March. http://www.newsweek.com/id/185790 (accessed 8 April 2009).

Madslien, J. (2010) Dotcom bubble burst. BBC, 9 March. http://news.bbc.co.uk/2/hi/business/8558257.stm (accessed 23 October 2010).

Maney, K. (2009) His space. *Portfolio*, 18 March. http://www.portfolio.com/executives/2009/03/18/MySpace-CEO-DeWolfe-Q-and-A (accessed 22 March 2011).

Mansell, R. (2004) Political economy, power and new media. *New Media & Society*, 6, 1: 96–105.

Mansfield, H. (2009) Top 5 online electronic dance music retailers. *Examiner*, 2 August. http://www.examiner.com/electronica-music-in-national/top-5-online-electronic-dance-music-retailers (accessed 11 October 2010).

Marshall, P. D. (2004) *New Media Cultures*. London: Arnold.

Massey, D. (1993) Power-geometry and a progressive sense of place. In J. Bird, B. Curtis, T. Putnam, G. Robertson, & L. Tickner (Eds.), *Mapping the Futures: Local Cultures, Global Change*. London: Routledge.

Matos, M. (2010) How Justin Bieber gave SoundCloud a boost. *The Guardian*, 30 September. http://www.guardian.co.uk/music/2010/sep/30/soundcloud-justin-bieber-myspace/print (accessed 18 October 2010).

Mavise (2010) Mavise: database for TV companies and TV channels in the European Union and candidate countries. www.mavise.obs.coe.int (accessed 19 September 2011).

McCarthy, C. (2008) Facebook 'is beating MySpace in popularity contest.' ZDNET, 23 June. http://www.zdnet.com.au/news/software/soa/Facebook-is-beating-MySpace-in-popularity-contest-/0,130061733,339290024,00.htm (accessed 4 March 2010).

McLeod, K. (2001) Genres, subgenres, sub-subgenres and more: musical and social differentiation within electronic/dance music communities. *Journal of Popular Music Studies*, 13, 59–75.

McStay, A. (2010) *Digital Advertising*. London: Palgrave.

McWilliams, J. (2009) How Facebook beats MySpace. *The Guardian*, 23 June. http://www.guardian.co.uk/commentisfree/cifamerica/2009/jun/23/facebook-myspace-social-networks (accessed 4 March 2010).

Mediati, N. (2010) Privacy in iTunes Ping. *PC World*, 2 September. http://www.pcworld.com/article/204773/privacy_in_itunes_ping.html (accessed 5 December 2010).

Mendelson, A. L., & Papacharissi, Z. (2010) Look at us: collective narcissism in college student Facebook photo galleries. In Z. Papacharissi (Ed.), *The Networked Self: Identity, Community and Culture on Social Network Sites*. (pp. 251–273). New York: Routledge.

Michaels, S. (2008) Gorillaz most popular band on MySpace. *The Guardian*, 24 December. http://www.guardian.co.uk/music/2008/dec/24/gorillaz-myspace-friends/print (accessed 9 April 2009).

Midtsjø, L. (2009) Ny milepæl for Facebook i Norge. *Kampanje*, 23 January. http://www.kampanje.com/medier/article5240392.ece (accessed 23 March 2011).

Milmo, D. (2001) News Corp axes more internet jobs. *The Guardian*, 16 January. http://www.guardian.co.uk/media/2001/jan/16/citynews.newmedia (accessed 3 April 2009).

Mjøs, O. J. (2010a) *Media globalization and the Discovery Channel networks*. New York: Routledge.

Mjøs, O. J. (2010b) News Corporation's MySpace.com and the digital challenges to audiovisual regulations. In J. Gripsrud & H. Moe (Eds.), *The Digital Public Sphere: Challenges for Media Policy*. Gothenburg: Nordicom.

Mjøs, O. J., Moe, H., & Sundet, V. S. (2010). The functions of buzzwords: a comparison of Web 2.0 and telematics. Paper presented at the Norwegian Media Research Association's 14th Conference.

Mohr, T. (2009) Music: the warm sounds born of extreme darkness and bitter cold (includes free MP3s!). *The Huffington Post*, 14 October.

Molz J. G. (2006) 'Watch us wander': mobile surveillance and the surveillance of mobility. *Environment and Planning A*, 38, 2: 377–393.

Moore, M. (2008) MySpace Music to offer millions of free songs. *Daily Telegraph*, 25 September. www.telegraph.co.uk/connected/main.jhtml?xml=/connected/2008/09/25/dlmyspace125.xml (accessed 8 April 2009).

Morley, D. (1991) Where the global meets the local. *Screen*, 32, 1: 1–15.

Morley, D. (2000) *Home Territories: Media, Mobility and Identity*. London: Routledge.

Morley, D. (2006) Globalisation and cultural imperialism reconsidered: Old questions in new guises. In J. Curran & D. Morley (Eds.), *Media and Cultural Theory* (pp. 30–43). London: Routledge.

Mosnes, K. (2011) *Øving er for Drittband*. Bergen: Kapabel.

MSNBC (2010) MySpace users can now sync posts to Facebook. 30 August. http://www.msnbc.msn.com/id/38924953/ns/technology_and_science-tech_and_gadgets/# (accessed 19 October 2010).

Murdoch, R. (2006) Chairman's Address to the 2006 Annual Stockholders' Meeting. 20 October. http://www.newscorp.com/news/news_316.html (accessed 6 May 2009).

Murdoch, R. (2008) Rupert Murdoch has potential. *Esquire*, 11 September. http://www.esquire.com/features/75-most-influential/rupert-murdoch-1008 (accessed 26 March 2009).

MySpace.com (2009a) Online advertising. https://advertise.myspace.com/onlineadvertising.html (accessed 26 March 2009).

MySpace.com (2009b) MyAds Beta. https://advertise.myspace.com/musicians.html ?sem=total&aud=band&ctype=search&place=Google&semcamp=bandpromotion_b&semad=bandpromotion&HBX_PK=bandpromotion&HBX_OU=50&pr=QGCpC05uA0tsioeN66ytOw%3D%3D (accessed 9 April 2009).

Naughton, J. (2006) MySpace or his space? Does Rupert get the problem? *The Observer*, 17 September. http://www.guardian.co.uk/technology/2006/sep/17/comment.media (accessed 8 April 2009).

Nettby (2010) Av en god begynnelse blir det en god slutt! 26 October. http://www.nettby.no/community/article.php?id=2758078&community_id=19 (accessed 26 October 2010).

New York Times (2008) www.nytimes.com/auth/login?URI=/2008/09/17/dining/17diet.html&OQ=_rQ3D5Q26refQ3DhealthQ26orefQ3DsloginQ26orefQ3DsloginQ26orefQ3DsloginQ26orefQ3Dslogin&REFUSE_COOKIE_ERROR=SHOW_ERROR (accessed 17 September 2008).

New York Times (2009) Ex-Chief of AOL to run MySpace. *The New York Times*, 1 April. http://www.nytimes.com/2009/04/02/business/media/02digital.html?_r=1&scp=5&sq=myspace%20china&st=cse (accessed 9 April 2009).

News Corporation (2005) News Corporation to acquire Intermix Media, Inc. 18 July. http://www.newscorp.com/news/news_251.html (accessed, 24 October).

News Corporation (2006) Annual report. http://www.newscorp.com/investor/annual_reports.html (accessed 30 August 2010).

News Corporation (2007) NBC Universal and News Corp. announce deal with internet leaders AOL, MSN, MySpace and Yahoo! To create a premium online video site with unprecedented reach. http://www.newscorp.com/news/news_329.html (accessed 8 April 2009).

News Corporation (2008) FORM 10-K. Annual report. 13 August. http://investor. newscorp.com/sec.cfm?DocType=&DocTypeExclude=&SortOrder=FilingDat e%20Descending&Year=&Pagenum=5 (accessed 9 April 2009).

News Corporation (2009) Corporate profile. Investor relations. http://www.newscorp.com/investor/index.html (accessed 2 April 2009).

Nicole, K. (2007) YouTube launches in Australia & New Zealand. http://mashable. com/2007/10/22/youtube-australia-new-zealand/ (accessed 5 May 2010).

Nielsen Online, (2009) Global faces and networked places: A Nielsen report on social networking's new global footprint. March. blog.nielsen.com/nielsenwire/ wp-content/ . . . /Nielsen_globalfaces_mar09.pdf (accessed 20 July 2011).

Nielsen Online (2010a) Led by Facebook, Twitter, Global Time Spent on social media sites up 82% year over year. 22 January. http://blog.nielsen.com/nielsenwire/global/led-by-facebook-twitter-global-time-spent-on-social-media-sitesup-82-year-over-year/ (accessed 21 July 2011).

Nielsen Online (2010b) Global audience spends two hours more a month on social networks than last year. 19 March. http://blog.nielsen.com/nielsenwire/global/ global-audience-spends-two-hours-more-a-month-on-social-networks-thanlast-year/print/ (accessed 19 October 2010).

Nielsen Online (2010c) Facebook and Twitter post large year over year gains in unique users. 4 May. http://blog.nielsen.com/nielsenwire/global/facebook-andtwitter-post-large-year-over-year-gains-in-unique-users/ (accessed 19 October 2010).

Nielsen Online (2010d) Social media dominates Asia Pacific internet usage. News Release. *Nielsen*, 30 June. www.nielsen-online.com/pr/APAC_smrpt_mr-jun10. pdf (accessed 2 November 2010).

Olson, P. (2008) Time Warner bags Bebo. *Forbes*, 13 March. http://www.forbes. com/2008/03/13/bebo-time-warner-markets-equity-cx_po_0312markets10. html (accessed 4 April 2009).

O'Reilly, T. (2005) What is Web 2.0? Design patterns and business models for the next generation of software. O'Reilly Network.

Palmer, M. (2010) A future alongside Facebook. *Financial Times*, 24 February. http://cachef.ft.com/cms/s/0/0bda8d80–2187–11df-830e-00144feab49a. html#axzz1HRSKDrnV (accessed 23 March 2011).

Papacharissi, Z. (2009) The virtual geographies of social networks: a comparative analysis of Facebook, LinkedIn and ASmallWorld. *New Media & Society*, 11, 1–2: 199–220.

Patchin, J. W., & Hinduja, S. (2010) Trends in online social networking: adolescent use of MySpace over time. *New Media & Society*, 12, 2: 197–216.

Pentel, Z. (2010) 5 superb social media tools for musicians. http://mashable. com/2010/01/04/social-media-tools-bands/ (accessed 3 December 2010).

Pomerantz, D. (2008) In pictures: web strategies of the big studios. *Forbes*, 30 March. http://www.forbes.com/2008/04/30/hollywood-internet-studios-biz-cz_ dp_0430studios_slide_6.html?thisSpeed=20000 (accessed 28 March 2009).

Pospisil, J. (2006) *Hacking MySpace: Customizations and Mods to Make MySpace Your Space*. Indianapolis, IN: Wiley.

Rantanen, T. (2005) *The Media and Globalization*. London: Sage.

Reynolds, S. (1998) *Energy Flash: A Journey Through Rave Music and Dance Culture*. London: Picador.

Reynolds, S. (1999) *Generation Ecstasy: Into the World of Techno and Rave Culture*. New York: Routledge.

Reynolds, S. (2008) *Energy Flash: A Journey Through Rave Music and Dance Culture*. New edition. London: Picador.

Rheingold, H. (1993/2000) *The Virtual Community: Homesteading on the Electronic Frontier*. MIT Press edition. Cambridge, MA: MIT Press.

Riley, D. (2007) MySpace to announce Self-Serve hyper targeted advertising network. 4 November. http://www.techcrunch.com/2007/11/04/myspace-to-announce-self-serve-advertising-network/ (accessed 8 April 2009).

Robertson, R. (1995) Globalization: time-space and homogeneity—heterogeneity. In M. Featherstone, S. Lash, & R. Robertson (Eds.), *Global Modernities* (pp. 25–44). London: Sage.

Robins, K., & Webster, F. (1988) Cybernetic capitalism: information, technology, everyday life. In V. Mosco & J. Wasko (Eds.), *The Political Economy of Information* (pp. 44–76). Madison, WI: University of Wisconsin Press.

Roe, K., & De Meyer, G. (2001) One planet—one music? MTV and globalization. In A. Gebesmair & A. Smudits (Eds.), *Global Repertoires: Popular Music within and Beyond the Transnational Music Industry* (pp. XI, 176 s.). Aldershot: Ashgate.

Rogers, E. (2003) *Diffusion of Innovations* (5th ed.). New York: Free Press.

Rosen, J. (2005) Scandinavian star on a pop streak. *The New York Times*, 3 May. http://www.nytimes.com/2005/05/02/arts/02iht-annie.html (accessed 24 September 2010).

Rosenbush, S. (2005) Hey, come to this site often? *Business Week*, 13 June. http://www.businessweek.com/magazine/content/05_24/b3937077_mz063.htm (accessed 13 April 2009).

Rosoff, M. (2009) Vevo CEO confirms it's all about business. 10 December. http://news.cnet.com/8301–13526_3–10413316–27.html (accessed November 2010).

Rubin, H. J., & Rubin, I. (1995) *Qualitative Interviewing: The Art of Hearing Data*. Thousand Oaks, CA: Sage.

Sabbagh, D. (2008) AOL pays $850 in cash for Bebo as cornerstone of international strategy. Available at: http://business.timeonline.co.uk/tol/business/industry_sectors/media/article3548913.ece (accessed 26 August 2011).

Sayer, P. (2007) Google launches YouTube France: YouTube expands reach with French version. 19 June. http://www.pcadvisor.co.uk/news/index.cfm?NewsID=9772 (accessed 5 May 2010).

Schifferes, S. (2006) Has the dotcom boom returned? *BBC*, 10 October. http://news.bbc.co.uk/1/hi/business/6036337.stm (accessed 2 April 2009).

Schiller, H. (1969) *Mass Communications and American Empire*. New York: Kelley.

Schiller, H. (1985) Electronic information flows: new basis for global dominations? In P. Drummond & R. Paterson (Eds.), *Television in transition: papers from the first International Television Studies Conference* (pp. 11–20). London: BFI.

Schiller, H. (1992) *Mass Communications and American Empire* (2nd updated ed.). Boulder, CO: Westview Press.

Schiller, H. (1998) Striving for communication dominance: a half-century review. In D. K. Thussu (Ed.), *Electronic Empires: Global Media and Local Resistance* (pp. 17–26). London: Arnold.

Schneider, A. P. (2004) Facebook expands beyond Harvard: Stanford, Columbia join network, with Yale next in line. *Harvard Crimson*, 1 March. http://www.thecrimson.com/article/2004/3/1/facebook-expands-beyond-harvard-harvard-students/ (accessed 18 July 2011).

Schnitt, B. (2009) Debunking rumors about advertising and photos. 24 November. http://blog.facebook.com/blog.php?topic_id=212696506250 (accessed 3 March 2010).

Schonfeld, E. (2010) YouTube helps Vevo overtake MySpace Music in the U.S. (plus, top ten music properties). 13 January. http://techcrunch.com/2010/01/13/youtube-vevo-overtake-myspace-music/ (accessed 14 October 2010).

Schwartz, J. (2001) Giving web a memory cost its users privacy. *The New York Times*, 8 September. http://www.nytimes.com/2001/09/04/business/giving-web-a-memory-cost-its-users-privacy.html?scp=1&sq=Giving (accessed 12 April 2010).

Schwartz, J. (2010) Once-fading MySpace focuses on youthful reincarnation. 10 March. http://www.usatoday.com/tech/techinvestor/corporatenews/2010–03 –10-myspace10_CV_N.htm (accessed 18 March 2010).

Scott-Joynt, J. (2005) What MySpace means to Murdoch. *BBC*, 19 July. http://news.bbc.co.uk/2/hi/business/4697671.stm (accessed 2 April 2009).

Sellers, P. (2006) MySpace cowboys. *CNN*, 29 August. http://money.cnn.com/magazines/fortune/fortune_archive/2006/09/04/8384727/index.htm (accessed 13 April 2009).

Sheller, M., & Urry, J. (2006) The new mobilities paradigm. *Environment and Planning A*, 38, 2: 207–226.

Sherwin, A. (2006) Amateur 'video bloggers' under threat from EU broadcast rules. *The Times*, 17 October. http://www.timesonline.co.uk/tol/news/world/europe/article603123.ece (accessed 4 June 2009).

Shklovski, I., & boyd, d. (2006) Music as cultural glue: supporting bands and fans on MySpace.

Siklos, R. (2005) News Corp. to acquire owner of MySpace.com. *The New York Times*. http://www.nytimes.com/2005/07/18/business/18cnd-newscorp.html (accessed 2 April 2009).

Skatebård (2009) interview, March

Slatalla, M. (1998) Cookies may annoy but they don't hurt. *The New York Times*, 2 April. http://www.nytimes.com/1998/04/02/technology/fundamentals-user-s-guide-cookies-may-annoy-but-they-don-t-hurt.html?scp=1&sq=Cookies%20May%20Annoy%20But%20They%20Don't%20Hurt.%22%20%20&st=cse (accessed 13 April 2010).

Smith, E. (2010) MTV overtakes Vevo as top online music destination. 8 September. http://blogs.wsj.com/speakeasy/2010/09/08/mtv-overtakes-vevo-as-top-online-music-destination/ (accessed 30 November 2010).

Smith, J. (2008) Now you can help translate Facebook into any language. 2 April. http://www.insidefacebook.com/2008/04/02/now-you-can-help-translate-facebook-into-any-language/ (accessed 20 July 2011).

Sparks, C. (2007) What's wrong with globalization? *Global Media and Communication*, 3, 2: 133–155.

Spurgeon, C. (2008) *Advertising and New Media*. London; New York: Routledge.

Sreberny, A. (2000) The global and the local in international communication. In J. Curran & M. Gurevitch (Eds.), *Mass Media and Society* (pp. 93–119). London: Arnold.

Steel, E., & Vascellaro, J. E. (2010) Facebook, MySpace confront privacy loophole. 21 May. http://online.wsj.com/article/SB100014240527487045131045752567 01215465596.html (accessed 10 November 2010).

Stone, B. (2007a) MySpace, chasing YouTube, upgrades its offerings. *The New York Times*, 26 June. http://www.nytimes.com/2007/06/27/technology/27video.html (accessed 26 June 2009).

Stone, B. (2007b) MySpace to discuss effort to customize ads. *The New York Times*, 18 September. http://www.nytimes.com/2007/09/18/technology/18myspace.html (accessed 22 September 2008).

Stone, B. (2007c) Microsoft buys stake in Facebook. 25 October. http://www.nytimes.com/2007/10/25/technology/25facebook.html?_r=1 (accessed 5 March 2010).

Story, L. (2007) The evolution of Facebook's Beacon. *The New York Times*, 29 November. http://bits.blogs.nytimes.com/2007/11/29/the-evolution-of-face-books-beacon (accessed 1 October 2008).

Story, L., & Stone, B. (2007) Facebook retreats on online tracking. *The New York Times*, 30 November. www.nytimes.com/2007/11/30/technology/30face.html?pagewanted=print (accessed 1 October 2008).

Straubhaar, J. (1991) Beyond media imperialism: asymmetrical interdependence and cultural proximity. *Critical Studies in Mass Communication*, 8, 1–11.

Straubhaar, J. D. (2007) *World Television: From Global to Local*. Los Angeles: Sage.

Straw, W. (1991) Systems of articulation, logics of change: communities and scenes in popular music. *Cultural Studies*, 5, 3: 368–388.

Stross, R. (2008) *Planet Google: One Company's Audacious Plan to Organize Everything We Know*. New York: Free Press.

Sullivan, M. (2007) Is Facebook the new MySpace? *PC World*, 24 July. http://www.pcworld.com/article/134635/is_facebook_the_new_myspace.html (accessed 24 March 2010).

Sweney, M. (2006) MySpace targets European expansion. *The Guardian*, 20 June. http://www.guardian.co.uk/technology/2006/jun/20/news.citynews1 (accessed 22 March 2011).

Syvertsen, T. K. (2001) Kommersialisering, globalisering og konvergens: Utfordringer for mediepolitikk og medieregulering [commercialization, globalization and convergence: challenges for media policy and media regulation], Report from the Norwegian Power and Democracy Study, Report 31, July. http://www.sv.uio.no/mutr/publikasjoner/rapp2001/Rapport31.html. (2001) (accessed October 2007).

Takahashi, T. (2010) MySpace or Mixi? Japanese engagement with SNS (social networking sites) in the global age. *New Media & Society*, 12, 3: 453–475.

Teather, D. (2009) MySpace is forced to slash workforce as social network users flock to Facebook. 23 June. http://www.guardian.co.uk/technology/2009/jun/23/myspace-facebook-job-cuts-redundancy (accessed 4 March 2010).

Tenold, S. (2010) *Making Waves: Bergensbølgen and the Branding of Music Locality*: Norwegian School of Economics and Business Administration.

The Sidney Morning Herald. (2006) New rock stars use web videos to win fans. *Reuters News*, 29 August. http://www.smh.com.au/news/web/new-rock-stars-use-web-videos-to-win-fans/2006/08/28/1156617265516.html?page=fullpage#contentSwap1 (accessed 5 May 2010).

Thorkildsen, J. (2009) MySpace legger ned i Norge. *Dagbladet*, 5 March. http://www.dagbladet.no/2009/03/05/kultur/musikk/tekno/myspace/5156064/ (accessed 6 April 2009).

Thornton, S. (1995) *Club Cultures: Music, Media and Subcultural Capital*. Cambridge: Polity Press.

Thussu, D. K. (2000/2006) *International Communication: Continuity and Change* (2nd ed.). London: Hodder Arnold.

Thussu, D. K. (2005) The transnationalization of television: the Indian experience. In J. K. Chalaby (Ed.), *Transnational Television Worldwide: Towards a New Media Order* (pp. 156–172). London: I. B. Tauris.

Thussu, D. K. (2007a) *Media on the Move: Global Flow and Contra-flow*. London: Routledge.

Thussu, D. K. (2007b) The 'Murdochization' of news? The case of Star TV in India. *Media, Culture and Society*, 29, 4: 593–611.

Timms, D. (2006) Murdoch unveils plans for myspace.com. *The Guardian*, 10 January. http://www.guardian.co.uk/media/2006/jan/10/newscorporation.rupertmurdoch (accessed 4 March 2010).

Tomlinson, J. (1991) *Cultural imperialism: a critical introduction*. London: Continuum.

Tomlinson, J. (1999) *Globalisation and Culture*. Cambridge: Polity.

Topping, A. (2010) Twitter power: how social networking is revolutionising the music business. *The Guardian*, 5 September. http://www.guardian.co.uk/media/2010/sep/05/twitter-power-social-networking-music/print (accessed 18 October 2010).

Tunstall, J., & Machin, D. (1999) *The Anglo-American Media Connection.* Oxford: Oxford University Press.

Turkle, S. (1995) *Life on the Screen: Identity in the Age of the Internet.* New York: Simon & Schuster.

Turow, J. (1997) *Breaking up America: Advertisers and the New Media World.* Chicago: University of Chicago Press.

Turow, J. (2009) *Media Today: An Introduction to Mass Communication.* New York: Routledge.

Twitter Blog (2009) Coming soon: Twitter in more languages. 8 October. http://blog.twitter.com/2009/10/coming-soon-twitter-in-more-languages.html (accessed 1 November 2010).

Twiturm (2010) About Twiturm. http://www.twiturm.com/about (accessed 3 December 2010).

Urry, J. (2000) *Sociology beyond Societies: Mobilities for the Twenty-First Century.* London: Routledge.

Urry, J. (2003) *Global complexity.* Cambridge: Polity Press.

Urry, J. (2005) The Complexities of the Global. *Theory Culture & Society,* 22, 5: 235–254

Urry, J. (2007) *Mobilities.* Cambridge: Polity.

USA Today (2006) Fox ffers shows on MySpace, Fox TV station sites. *USA Today,* 3 October. http://www.usatoday.com/tech/news/2006–10–03-fox-myspace_x.htm?POE=TECISVA (accessed 8 April 2009).

Van Buskirk, E. (2007) Arctic Monkey frontman collaborates with Final Fantasy on side project. *Wired,* 22 October. http://blog.wired.com/music/2007/10/arctic-monkey-f.html (accessed 10 April 2009).

Van Buskirk, E. (2010) YouTube globalization continues with four new languages. *Wired,* 25 August (accessed 2 November 2010).

Van Dijck, J., & Nieborg, D. (2009) Wikinomics and its discontents: a critical analysis of Web 2.0 business manifestoes. *New Media & Society,* 11, 4: 855–874.

Van Doorn, N. (2010) The ties that bind: the networked performance of gender, sexuality and friendship on MySpace. *New Media & Society,* 12, 4: 583–602.

Van Duyn, A., & Chaffin, J. (2006) News Corp plans China MySpace. *Financial Times,* 19 September. http://www.ft.com/cms/15647e34–4845–11db-a42e-0000779e2340.html (accessed 23 March 2011).

Vascellaro, J. E. (2008) MySpace aims for trickier markets. *The Wall Street Journal,* 13 December. http://online.wsj.com/article/SB119749126310624423.html?mod=dist_smartbrief (accessed 6 April 2009).

Vincent, F. (2007) *MySpace for Musicians: The Comprehensive Guide to Marketing Your Music Online.* Boston, MA: Cengage Learning.

Waisbord, S. (2004) McTV: understanding the global popularity of television formats. *Television & New Media,* 5, 4: 359–383.

Warsaw Business Journal, W. B. (2009) MySpace quits Poland after just fi ve months of operations. 16 March. http://www.wbj.pl/article-44782-myspace-quits-poland-after-just-five-months-of-operations.html (accessed 23 March 2011).

Wasko, J., & Erickson, M. (2009) The political economy of YouTube. In P. Snickars & P. Vonderau (Eds.), *The YouTube Reader* (pp. 372–387). Stockholm: National Library of Sweden.

Wauters, R. (2008) MySpace gives up on the Netherlands. *Techcrunch,* 26 October. http://www.techcrunch.com/2008/10/26/myspace-gives-up-on-the-netherlands/ (accessed 6 April 2009).

Wauters, R. (2009) China's social network QZone is big, but is it really the biggest? *Techcrunch,* 24 February. http://techcrunch.com/2009/02/24/chinas-social-network-qzone-is-big-but-is-it-really-the-biggest/ (accessed 3 November 2010).

Web 2.0 Conference (2004) http://www.web2con.com/web2con/ (accessed 5 August 2010).

Webb, A. (2006) Making a song and dance. *The Guardian*, 25 May. http://www.guardian.co.uk/music/2006/may/25/internet.netmusic/print (accessed 24 April 2009).

Wellman, B., Quan-Haase, A., Boase, J., & Wenhong, C. (2003) The social affordances of the internet for networked individualism. *Journal of Computer-Mediated Communication*, 8, 3.

Wellman, B., & Gulia, M. (1999) Virtual communities as communities: net surfers don't ride alone. In M. A. Smith & P. Kollock (Eds.), *Communities in Cyberspace* (pp. 167–194). London; New York: Routledge.

Wikipedia (2010) YouTube. http://en.wikipedia.org/wiki/YouTube (accessed 5 May 2010).

Wikström, P. (2009) *The Music Industry: Music in the Cloud*. Cambridge: Polity Press.

Wray, R. (2010) Ten years after the crash, the dotcom boom can finally come of age. *The Guardian*, 14 March. http://www.guardian.co.uk/business/2010/mar/14/technology-dotcom-crash-2000 (accessed 23 October 2010).

Yahoo! Europe (2005) Response to the Commission's Issues Papers for the Liverpool Audiovisual Conference. http://ec.europa.eu/avpolicy/docs/reg/modernisation/issue_papers/contributions/ip1-yahoo.pdf (accessed 4 June 2009).

Zuckerberg, M. (2007) Thoughts on Beacon. 5 December. http://blog.facebook.com/blog.php?post=7584397130 (accessed 3 March 2009).

Index

For Product Safety Concerns and Information please contact our EU
representative GPSR@taylorandfrancis.com Taylor & Francis Verlag GmbH,
Kaufingerstraße 24, 80331 München, Germany

Printed and bound by CPI Group (UK) Ltd, Croydon, CR0 4YY
02/05/2025
01859445-0001